THE PIONEERS OF MAINE
AND
NEW HAMPSHIRE

The Pioneers of Maine and New Hampshire

1623 to 1660

A Descriptive List, drawn from Records of the Colonies, Towns, Churches, Courts and Other Contemporary Sources.

BY

CHARLES HENRY POPE

Author of the Pioneers of Massachusetts, Pope, Cheney, Tobey, Merriam and Hooper Genealogies, etc.

WITH FOREWORD
BY
JAMES PHINNEY BAXTER, A. M., LITT. D.

JANAWAY PUBLISHING, INC.
Santa Maria, California

Notice

In many older books, foxing (or discoloration) occurs and, in some instances, print lightens with wear and age. Reprinted books, such as this, often duplicate these flaws, notwithstanding efforts to reduce or eliminate them. The pages of this reprint have been digitally enhanced and, where possible, the flaws eliminated in order to provide clarity of content and a pleasant reading experience.

Copyright © 1908, Charles Henry Pope

Originally published
Boston:
1908

Reprinted by:

Janaway Publishing, Inc.
732 Kelsey Ct.
Santa Maria, California 93454
(805) 925-1038
www.janawaygenealogy.com

2014

ISBN: 978-1-59641-322-1

Made in the United States of America

FOREWORD

It is encouraging to note the progress which the study of genealogy has made within the last decade, which may be said to mark an epoch in the family history of New England. Books like those which Mr. Pope has compiled are invaluable as aids to this study, since they furnish important clues to the genealogist, which he could not obtain except by long research in public and private archives alone familiar to experts like Mr. Pope.

The Pioneers of Maine and New Hampshire aims to give such particulars as are accessible of the founders of these states, and, in many cases, all the particulars which exist; many, it is true, most meagre; but any one who has sought through scores of obscure registers and volumes difficult to reach, knows what the finding of a single name sometimes means to him, for it often settles a mooted point which nothing else can do.

An examination of "The Pioneers" will convince students of the extent and value of Mr. Pope's researches, and insure him their gratitude. These students are not at all confined to New England, but are scattered over the entire Union, for it is in our old colonial settlements that the roots of American Family History are to be found.

JAMES PHINNEY BAXTER.

PIONEER TOWNS AND PLANTATIONS OF MAINE AND NEW HAMPSHIRE, 1623-1660

Agamenticus, Accomenticus (York)
Biddeford
Black Point (Scarborough)
Bloody Point (Dover)
Cape Porpoise (Arundel, Kennebunkport)
Casco, Bay and settlement (Portland)
Dover
Exeter
Falmouth (Portland)
Gorgeana (York)
Great Island (Portsmouth)
Hampton
Isles of Shoals
Kennebunk
Kittery
Machias
Ogunquit (Wells)
Pemaquid
Penobscot (Castine)
Piscataqua, River and region
Portsmouth
Richmond Island
Saco
Scarborough
Strawberry Bank (Portsmouth)
Wells
York

AUTHORITIES QUOTED
With Abbreviations

Aspinwall, William, Notary, His Note-Book,	A.
Baxter, James Phinney, A.M., Litt.D., Manuscripts relating to early history of Maine, printed in Me. Hist. Coll. Other manuscripts, unpublished, quoted without specification.	Bax. MSS.
Trelawney Papers (The Richmond's Island Colony),	Trel.
Bradford, William, Gov. Plymouth Colony, History,	B.

AUTHORITIES QUOTED—Continued

Champernowne, Francis, Sketch of,	Champ.
Dover, N. H. Historical Collections,	Dov. Hist. Col.
Emmerton and Waters Gleanings in England,	Em. & Wat.
Essex County Court Records,	Es. Ct. Rec.
Essex County Files,	Es. Files
Essex County Probate Records,	Es. Prob.
Essex Historical Society Collections,	Es. Coll.
Exeter, N. H., History, Bell,	Ex. Hist.
Genealogical Advertiser, The,	Gen. Adv.
Hampton, History, Dow,	Hamp. Hist.
Hobart, Rev. Peter, Diary,	Hob.
Hubbard, William, History of New England,	Hub.
Lechford, Thomas, Note Book,	L.
Lygonia Assembly, Records,	Lyg. Ass. Rec.
Maine Court Records,	Me. Ct. Rec.
Maine Historical Society Collections,	Me. Hist. Coll.
Maine Wills,	Me. Wills
Mason, John, Sketch of,	Jo: Ma:
Massachusetts Archives,	Mass. Arch.
Massachusetts Colonial Records,	Mass. Col. Rec.
Massachusetts Historical Society, Collections,	Mass. Hist. Coll.
New Hampshire Historical Society, Collections,	N. H. Hist. Coll.
New Hampshire Wills (quoted without specification),	
Norfolk County (old) Court Files,	Norf. Files
Norfolk County Records,	Norf. Rec.
Parliamentary Papers, Domestic Series,	Parl. Dom. Ser.
Pioneers of Massachusetts, Charles Henry Pope,	P. of M.
Piscataqua Court Files,	Pisc. Files

Piscataqua Court Records,   Pisc. Rec.
Register; The N. E. Hist.-Gen.
    Soc.,   Reg.
Sewall, Judge Samuel, Diary,   S.
Waters, Henry F., A.M.,
    Gleanings in England,   Wat.
Winthrop, John, Gov. Mass.
    Bay Colony, History,   W.
York County Deeds,   York De.
York County Files,   York Files

Beside the extant records of the towns in Maine and New Hampshire, 1623-1661, and the churches therein.

OTHER ABBREVIATIONS

Acct.	Account	d.	Died
Ae.	Aged	Dism.	Dismissed
Atba.	Able to bear arms	Eng.	England
Adm.	Admitted	Es.	Essex (the county of)
Admin.	Administer, administration	Est.	Estate
		Exam.	Examination
App.	Appointed	Exec.	Executor, executrix
Appr.	Apprentice, apprenticed	Folg.	Following
Appl.	Applied, applied for	Frm.	Freeman, (citizen)
Arch.	Archives or official documents	Gen.	General
		Gent.	Gentleman
Asst.	Assistant, magistrate	Gov.	Governor
Bapt.	Baptized	Grad.	Graduated
Beq.	Bequeathed, bequests	Gr. ch.	Grand-child
b.	Born	Gr, gr. ch.	Great-grand-child
Bro.	Brother	Gr.	Granted
bur.	Buried	Gr. st.	Grave-stone
Cert.	Certified	Inv.	Inventory
Ch.	Child, children	Mag.	Magistrate
Chh.	Church	m.	Married
Col.	Colony, colonial	Mdx.	Middlesex (county)
Co.	Company, county	Memb. chh.	Member of church
Conn.	Connecticut	Norf.	Norfolk (county)
Dau., daus.	Daughter, daughters.	Nunc.	Nuncupative, i. e., oral
Dec.	Deceased	Ord.	Ordained
De.	Deeds	Org.	Organized
Def.	Defendant	Plym.	Plymouth
Depos.	Deposed or deposition	Prob.	Probate, probated
Dep.	Deputy, representative	Prop.	Proposed

Propr.	Proprietor	Rem.	Remained, removed
Q. V.	Quod vide (which see)	Res.	Resided, residence
Recd.	Received	Ret.	Returned
Rec.	Records	Suff.	Suffolk (county)
Ref.	Referred		

Brackets, [ ], are used in two ways: 1. They enclose the authority or source of a statement, or a reference to some book or document which may well be read in the connection. 2. They are also used to enclose words or statements which are believed to be correct, but for which the writer has not found absolute documentary evidence.

SPECIAL DIRECTIONS FOR SEARCHERS

1. **Observe many variations of surnames.** One must sometimes look on several pages before discovering a desired name. Not only did public recorders vary the orthography, but a man sometimes spelled his own name in two or more ways.

2. **Always consult the other names mentioned in an article and the Index of Other Names.**

3. **Note the Abbreviations** employed, since many lines of original record have sometimes been compressed into one word or line in this volume.

4. **The source from which a statement has been drawn** can be inferred in most cases from its nature; as proprietorship and town office from town records; church membership, dismission, etc., from those of the churches; purchase and sale of lands from county Records of Deeds; depositions, giving age, etc., from records or files of the Courts or Colonies; designations of trade, occupation or social position were usually given in deeds, but sometimes in records of admission to churches; wills and administrations of estates in Probate Records or those of the County or Colony. When an item was found in an unusual place, the source has been noted.

5. The dates are given as they were recorded. March 25 was New Year's Day in England and her colonies in the seven-

teenth century. It is at once a blunder and a crime to alter such dates to suit a calendar which our Forefathers did not use. Their "style" was just exactly "old style," not at all "new." From January 1 to March 25, during which some other nations used the new year number, they often wrote a double date; as "3 February, 1621-2"; but February was still "moneth 12," and even 24 March was in the old year, although the month, by anticipation of "day 25," was "moneth 1."

6. **Maine and New Hampshire** are treated as one because in the origin of their settlements and their political history during the period covered they were so nearly one people.

Pioneers of
MAINE AND NEW HAMPSHIRE
1623 to 1660.

ABBINGTON,
William, residence not stated, defendant in a lawsuit at Strawberry Bank in 1642.

ABBOT, ABBOTT, ABBET, ABBIT,
Walter, Strawberry Bank, agent for Peter Garland in court 10 (7) 1645. Wife Sarah a witness in court in 1648. Kept the ordinary 2 (8) 1651. Lawsuits in 1654 and 1655. Took oath of allegiance July 21, 1657. Thomas, of Piscataqua, who deposed 8 (10) 1652, ae. about 18 or 19, as to the conduct of his master, Mr. John Bets, toward Robert Knight, [Mass. Arch. 38 B, 143,] was his son; with wife Sarah he sold land 8 Jan. 1663.
Will, dated May 15 and 16, prob. June 26, 1667, beq. to wife Sarah; son Peter, (a double portion;) dau. Wills, sons William, Walter and John, daus. Mary and Elizabeth, gr. ch. Thomas and Joseph Abbot and Sarah Wills.
See also Connell, Clifton, Drake, Green, Sherburne.

ABBY, ABBIE,
Thomas, residence not stated, one of the witnesses to the transfer of land at Black Point 30 June, 1637.
See also Green.

ABOURN, see Haborne.

ACKORMUCKE, see Meckermecke.

ADAMS,
Abel, Portsmouth, a servant of dame Hunkins, deposed 2 April, 1660, aged 40 years. [P. Court Files.]
Charles, Dover (Durham,) taxed Oct. 19, 1648. Bought house and land of John Aulte 10 April, 1645. Joined in petition to Gen. Court 10 Oct. 1665.
He m. Temperance, dau. of Philip Benmore, and inherited land in Kittery of him which he sold March 6, 1692; the widow confirmed the sale March 30, 1696. Estate settled by son Charles April 1, 1695.
Philip, York, took oath of allegiance to Mass. govt. 22 Nov. 1652. Proprietor, 1654.
Elizabeth, widow, (husband's name not given,) York, made will 6 June, prob. 18 Oct. 1710; beq. to dau. Sarah Black and grandchildren Daniel and Elizabeth Black, Nathaniel Adams and Samuel Johnson.
See also Abbot, Mackworth, Pormort.

AGNEW,
Niven, Oyster River, Kittery, juryman, 11 Nov. 1659. [P. Court Files.]
He made will, proved Sept. 16, 1687; beq. to friend John Taylor for his dau. Mary T., and to Peter Grant for his dau. Elizabeth G.; debts to be paid which were owing by his "predecessor" James Barrow.
See also Taylor.

ALLCOCK, ALLCOCKE, ALCOTT, ALCOCK,
John, planter, housekeeper, York, Agamenticus, his servant John Smith ran away and was returned to him by order of court Sept. 9, 1640. Rented land of William Hooke 16 June, 1643. Was a juror in 1647; a witness of George Parker's deed 23 Nov. 1648; bought land at Cape Neddicke Beach 16 July, 1650.
Took oath of allegiance to Mass. govt. and was appointed

sergeant 22 Nov. 1652. Proprietor. Mortg. land 20 Nov. 1666, to John Bray, shipwright, of Kittery.

His eldest son Joseph, aged about 20 years, testified at Kittery in Gunnison case in 1654; John, son of Joseph, sold land 3 Nov. 1687, which his grandfather, "farmer Allçock" had formerly owned. [York De. VI.]

See also Amerideth, Brooks, Harker, Jewell, Moulton, Raynes.

ALGER, AUGER,

Andrew, Casco, came in the service of John Winter with Capt. Hawkins in 1653, sharing the profits of the fishing. [Trel.] Resided at Biddeford and had share of marsh, 1653. Signed a petition with Jocelyn and others for fair trial and rights. With brother Arthur bought land of Indians and sold some of it July 15, 1662. "3 of his men" are mentioned by George Cleve in 1645 as coming to borrow scales and weights to weigh fish with. A daughter of his m. John Palmer about 1669 and recd. marriage portion of 50 acres of land at "Dunston," Scarboro. A petition for confirmation of this title was made to Andros. [Bax. MSS.]

Arthur, Casco, signed petitions in 1653. Gyles Roberts, in his will in 1666, calls him "brother." Arthur, Jr. took oath of allegiance to Mass. Bay govt. at Spurwink, July 13, 1658.

His wife Ann married as her second husband Samuel Walker, of Woburn, Mass. and deeded land to her sons Isaac and Ezekiel Alger in 1702.

Thomas, from Newton Ferrers, Eng. came to Casco; worked for John Winter a year, about 1630. See Rouse. [Trel.]

Trustrum, Casco, 1637 "a quiett man," sent money home to his wife in England through his employer, Winter. [Trel.]

See also Plaisted, Roberts.

ALLEN, ALLIN, ALLING,

Arnold, Spurwink, juror, 15 Sept. 1640.

Charles, Dover, sued by Henry Tibbet in 1659 for using certain lands of his. Portsmouth, proprietor, 1660.

Mary, residence not stated, deposed 26 Jan. 1645, before Henry Jocelyn relative to George Cleve in England.

William, boat master, Richmond Island, in the employ of Winter, "deserted" (i. e., left his employer) in 1640. [Trel.]

ALLERTON,
Isaac, of Plymouth, Mass. prominent member of that colony, also traded at Machias, then the eastern trading-post on the Maine coast, in 1633. See Vines.

AMBROSE, AMBROSS,
Henry, house-carpenter, Hampton, 1640; removed to Charlestown, Mass.
See Chase, Dalton, Thing.

AMERIDETH, MERIDA,
John, cooper, from Dartmouth, Eng. settled at Kittery. Lawsuit in Dover Court in 1648. He married Joanna, dau. of James Treworgy. He d. 26 Jan. 1690-1; beq. estate in Eng. to wife Joane for her life afterward to go to son and dau. John and Joanna Alcock, then to their ch. Joseph and Joanna Alcock; land in Kittery to same, then to gr. ch. Joseph and Joanna Alcock; money to be paid by "cozen" John Shapleigh to gr. ch. Abigail and Mary Alcock.
See also Tucker.

AMIRE, AMRY,
John, cooper, from Chudleigh, Eng. came to Richmond Island upon a "covenant" with Trelawney. Wrote to him 2 July, 1638. Money was paid to his wife in England on account. Soon after he left the island.

ANDREW, ANDREWS,
Edmund, blacksmith, Yalmpton, co. Devon, Eng. cov-

enanted 22 Nov. 1642, with Trelawney and Winter, to come to New Eng. and work at their plantation, Richmond Island, for 3 years. Was charged with a suit of "cammas" in 1643.

James, Senior, in a petition to Andros for confirmation of land title deposed April 14, 1688, that he "hath bine and Now is possessed of a Certaine parrsell of Massh neare thirty five years since Lyinge and being on the North Est Side Amisscongon River & Adjoyning thare too: near prsumsgate ffalls." &c. Edward Tyng attested to the correctness of the claim. [Bax. MSS. VI.]

John, Kittery, one of the inhabitants who attended court there June 25, 1640. With wife Joan sold house and land adjoining that of John Simmonds 21 March, 1648. Took oath of allegiance to Mass. Bay govt. 16 Nov. 1652. Deposed in the Gunnison case 24 April, 1654, ae. about 54 years. [Bax. MSS. I.] The wife Joane deposed 25 Feb. 1660, ae. about 40 years. [York De. II.] Ch. Sarah, Joane and John. He died before July 4, 1671, when the court made the widow Joane admx.

After his death she m. 2, — Atwell, and with son John Andrews, sold land 8 April, 1675.

Samuel, ae. 37, with wife Jane, ae. 30, and daus. Jane, ae. 3, and Elizabeth, ae. 2, and Elen Lougie, servant, ae. 20, came in the Increase, April 14, 1635. He was one of four "sent away" by Robert Cordell, goldsmith, Lombard St. London. Taxed at Saco 7 (7) 1636. Res. at Charlestown. "Having had the command of ships upon several voyages," he and Mr. Jonas Clarke were appointed 13 Oct. 1654, to take observations at the northerly bounds of Mass. plantation. [Arch. Col. 23.]

Inv. of his est. taken by Nicholas Davison and two other Charlestown men the last of Oct. 1659, shows merchandise; gives list of debts due from persons at Oyster Bay, L. I. Huntington, Hampstead, Stanford, Stratford, various Indians, etc. House, land given him by the town, etc. No clue as to family in the document.

He d. before Aug. 1, 14 Charles I, when the widow Jane

recd. a confirmatory deed of 100 acres of land on which her husband formerly built a house, etc. on the west side of Saco river. Confirmed by selectmen of Saco 26 (4) 1654. The widow married Arthur Mackworth, q. v.

Thomas, Mr. petitioned the court at Saco 25 March, 1636, relative to the debt of John Stratten. It seems probable that this is the Watertown, Mass. resident. [See P. of M.]

See also Blackappe, Felch, Mackworth, Neale, Reading, West.

ANGIER, ANGER, AINGER,

Samson, fisherman, York, juryman Oct. 16, 1649; bought land 24 June, 1650. Took oath of allegiance to Mass. govt. 22 Nov. 1652. With wife Susanna sold land 23 Aug. 1668; with wife Sarah sold land to Jasper Pullman, fisherman, 14 Aug. 1675.

Will dated 13 May, 1691, prob. 10 Jan. 1693-4, beq. all to wife Sarah.

John, Kittery, gave due bill to Roger Playstead 15 Oct. 1655.

ASHLEY,

William, Wells, constable, allowed by court July 4, 1659.

ATKINS, ADKINS,

Thomas, an early settler at Sagadahock, mouth of the Kennebec river. Sold a tract to William Cocks, westward of the mouth of the river. His dau. Elizabeth, born about 1645, lived at home about 12 years till she married. As "Elizabeth Davis of Beverly," she testified to these facts at Salem, July 25, 1709. [Es. De.]

His land was in the present town of Phippsburg, Me.

See also Cox.

ATKINSON, ATKERSON,

Joseph, Piscataqua, before the court in 1652. Took oath of fidelity to Mass. govt. July 2, 1657. Had a bill against

Portsmouth 4 Feb. 1600-1. His estate admin. Sept. 24, 1678; "children."
See also Lloyd, Phillips, Wheelwright.

ATWELL, ATWILL,
Benjamin, Richmond Island, was paid in 1640 for ducks he had shot. [Trel.] He and son John legatees of Richard Martin.
See also Andrew, Martin.

AUGER, see Alger.

AVERY,
Thomas, Portsmouth, proprietor, 1660.

AULT, AULTE, AWLT, ALLT,
John, planter, yeoman, Dover, brought suit 10 (7) 1645 against Capt. Thomas Wiggin for wages due to his wife Remembrance before she arrived at Pascataquacke, being 14 Dec. 163[5]; it was proved by the testimony of Henry Tybote that her time of service began March 1 before she came. Suit gained. This shows the wife to be that Remembrance Tybote, ae. 28 years, who came in the James, in company with [her brother?] Henry and his family.
Taxed in Dover in 1648. Constable and grand jury man in 1650. Frm. Jan. 26, 1656. He deposed March 2, 1677-8, ae. about 73 years. [Norf. Rec.] He and wife Remembrance deeded lands 17 June, 1667, to their son Thomas and dau. Rebecca Edgerly.
See also Branson, Tibbetts.

AUSTIN, ASTEN,
Francis, a pioneer at Dedham, Mass.; his lot passed to Francis Chickering before (7) 1640.
Francis, proprietor at Hampton in June, 1640. He d. before July 13, 1642, when his widow [Isabella] had a grant of land. She m. second, Thomas Leavitt of Exeter and Hampton.
See also **Davis, Gooch, Leavitt, Topp.**

Joseph, planter, Dover, had case in court in 1647; taxed Oct. 19, 1648. Bought one quarter of a sawmill of Richard Waldron 20 Sept. 1649. He deposed 27 June, 1661, ae. about 45 years. [P. Files.]

His will dated 25 Jan. 1662, was probated July 1, 1663, by widow Sarah; beq. to wife and children; son Thomas to have a double portion; brother Peter Coffin one of the overseers.

Note Matthew, who deposed 5 June, 1665, regarding sale of land at York, about 1660, aged about 45 years.

Samuel, Dover, proprietor, 1649. Sold land to Wm. Furber 15 Dec. 1650, Constable. Rem. to Wells. With wife Elizabeth sold house and land 25 Sept. 1655. His wife died and he m. 2, Sarah, widow of William Storer. Deeded land to son in law Samuel Storer 8 Oct. 1674.

BABB,

Philip, Hog Island, Kittery, took oath of allegiance to Mass. govt. 16 Nov. 1652. Constable for Isles of Shoals except Starr Island, 1652. Signed petition for incorporation of the islands 18 (3) 1653. Was one of the commissioners for settling minor cases there.

He died, and admin. of his estate was granted April 24, 1670-1, to Nathaniel Fryer. His wife died soon and their child Philip, "five years old next Michelmas," was apprenticed to Joseph Hall June 27, 1676.

Thomas, of Wapping, Eng. master of a ship which made voyages hither, [Trel.] was mentioned in records of court at Saco, March 6, 1636-7.

BABSON,

Stephen, gave bonds for another person in York court June 30, 1656.

BACHILER, BACHELLER, BATCHELDER, BATCH-
    ILOR, etc.

Alexander, merchant, Portsmouth; authorized May 17, 1652, "to keep the ferry from Great Island unto the rendezvous or the Great house"; suit in court in 1656; grand jury man 30 June, 1657; took oath of fidelity July 2, 1657. Admin. of his estate was granted 26 June, 1660, to his widow Ann. Her will dated 5 Nov. 1660, prob. June 26, 1661, beq. to son John or to his widow and "theyre Joynt children"; to James Leech, his wife and their 4 children; to Jane Furson, widow Mary Walford, servants Richard Peirce and Tho. Paine.

Nathaniel, son of Nathaniel and Hester (Mercer), place and date of birth unknown, came to this country before 1647, certainly, as in that year his grandfather, Rev. Stephen, gave property at Strawberry Bank to him in partnership with his cousins John and William Sanborn. He was then and for the rest of his life a resident of Hampton, N. H. Planter, yeoman, so he was designated in deeds; constable and otherwise in public business. He owned considerable land. Mortg. a tract 22 March, 1664, to his father in law John Smith and his brother in law, John, Jr., to secure to them the payment of their legacies by the will of Mrs. Ruth Dalton, of whose estate he was executor.

He m. 10 (10) 1656 Deborah, dau. of John and Deborah Smith; ch. Deborah b. 12 (8) 1657, (m. Joseph Palmer,) Nathaniel b. 24 (10) 1659, Ruth b. 9 (3) or (6) 1662, (m. James Blake, of Dorchester, Mass.) Hester b. 22 (12) 1664, (m. Samuel Shaw,) Abigail b. 28 (10) 1667, (m. John Dearborn,) Jane b. 8 (11) 1670, (m. Benjamin Lamprey,) Benjamin b. 19 (7) 1673, Stephen b. 8 (1) 1675-6, Mercy b. 11 (10) 1677, (m. Samuel Dearborn,) Mary b. 18 (7) 1679, Samuel b. 10 (10) 1680-1, Jonathan, Theodate, (m. Morris Hobbs,) Thomas, Joseph b. 9 (6) 1687, Mary b. 17 (8) 1688.

His first wife d. 8 (12) 1675-6; he m. 2, 31 (8) 1676, Mary (Carter) widow of John Wyman of Woburn, Mass.; he m. 3, 23 Oct. 1689, Elizabeth, widow of John Knill.

He d. 17 (10) 1710, "aged about 80 years."

Rev. Stephen, b. about 1561, matr. St. John's coll. Oxford, Nov. 17, 1581, B. A. Feb. 3, 1586-7, vicar of Wherwell, Hants, 26 Jan. 1587-8 to 1601; came in the William and Francis June 5, 1632, ae. 71, with wife Helen and others of his family. Settled at Saugus, (Lynn). Frm. May 6, 1635. Entered at once upon church life, drawing down the suspicions and oppositions of some in power for such independency. Undertook a scheme for founding a plantation at Yarmouth, but the winter season and the poverty of his associates caused the brave attempt to fail. Rem. to Newbury; thence in 1638-9 joined in the settlement of Hampton, N. H. to which he is said to have given the name, and whose first minister he became. He was on the ground before Oct. 9, 1638 with others, planning for the settlement, and was the real leader of the enterprise.

After earnest service, mingled with injudicious (if not erring) conduct, which brought conflicts with his associates and the Mass. government, he rem. to Strawberry Bank, (Portsmouth,) whence he returned to England not far from 1647. Deeded land 8 (7) 1647, to his three grandsons, John and William Sanborne and Nathaniel Bachiler, Jr.

Admin. of his estate in N. H. granted in Pisc. Court March 26, 1673, to "Wm. Richards, husband unto Mary ye daughter of Mr Steven Batchelor deceased."

He m. first ——; he m. 2, Helen ——, who was ae. 48 in 1631, when he visited ch. at Flushing; she came hither and died; he m. 3, widow Mary ——, at Strawberry Bank, from whom he separated, leaving her here to a sad and unsavory life. Ch. Theodate, (m. Christopher Hussey,) Deborah, (m. Rev. John Wing,) Stephen, (ae. 16 on entering Oxford in 1610,) Ann, (ae. 20 in 1630; m. John Sandburn,) Nathaniel, (m. Hester Mercer; son Nathaniel came here early and was a citizen of Hampton; Mary (m. Wm. Richards.) [See W., Reg. XVII, XXXVII, XLV, XLVII and Genealogy.]

See also Colcord and Woodward.

BADIVER,
John, Casco, worked for Winter a year about 1630.

BAGNALL,
Walter, first grantee of Richmond Island. Was mur-

dered by the Indians in 1631; Winthrop speaks severely of the man's character and treatment of the Indians; yet the Gen. Court ordered a boat, sufficiently manned, to be sent to investigate the case, Aug. 7, 1632, and to bring the guilty persons to Boston for trial, if they could be found.

BAILEY, BALY, BAYLEY, BEYLY, BEILL,

Jonas, Richmond Island, in employ of Winter, 1639-1643. [Trel.] Took oath of allegiance to Mass. govt. July 13, 1658. He deposed July 2, 1660, ae. about 53 years; was servant to Trelawney about 20 years before. [York De. I.] Resided at Blue Point alias Scarborough.

Will dated 11 Nov. 1663, prob. 9 Feb. 1663-4; beq. to wife Ellnor; brother Nicholas Baly; to "man" Henry Burt; to Francis Neale, Sen. and Jun.; godson Samuel Neale; Elizabeth Bryers, John Bryers, young John and two daughters; John Jackson, Mr. Robert Jordan's 6 sons and Andrew Brown. To be buried near wife Elizabeth.

John, fisherman, Isles of Shoals, bought a house 27 June, 1659, and conveyed it to his son in law Michael Endell, fisherman, 17 May, 1662.

See also Endell, Way.

BAKER, BECKER,

Edmund, from Newton Ferrers, Eng. came to Casco and lived one year, about 1630. [Trel.]

John, husbandman, Boston, adm. chh. 26 (1), frm. 18 May, 1642. Was dism. 6 (7) 1646, to the church of Gorgeana. [W.] Perhaps he was the J. B. who was a juryman in Maine court in 1640. Fined in Piscataqua court in 1645 for threatening words against Wm. Furber, and for running after Indians with a drawn sword, etc. Taxed at Dover Oct. 19, 1648. Testified in Norf. court in 1649. Not unlikely he is the J. B. who resided at Cape Porpoise, and took the oath of allegiance to Mass. govt. 5 July, 1653. Was prosecuted for abusive speeches against ministers and for upholding private meetings and preaching in them, to the disturbance of public assemblages.

BALCH,

    Freeborn, (presumably son of John, of Salem) residence not stated, testified in Piscataqua court 19 Aug. 1657, ae. 23 years, that he saw Henrie Thorner, ship-carpenter, of Wapping, killed by the rolling of masts which his men were putting into the water at Oyster River.

BALL,

    Edward, Portsmouth, in the employ of Stephen Ford, deposed 18 June, 1660, ae. about 30 years. [P. Files.] He was reproved by York court July 2, 1661, for living from his wife, and he promised to go to her if she came not to him.

    John, fisherman, York, juryman in court held at Gorgeana March 15, 1649. Had grant of land with Way, Stover and Powell at Cape Neddicke, for fishing trade, 3 July, 1649. Residing at Kittery, he bought land at Eagle Point 20 April, 1667.

    Richard, Winter Harbour, rem. to Cape Porpoise; took oath of allegiance to Mass. govt. at Wells 5 July, 1653. Sold Long Island 11 Dec. 1655.

    See also Powell, Spurrell, Way.

BALLEW, BELLEW, BELEW,

    William, Dover, witnessed a deed of Thomas Larkham in 1642. Sold a house and 20 acres of land on the north side of Back river 28 (6) 1645. One of the arbiters in Beard's case in 1647. Taxed in D. in 1648.

BANKS, BANCKS, BANKES, BANCKES,

    Richard, planter, York, had 20 acres of land laid out to him by the attorney of Wm. Hooke, July 19, 1645. Witnessed the grant of mill privilege to Rishworth in 1651. An Assistant at a court held at Mr. Gullison's 7 Nov. 1652. Took oath of allegiance to Mass. govt. 22 Nov. 1652. He is believed by family historians to have been the Richard Bankes who took the oath of fidelity to Plymouth Colony at Scituate (list not dated). See study of Kent families of this name in Reg. LI. Proprietor; town officer. Sold land 7 May, 1664.

BAREFOOTE,
Walter, Captain, gent. Kittery, bought land and house of Capt. Champernowne, 1658; later home, Newcastle. A partisan of Charles II and of the Masons; an official in the Provincial govt., involved in many conflicts, 1679-1688. Will 3 Oct. prob. 8 Oct. 1688; sister Sarah, wife of Thomas Wiggin (Jr.); cousin John Lee and others.

BARKELEY,
James, placed himself as a covenant servant for 4 years with Maj. John Johnson of Portsmouth 6 Sept. 1659.

BARLOW, BARLEY,
George, Exeter, signed the combination 5 (4) 1639. Had town grant of 40 acres of land in 1641. Joined with others in setting up a sawmill, 1649-50. Lawsuit in Norf. court in 1648. [Wife] Sysley fined in 1649 for not appearing as a witness. Rem. to East Saco; took oath of allegiance to Mass. govt. 5 July, 1653. Sometimes preached. See also Bursley, Listen.

BARNARD, BARNETT,
Bartholomew, Agamenticus, witness to deeds in 1636 and 1643; chosen a deputy to attend court at Saco June 25, 1640. Sold land near Henry Lynn's house 26 Nov. 1646.
See also Davis.

BARRETT,
John, Sen. planter, Wells, took oath of allegiance to Mass. govt. 4 July, 1653. John, Jr. took oath at Wells next day. He bought lands of Rishworth, which the selectmen confirmed to him 2 July, 1657. [York De. I.] Ensign. Rem. to Cape Porpoise; bought land 16 June, 1666. His wife Mary was a daughter of Edmund Littlefield and a legatee. Will prob. 4 July, 1664, beq. to wife Mary and son John.

BARTLETT,
Nicholas, fisherman, Cape Porpoise, bought 100 acres

of land at Casco Bay of George Cleve Dec. 26, 1651. Rem.
to Salem; sold the land to John Higginson, Jr. of S. 3 Feb.
1699. [York De. VI.]
See also Heard.

BARTON,
Edward, plaintiff in court at Gorgeana in 1650. [Strawberry Bank,] juryman in 1650. Before the court in 1651, charged with beating his wife. Took oath of fidelity July 2, 1657. Rem. to Cape Porpoise. He d. in 1671. Admin. granted July, 1671.
See also Crockett.

BATEMAN,
Edward, "of Kennebec," sold land before 1650 to James Phipps and John White. [See White.]

BATSON, BATSONS,
Nicholas, mariner, of late belonging to Capt. Cromwell, bought a vessel of Chr. Lawson of Boston about 20 (5) 1646. [A.]

Stephen, Cape Porpoise. With wife Elizabeth, apprenticed daughter Margery to Capt. Richard Bonithon and Lucretia, his wife, till she should be 21 years of age; done in court at Saco, April 4, 1637. Had a grant of land 21 Oct. 1645. A small river still bears his name. Took oath of allegiance to Mass. govt. 5 July, 1653. Sold 20 Sept. 1662, a log house, 300 acres of land on the main land, stage, cattle and other property on Stage Island; Arthur Batten and Margery Kindall, witnesses. Sold land to son John 8 Feb. 1672-3. Rem. before this date to Wells.

Will dated March 8, 1673; he d. June 30, 1676; inv. returned Aug. 21, 1676. Calls himself "antient"; beq. to son John, daus. Margery Young, Mary Brookehouse, Elizabeth Ashley; gr. ch. John Trott; Sarah Ashley and Mary Trott.
See also Cole.

BEADLE, BEEDLE,
Robert, Kittery, had grant of land from Thomas Gorges 20 May, 1641. See Simmons.

BEAN, BEANE, BENE,
John, Exeter.
Children, (parent not stated): Mary b. 18 June, 1655, Henry b. 5 March, 1662-3; (of John,) John b. 15 Aug. 1661, Daniel b. 23 March, 1662, Samuel b. 23 March, 1665-6, John b. 13 (8) 1668. [Norf. co. rec.]

BEANTON,
George, took oath of allegiance at Gorgeana 22 Nov. 1652.

BEARD,
Thomas, carpenter, Dover, had a lawsuit in 1641; bought house, 4 acres of upland and 6 acres of marsh 9 (10) 1644. [Suff. De.] Sold pipe staves etc. to Chr. Lawson; account settled by arbitration 14 (2) 1648. [A.] With wife Mary sold land 3 Feb. 1664.

Ch. William b. and d. 1664, Hannah b. 24 Oct. 1666. [Dov. Hist. Coll.] He took as an apprentice for 5 years Oct. 20, 1662, Thomas Coomes, whose passage had been paid from New Foundland to New England in the ship Joan. [P. Files.]

Will dated 16 Dec. 1678, prob. 25 March, 1679, beq. to wife Marie; daus. Marie Beard, Martha Bunker [or "Brimhor"] and Elizabeth Watson; sons Joseph and Thomas Beard.

Note. Compare with Thomas Beard, shoemaker of Massachusetts. See also will of Margaret Beard, widow, of Charterhouse Yard, parish of St. Sepulchres, London, 9 March, 1664, beq. to son Thomas B., then believed to be in parts beyond the seas. [Reg. XLII, 400.]

William, Dover, had lawsuit in Pisc. court in 1641; taxed, 1648. Signed petition of inhabitants in 1665.

He d. about 1 Nov. 1675; admin. of estate granted June
27, 1676, to widow Elizabeth with Richard Burnham and
Stephen Jones. Property to be divided between the widow
("and hir heyers") and Edward Leathers.
See also Cutt and Ballew.

BECK, BECKS, BEX,
  Caleb, Portsmouth, proprietor, 1660. Admin. of estate
granted to widow Hannah March 11, 1694-5.
  Henry, Dover, proprietor, signed the combination in
1640. Taxed in 1648. Juryman, 1652.
Land assigned at Portsmouth Jan. 13, 1652 and in 1660.
With wife Ann, Jan. 6, 1679, conveyed homestead to son
Thomas, conditioned on life care of self and wife. Admin.
of his estate granted to widow Elizabeth April 26, 1686. See
also Bolles.

BENILL,
  John, [Portsmouth,] his wife Jone recd. per Richard
Sealy, 26 Oct. 1657, fish to the value of 16 li. 3 s. of Henry
Brooken. [P. Files.]

BENDALL,
  Philip, servant to Richard Cutt, before Pisc. court 26
July, 1660.

BERRIFFES,
  William, railed in a plantation on the point of the neck
of land, near a creek called Salt Creek in Piscataqua river,
and called it The Farm, before 6 (10) 1645, when it was
sold by Francis Williams. [Suff. De. I.]

BERRY, BERRIE, BURY,
  Ambrose, planter, Saco, taxed in 1636; had lawsuit in
Maine court May 7, 1637. Bought land of Vines 20 April,
1642. [York De. VII.] Residing at Cape Porpoise, he took

the oath of allegiance to Mass. govt. 5 July, 1653. Had share of marsh at Biddeford July 12, 1653. Ambrose, mariner, Boston, Mass. gave liberty 18 Sept. 1686, to John Hill of Saco, to set up two dams for the stopping of water for the use of a mill or mills upon his land adjoining Bulley's Creek in Saco.

John, Hampton. Wife Susanna; ch. John b. 14 Jan. 1659.

William, Strawberry Bank, sold house and land to Anthony Ellins 10 July, 1648. Grand jury man 8 (8) 1650; constable.

His widow Jane was appointed admin. of his estate 28 June, 1654. She m. 2, Nathaniel Drake, and with him deeded land on Great Island 9 Dec. 1669. James Berry, a son and John Berry and Joshua Foss, gr. ch. agreed June 13, 1717, on the division of certain lands which had been granted to William Berry about 60 years before.

See also Lock, Withers.

BEST,
Edward, shipman, Richmond Island, left the service of Winter in 1638. [Trel.]

BESTONE, BEESON,
Thomas, Kittery, proprietor about 1642. [Deposition of Robert Mendum.] Witness to Crockett's deed in 1647.

BICKFORD, BIGFORDE,
John, Isles of Shoals in 1642. [Trel.] Taxed at Dover Oct. 19, 1648. Grand jury man in 1650. Signed petition of I. of S. people for incorporation in 1653. Benjamin also signed. Licensed victualer in 1657. A John Bickford signed (with mark) a petition of Dover people to Gen. court 10 Oct. 1665.

Admin. of his estate was granted 24 June, 1662, to Philip Tucker.

"Old Bickford," fisherman, at Richmond Island in employ of Winter; sent home to England, sick, in 1637.

Priscilla, maid servant of Winter, 1636-7; money paid to her mother in England. [Trel.]
See also Williams.

BIGGS,

Thomas, yeoman, Exeter, 1643; may be the Thomas ae. 13, who came in the Blessing to Boston in July, 1635, lawsuits in 1644 and 1651; won a suit against neighbors for slandering himself and wife Hester in 1647. Had grant of land for a sawmill at Pascasuck river, and other lands at Lamprell river; sold these 8 May, 1652, to Edward Gyllman. Wife Hester joined him in a deed of land 22 Oct. 1663.
See also Hall.

BILLINE, BILLING,

John, fisherman, Pascataquack, Kittery, equal partner of John Lander in house, land, swine, shallop, etc. 10 Jan. 1639. [York De. I.] His son John made over to his mother, Elizabeth Thomas, 12 Aug. 1661, all his right and title in land and cattle for her life; then to return to himself; deed confirmed 23 June, 1680. [York De. III.] Perhaps this son is the J. B. inventory of whose estate was taken Dec. 3, 1690. [York De. V.]
See Lander.

BINNS, see BYNNS.

BLACKAPPE,

Henry, witness to a deed of Andrews in Kittery in 1648.

BLACKWELL,

Jeremiah, came in the ship Truelove to New England xix Sept. 1635, aged 18 years. We find him at Exeter, proprietor, in 1639.

BLAISDELL, BLEASDELL,

Ralph, one of the deputies of Agamenticus June 25, 1640.

BLAKE,

Jasper, fisherman, seaman, Hampton. He recd. a deed of gift of land 10 Oct. 1657, from his "kinsman," Rev. Timothy Dalton.
Wife Deborah; ch. Timothy b. 16 (8) 1649, Deborah b. 15 (11) 1651, (m. Eleazer Elkins,) John b. 31 (8) 1656, Sarah b. 14 (12) 1658, d. 29 (7) 1660, Sarah b. 30 (4) 1661, Jasper b. 16 (9) 1663, Samuel b. 6 (4) 1666, [Norf. Rec.], Dorothy b. 17 (7) 1668, Philemon b. 23 (3) 1671, Maria b. 1 (1) 1672-3.
He d. Jan. 5, 1673-4. Will dated 18 July, 1673, prob. 14 (2) 1674, beq. to wife Deborah, children Timothie, Israel, Deborah, John, Jasper; provision made for "small children." "Cossen" Samuel Dalton, overseer.
The widow d. 20 (10) 1678. [Hamp. De. II, 324.]
See also Bachiler, Dalton.

BOAD, BODE, BOADE,

Henry, gent. Saco, brought suit in court Feb. 7, 1636; juryman, 1640. Rem. to Wells; selectman, 1646. [York De. I.] There is a letter from him to Gov. John Winthrop in the Winthrop Collection [Mass. Hist. Coll. 5th series vol. 1], dated Gorgeana, Jan. 29, 1648, endorsed "Cosin Boad." Petition for the rights of the people of the Eastern part of New England May 6, 1653. [Bax. MSS.] Took oath of allegiance to Mass. govt. 5 July, 1653. Commissioner for small cases. Letter to General Court of Mass. regarding affairs in Maine, May 6, 1653. [Bax. MSS.] Made contracts 12 (4) 1655 with Harl. and Wm. Symonds for management of farm.
Will signed 8 Jan. 1654, prob. 16 July, 1657, beq. to wife Ann, whom he made executrix; appointed his "cossons Mr. John Winthrope Esqr. and Tymothy Daulton minister of Hampton" overseers. [York De. I.] The widow m. 2, Samuel Winesley of Salisbury; contract 6 Oct. 1657. [Norf. Rec.] They sold the farm to Harl. Symonds 16 (10) 1657.
See also Rishworth.

BOLLES, BOWLES, BOLES, BOULES, BOOLS, [BOLEN?]

Joseph, gent., Wells, testified before Maine court in 1640. His land at Cape Porpoise adjoined that of Morgan Howell in 1648. Subscribed to the oath of allegiance to Mass. govt. July 4, 1653. [Mass. Arch. 3, 219.] Clerk of the writs. The selectmen of Saco asked Dr. Childs to confirm the title to his land in 1654. [York De. I.] He sold land to Peter Hill 1659.

Will dated 18 Sept., prob. 29 Nov. 1678, beq. to wife Mary, sons Thomas, Samuel and Joseph, daughters Frost, Becke, Locke, Chadbourne, and Mercy B. Inventory in York De. V.

The record of marriage license of Nicholas Frost to "Mary Bollen of Monckleigh, gent." taken with the foregoing statements and the bequests of Morgan Howell, may point to Monckleigh, Devonshire, Eng. as the home of this family. But see the references in article of William S. Appleton [Reg. LII, 185] to the will of John Bolles of Clerkenwell, Mdx. co. Eng. in 1665, bequeathing to "my brother Joseph Bolles living in New England"; Mr. Appleton connects them with the Bolles family of Osberton, Northhamptonshire.

See also Howell.

BOLTER, BOALTER, BOULTER,

Nathaniel, Hampton, proprietor, sold land before July 8, 1644. [Norf. Rec.] Rem. to Exeter; signed petitions of inhabitants Sept. 7, 1643 and 29 (3) 1645. [Mass. Arch. 112, 8 and 39.] but returned to Hamp. Contracted to deliver pipe staves to Wm. Hilton of Dover "in May next, 1645." [Mass. Arch. 39, 70.] Signed petition in 1645. Was before Gen. Court of Mass. 2 May, 1649. Exchanged land with John Marian 24 (1) 1654. Deposed in 1685, ae. 60.

He m. Grace, dau. of Richard Swaine; ch. Mary b. 15 May, 1648, Temperance b. 8 (11) 1650, Nathaniel b. 4 (1) 1653, d. 1 June, 1689, Joshua b. 1 (3) 1655, Joshua b. 23 (11) 1656, Rebecca b. 12 (8) 1659, Joseph d. 15 (9) 1661,

Grace b. and d. 1662-3, Hannah b. 27 (4) 1665, Elizabeth b. 27 (12) 1668-9, John b. 2 (10) 1672. He d. March 14, 1694-5. The inventory of his estate was taken April 16, 1695.

See also Swain, Sawers.

BOND,
    Nicholas, York, juryman in 1651; his land adjoined that of John Parker. Took oath of allegiance to Mass. govt. 22 Nov. 1652. He m. Jane, widow of Henry Simson, q. v.

BONE,
    Thomas, of Saltash, Eng. left the employ of Winter at Richmond Island in 1638. [Trel.]

BONITHON, BONYTHON, BONIGHTON,
    Captain Richard, Settled at Saco.

His name stands at the head of the list of Commissioners who held court at Saco 25 March, 1636, and the session was held at his house. His son John was before the court at the same meeting.

He had a tract of land by way of exchange from Robert Child 14 July, 1647, for his son in law Rich: Comeman, betwixt the river of Saco and Tho: Williams his house, etc. Witnesses Eliza and Lucretia Bonighton.

See also Batson, Child, Comeman, Foxwell, Lewis, Watts, Wiggin.

BOOTH,
    Robert, Exeter, discovered a piece of meadow about 3 miles south of the town in 1644, as he deposed. Sold house and lands to John Legat before 29 (5) 1650. Rem. to Wells; took oath of allegiance to Mass. govt. 5 July, 1653. He had liberty to "exercise his guift," i.e. to conduct religious meetings, until a minister could be procured. Was one of the commissioners of the town. Resided at West Saco, (Biddeford). Selectman, 1654. He deposed Aug. 13, 1668, aged

about 66 years, and Sept. 11, 1682, ae. about 80 years. [York De. I.] Deborah, his wife, witnessed a deed with him 21 July, 1650.

Will, unsigned, attested in court by witnesses 18 March, 1672-3, beq. to wife Deborah, daus. Mary Penewell, Ellner, Martha, and Rebecca, sons Symon and Robert; the mill to be divided between the sons.

BOWDEN, BOUDEN, BOADEN, BODEN,
 Ambrose, Sen., and Ambrose, Jun., took the oath of allegiance to Mass. govt. at Spurwink July 13, 1658.

 John, Black Point, was paid by Winter in 1640 for ducks and geese. [Trel.] Juryman at Biddeford, 1653. He deposed June 18, 1660, about Mr. Jordan's giving Ambrose his choice of lands at a former time.

 William, Piscataqua, signed the combination in 1640. Lawsuit in 1642.

 See also Hatch.

BOYSEY,
 John, a witness to Samburne's sale to Cutts in 1650.

BRACKETT, BRAKITE,
 Anthony, Piscataqua, a witness before the grand jury in 1648; juryman in 1650. Had 30 acres of land assigned him at Portsmouth in 1652. Took oath of allegiance 2 July, 1657. He deposed 27 June, 1660, ae. about 47 years. Will Sept. 11, 1691, proved July 11, 1692; daus. Jane Haines, Eleanor Johnson; gr. daus. Kasia Brackett and Roose Johnson; gr. son Samuel Brackett; son John executor.

 See also Mitten.

BRADBURY, BRADBERY,
 Mr. Thomas, mentioned in a letter of Sir Ferdinando Gorges, 11 Aug. 1636, "To my beloved Nephew Capt. William Gorges, Gouvenor of New Somersett in New England, or in his absence to Mr. Richard Vines, or Mr. Thomas

Bradbury, or any of them, give these." As an agent of Gorges he sold land to Edward Johnson 5 May, 1636. Rem. to Salisbury, Mass.; proprietor, 1639, frm. May 13, 1640, judge, schoolmaster, clerk of the writs, county recorder, deputy. He m. Mary, dau. of John Perkins; ch.: Wymond b. 1 (2) 1637, Judith b. 2 (8) 1638, (m. Caleb Moody,) Thomas b. 28 (11) 1640, Mary b. 17 (1) 1642, (m. John Stanyan,) Jane b. 11 (3) 1645, (m. Henry True,) Jacob b. 17 (4) 1647, William b. 15 (7) 1649, d. 4 Dec. 1678, Elizabeth b. 7 (9) 1651, (m. John Buss,) John b. 20 (2) 1654, d. 2 Nov. 1678, Ann b. 16 (2) 1656, d. in 1659, Jabez b. 27 (4) 1658, d. 28 April, 1657. He d. March 16, 1694-5; will dated 14 Feb. 1693-4, prob. March 26, 1695; aged and weak; beq. to grandchildren Thomas and Jacob B., who should pay to their aunt True a certain sum and give a receipt to their bro. William about the admin. of their father's estate, and pay an annuity to their grandmother; to daus. Mary Stanion and Jane True; to grandchildren Elizabeth Buss; five pounds to the selectmen for the poor; wife Mary and dau. Judith Moody execs.

The wife was accused in 1692 of being a witch; was tried and sentenced, in spite of many testimonials as to her worthy character; but escaped execution by the turning of the tide of persecution. She died Dec. 20, 1700.

See also Wheelwright.

BRADSHAW, BRADSHEW,

Richard, Spurwink, received a patent for land at S. from Capt. Walter Neale, and settled on it. Sold it about 1630 to Richard Tucker, who again sold it to George Cleve. [Trel.]

See also Cleve, Tucker.

BRAGDON,

Arthur, planter, York, constable in 1640; witnessed a deed July 3, 1647; took oath of allegiance to Mass. govt. 22

Nov. 1652, and was appointed lieutenant of the militia. Town officer. His wife Mary witnessed a deed with him in 1661. Sold land 1 Nov. 1668, to Andrew Rainking, planter, of the same place. He deposed 5 June, 1665, ae. about 67 years; deposed again 6 July, 1671, aged about 74 years, as to what he heard Mr. Tho. Rogers say before he went to England, which was in 1643. [York De. vol. 1, Part II, folio 14.]

Made deed of gift to son Thomas 25 May, 1678, conditioned on life maintenance for himself and wife. [York De. V.]

He died during the year. Inventory of his estate was filed 2 Oct., 1678.

See also Maxwell.

BRAND, BRANDE,
Andrew, (sic legitur,) took oath of allegiance to Mass. govt. at Spurwink 13 July, 1658.
See also Trickey.

BRANDE, BRAWNE,
Michael, Pascataquack, bought house of John Davis of Bloody Point 30 June, 1651. Resided at Kittery. Was one of those who gave testimony regarding one who spoke threatening words against the Commissioners of Mass. Bay, Nov. 15, 1652. [Bax. MSS.] In court in 1661. George, who, by wife Mary, had son Michael born at Dover 1 June, 1679, may be of his family. [Dov. Hist. Coll.]
See also Dixon.

BRANSON, BRONSON, BRANCEN, BRAUNSON,
George, Dover, had lawsuit in 1647; was taxed Oct. 19, 1648. Took oath of allegiance at York 22 Nov. 1652. Deposed in the Gunnison case in 1654, ae. about 44 years. [Bax. MSS. I.]

He was killed by his bull; inquest held July 2, 1657. John Ault and Richard York admin. on his estate.

BRAY,
Richard, Exeter, juror, propr., 1657. Admin. granted April 10, 1666, to widow Mary, and property divided to her and the two children, John and Mary.

BRETNALL,
John, Isles of Shoals, signed town petition 18 (3) 1653.

BROOKINS, BRAKIN, BROOKING, BROOKEN, BROOKINGS,
William, husbandman, Portsmouth, lot assigned him in 1652; grand jury man in 1655.
He m. Mary, dau. of Thomas Walford. Sold land on Great Island 2 June, 1667.
The inventory of his estate was taken Nov. 26, 1694 by John Savage and John Lang; filed by widow Mary.
See also Benill.

BROOK, BROOKS,
Thomas, alias Basil Parker, came early to the Piscataqua in the employ of the Shrewsbury Merchants, q. v. As T. B. he was an attendant at a court in Saco June 25, 1640. As B. P. he witnessed deeds of the Indian Sagamore Roles to Humphrey Chadburne in 1643 and 1646; was recorder of deeds in 1648. Edward Colcord sued the Shrewsbury Merchants in 1649 for wages due this man.
John Allcocke, as executor of his will, sold Dec. 31, 1652, land which "Tho. Brooks alias Basill Parker" had formerly owned in partnership with Peter Wyre.
See also Hilton, Hocking, Wiggin.

BROWN, BROWNE,
Andrew, planter, Black Point, in partnership with William Smith, bought land of Cleve 29 Sept. 1651. Took oath of allegiance to Mass. govt. at Spurwink 13 July, 1658. Rem. to Boston. Conveyed to John and Samuel B., sons of his son William B. of Boston, mariner, March, 1695-6, his tract

of land in Scarborough where he dwelt before the Indian war. A third son, William, sold his right in the same tract, after his father's death, 10 Jan. 1710. [York De. VII.]

Arthur, merchant, Casco, from about 1633. [Deposition.] Mentioned in records of Maine court April 4, 1637. Witnessed the transfer of land from Richard Vines to John Winter 30 June, 1637. Sold fish to Winter in 1642. [Trel.] Was one of the men — said to be of Winniganset — associated with Robert Morgan against whom Purchase brought suit in 1641.

John, Senior, Hampton, proprietor June, 1640. Signed petition in Howard case in 1643. Bought a house and lot 27 (5) 1643. Deeded one-half of his farm 31 Dec. 1666, to son John. Sold land 17 March, 1670-1. Gave land to son in law Isaac Marston 4 April, 1677. Wife Sarah; ch. Mary b. 13 (7) 1655, Thomas b. 14 (5) 1657. [Norf. Rec.]

John Browne, aged 98 years, died the 28 Feb. 1686. [Dov. Hist. Coll.]

John, New Harbor, Pemaquid, bought of the Indian sagamore Somerset or Samoset 15 July, 1625, a tract of land extending from Pemaquid Falls to the head of New Harbor, thence to the south end of Muscongus island, running into the country North and by east 25 miles, then twenty eight miles northwest and by west, then south and by west to Pemaquid. Witnessed by Matthew Newman and William Cox. Acknowledged before Abraham Shurt, July 24, 1626. [Me. Hist. Coll. V, 191-5.]

This deed was recorded at Charlestown, Mass. Dec. 26, 1720, upon request of James Stillson and Margaret Stillson. [Book of Eastern Claims.] His son John Brown, of Framingham, Mass. deposed Feb. 9, 1720, aged about 85 years, that he lived with his father at New Harbor, near Pemaquid till he was about 30 years old, and that during that time his brother in law Richard Pearse bought land of the Indians.

His dau. Margaret m. Alexander Gould, q. v.

Nicholas, Portsmouth, lawsuit in Court at Dover in 1647.

He d. in 1648; inventory rendered 10 May, 1648 at Boston by Francis Matthews, Nicho. Shapleigh, William Sevey, Humfrey Lux and John Rayes. One third of the estate appertains to John Seeley, who was app. admr.; 3 houses and lands at Pascataqua river; an apprentice boy's time 8 years; debts paid to Wm. Hinckson, Maj. Sedgwick, Mr. Foster, Mr. Knight, Richard Waldron, Henry Sherburne and Chr. Lawson. [Reg. VII, 174.]

See also Bailey, Cox, Davis, Lane, Newman, Pennell, Shurt.

BRUEN, BREWEN,

Obediah, draper, of Shrewsbury, Eng. bought a share in the Piscataqua patent May 4, 1640, of Richard Percyvall, draper, of Shrewsbury. This he occupied but little while. Rem. to Plymouth; was proposed for a freeman of that colony March 1, 1640-1, but did not remain. Rem. to Gloucester, Mass. Frm. May 19, 1642. Town officer, deputy, surveyor of the arms. Sold his Piscataqua property June 21, 1642. Was one of the commissioners to end small causes. Rem. to New London, Conn.

See also Larkham, Rowley, Shrewsbury, Knight, Scammon, Wingfield.

BUCKNALL,

George, Casco, witness of a deed of Cleve to Jordan in 1651.

Roger, Richmond Island, one of the partners in fishing in 1639.

Money paid his wife in England on his account by Mr. Trelawney.

BUCKNER, BUCKNEY,

Charles, Dover, chosen clerk of the writs 26 July, 1660. Rem. to Boston; he and wife Mary sold Dover property to Job Clement 12 April 1668.

BULLE, BULLY,

Nicholas, fisherman, Winter Harbor, West Saco, (Biddeford) bought house and land 27 June, 1650. Mortg. house, stage, flake-room and mooring-place May 2, 1664, as security for the delivery of a quantity of fish. "Nicholas Buly the younger," who had an allotment of land in 1653, may have been a son.

BULGAR, BULLGAR,

Richard, bricklayer, planter, Boston, was paid for work at the fort by Mr. Pynchon in 1632; adm. chh. 13 (2) 1634. Ch. John bapt. 20 (2) 1634. Had allotment of 30 acres in 1637.

He was dism. to the chh. at the Falls of Paschcataqua 6 (11) 1638. Settled at Exeter; signed the combination. Sold "one bull calfe of 5 months old for 3 li." to Richard Parker, 8 (5) 1639. [L.] Was elected lieutenant in 1641, town officer in 1664. Res. at Dover in 1640. [L.] Residing at Boston, he had deed of land at York from John and Joane Smith in 1646, for the use of Henry Walton of Portsmouth, R. I. [York De. I.] He rem. to Rhode Island. Solicitor general in 1656.

BUNKER,

James, Dover, in 1648 and 1649; in court Oct. 11, 1651; grand jury man, 1659. Will Oct. 14, 1697, proved June 24, 1698. "Well stricken in age." Wife Sarah, son James, Jr.; rest to "all our children."

See Swain.

BURDETT, BURHEAD,

Rev. George, minister, Salem, Mass., 1634, frm. Sept. 2, 1635. Rem. to Dover in 1638. [W.] Won the people away from Gov. Thomas Wiggin to himself, and succeeded in obtaining control of affairs for some time. But opposition arose against him, coupled with charges of criminal conduct, for which he was censured and fined. He rem. to Ac-

comenticus [York]; sent a letter to England in the packet of John Winter in 1640. [Trel.] Mr. Thomas Gorges coming to govern the colony, found Burdett very criminal in his practises, and prosecuted him; Burdett appealed from the fine which was laid upon him; returned to England, but was there committed to prison. [W.] His housekeeper, Ann Mesant, m. Mr. Edward Godfrey.
See also Godfrey, Johnson, Larkham, Shrewsbury.

BUNT, BUNTE,
George, boatswain, Richmond Island, he and his son in the employ of Winter in 1639; summoned to court in 1641. [Trel.]

BURNHAM, BURNAM,
Robert, yeoman, Boston, sold house-lot in 1648. Bought land at Oyster River May 12, 1657. [Suff. De.] Rem. to Portsmouth; juryman, 1659. Rem. to Dover; carpenter, clerk of train band; selectman, 1660. Wife Frances; ch. Robert, b. at Boston 25 (7) 1647; d. at Dover Feb. 25, 1663; Robert, b. at Dover Aug. 21, 1664; Elizabeth, b. at Bo. 27 (8) 1651. He d. June 12, 1691; will proved Sept. 29 folg.; wife Frances, sons Samuel and Jeremiah; some things at Chebacco, some at Oyster River.

BURGESS, BURGESSE, BURGIS,
Richard, York, bought land July 7, 1654. He and partners proprietors in 1665. [Bax. MSS.] Testified 4 (8) 1661, concerning a grant of land made to Crockett by Mr. Thomas Gorges "before he went for England," which was in 1643.
Richard, gave testimony June 5, 1651, in court at Gorgeana June 27, 1643. Was in the employ of Lieut. Davis in 1659.

BURRAGE, BURRIDG,
John, husbandman, in the employ of John Winter at Richmond Island in 1639; from Thorne Combe, co. Devon, Eng.; returned and came again with wife Avis on a 3 years

contract which is given in Trel. papers. His widow m. Thomas Hammatt. [York De. 1, 154.]
William, who testified 25 July, 1681, ae. 33 years, was a son. [Court Rec. 1661.]

BURSLEY, BURSLY, BUSLY,

Mr. John, Dorchester, Mass. proprietor, freeman May 18, 1631; probably the John Burseley who m. [Joane] daughter of Rev. Joseph Hull at Barnstable about Nov. 28, 1639; wife admitted to chh. of Barn. 22 July, 1643. Constable, 1645. Ch.: "A child," d. Jan. 25, 1640; Mary, bapt. July 29. 1643; John, b. and d. 1644; Johannah, bapt. March 1, 1645-6; Elizabeth, bapt. March 24, 1649; John, bapt. April 11, 1652.

John, believed the same, Kittery, brought suit to Pisc. Court, 1642. Rem. to Exeter; signed petition of inhabitants to Gen. Court 29 (3) 1645; bought houses and lands of George Barlow 25 March, 1648; July 26, 1649, specified cows that he gave in part payment, one of which "I had of my brother Jones." [A.] Submitted to Mass. Bay authority in 1652. [Bax. MSS.] Inv. of Mr. J. B. rendered at Plym. Court by John Smith and John Chipman Aug. 21, 1660.

See also Heard, Toby.

BUSH,

John, Cape porpoise, had lease of land from Cleve 20 (7) 1647; assigned the same to Rich. Moore 8 July, 1650, and he to Gregory Geoferey 19 May, 1652. Took oath of allegiance to Mass. Bay July 5, 1653. He and his "now wife Grace" sold land 17 Dec. 1663. Public worship was sometimes held at his house before a meeting house was built. He d. in 1670 and the widow m. Richard Palmer. [See Hist. Ken. Port.]

See also Turbat.

BYNNS, BINNS,

Jonas, Dover, taxed in 1648. Signed petition in 1654. [Mass. Arch. 3, 447.]

CADOGAN, CODAGONE, CORDAGINS,
Philip, Isles of Shoals, petitioned with others 18 (3) 1653 for better defences. [Mass. Arch. 3, 215.]
Rice or *Richard,* fisherman, Isles of Shoals, York, had suit in court in 1648; bought land 24 June, 1650. Lawsuit in 1656. His attorney, Bryan Pendleton, sold land for him 30 June, 1659. Took oath of allegiance to Mass. govt. 22 Nov. 1652.

CAMMOCK, CAMOCK, CAMMOCKE,
Captain Thomas, "a near kinsman of the Earl of Warwicks," [J. J.], gent. Wife Margaret.
After he and his associates had "lived, planted and built in New England two years," he received Nov. 1, 1631, a patent from the Council for New England for 1500 acres of land on the East side of the river of Blacke Poynte; Neale, Vynes and Joslyne were authorized to give him possession of the same. His eastern boundary was Spurwink river, as the land was laid out.
He was one of the Commissioners who held court at Saco 25 March, 1636.
He and his wife made a joint deed of all his land except 500 acres to Henry Jocelyn, Esq. 2 Sept. 1640; and the court recognized this deed as his will 18 Oct. 1643; the remainder of his property they gave to his widow.
See Jocelyn.

CAMMOND,
Abel, Piscataqua, signed the combination in 1640; he had a suit in court in 1642; one in York court in 1650.

CAMPION, CHAMPION,
Clement, mariner, Strawberry Bank, had a lawsuit Sept. 3, 1641. Carried freight from Casco to Isles of Shoals in 1643. [Trel.] Made voyage to Barbadoes in 1647. May 6, 1648, his accounts with Thomas Janverie were audited, covering the business of "the good ship the Constance, bound

for Virginia," of which he was "master, 27 Oct. 1637."
[A.] Sold house and land at Strawberry Bank to Thomas
Burton of London before 4 (11) 1650. Sold a house and
land at Charlestown to Nicholas Davison April 13, 1647.
[Suff. De.]
 Richard Wayte of Boston, admin. of his estate, sold land
to Richard Cutt 3 Aug. 1659.
 Richard, "Champion," of Clifton, Dartmouth Hardnes in
the county of Devon, came to Piscataqua about 1652. His
widow Elizabeth made Mr. Francis Champernoone her attorney for settlement of his estate 30 Sept. 1659.
 See Cutt.

CANNAGE,
 Matthew, Richmond Island, one of Winter's fishing company in 1634. [Trel.]

CANNEY, CANNING, KANNY,
 Thomas, Piscataqua, signed the combination in 1640. Living at Bloody Point, he was one of those residents who petitioned about 1642 to be included in the town of Dover. [Mass. Arch. 3, 438.] Constable in 1648. His wife Jane was in court in 1655 upon some matters affecting her husband and her son in law Jeremy Tibbits, husband of her daughter Mary. Sons Thomas, Jr. and Joseph. He joined in a petition to the Gen. Court 10 Oct. 1665. Rem. to York.

CARPENTER,
 Ambrose, Hampton, proprietor, June, 1640.

CARTER, CARTERE, CATER, CATTER,
 Richard, Senior, planter, Dover, proprietor; sold house and land 24 June, 1648. His servant James Michemore was in court in 1651 and 1655. Joined in petitions of inhabitants to Gen. Court Sept. 7, 1643. [Mass. Arch. 112, 8, 9,] and to Oct. 1665. His son Richard made marriage covenant with Mary Ricord of Portsmouth, spinster, 6 April, 1672.

Richard, Senior. Westgostuggoe, Casco Bay, sold a house and land about 1652 to John Mayne. Testimony to this was given 26 June, 1682, by Agnes Carter alias Maddiver, ae. about 82 years, Richard Carter, ae. about 37 years, and John Coussons, ae. about 86 years.
See Dalton.

CASS,
John, planter, Hampton, proprietor. Sold land to Anthony Taylor in 4 mo. 1648. Frm. 10 (8) 1651. Had deed of land and house 1 April, 1671, from his son in law John Redman, Jr.
Wife Martha, dau. of Thomas Philbrick; ch.: Martha b. 4 (8) 1649, Mary, Joseph b. 5 (8) 1656, Samuel b. 13 (5) 1659, Jonathan b. 13 (7) 1663, Elizabeth b. 4 (4) 1666, Mercy b. 1 (6) 1668, Ebenezer b. 17 (5) 1671, Abigail b. 11 (11) 1673-4.
He d. April 7, 1675. Will dated 4 (3) 1674, prob. 13 April, 1675; beq. to wife Martha; ch.: Joseph, Samuel, Abigail, Elizabeth, Mercy, Jonathan and Ebenezer; daus. Martha and Mary have already had their portions; brothers Philip Lewis and Thomas Philbrick execs.

CATE,
James, Portsmouth, carpenter, had a bill against the town 4 Feb. 1660-1. He died May 15, 1677; admin. granted to his widow Alice. Mary Partridge, ae. 59 or thereabouts, deposed 8 June, 1702, that she knew that Edward Cate was born about 47 years ago, first child of James and Alice Cate. Other children shown in Probate papers; John Cate; Rebecca, wife of John Urin; Sarah, wife of Peter Babb; Mary, wife of Samuel Whidden, and Elizabeth Cate.

CAULL,
Richard, before Piscataqua court Aug. 16, 1655.

CHADBOURNE, CHADBURNE,
Humphrey, Dover, bought land of "Mr. Roles, sagamore

of Newichawannock," May 10, 1643. [York De. I.] Bought
house and lot 18 (3) 1645. [Suff. De. I.] Rem. to Kittery. Took oath of allegiance to Mass. govt. 16 Nov. 1652.
Made the acquaintance of Indians at "Winepesocket" in June,
1654, who desired to make a league of friendship with the
English; this he reported to the Gen. Court of Mass. in a
letter, dated Oct. 9, 1654. [Arch. 30, 34.]
Will dated 25 May, 19 Charles II, 1667, prob. 13 Sept.
1667; beq. to wife Lucy; 3 daughters, Lucy, Alice and
Katharine; sons Humphrey, James and William; cousin
Mary Fosse and sister Spencer. Uncle Nicholas Shapleigh
and cousins John Shapleigh and William Spencer overseers.
Estate appraised at 1713 li. [York De. II.] The widow
married second, Thomas Wills, mariner; contract 25 March,
1669. [York De. IV.] She m. third, Elias Stileman.

William, carpenter, made agreement March 4, 1634, in
company with James Wall and John Goddard, to come to
Piscataqua and settle on lands of John Mason. Built a house
on his part of the land, and gave it to his son in law Thomas
Spencer. [See deposition of Wall.]

He seems to be the man who resided in Boston in 1644;
his child Mary, by wife Mary, being there born (10) 1644.
But if so he returned to Kittery, where he took the oath of
allegiance to Mass. govt. 16 Nov. 1652.

See also Bolles, Brooks, Heard, Otis.

CHAMPERNOWNE, CHAMPERNOON, CHAMPERNOUNE, CHAMPERNOWN,

Francis, gentleman, captain, son of Sir Arthur and
Bridget (Fulford) C. born in Dartington, co. Devon, in
Oct. 1614, came to New England about 1639. His father
had received a commission in 1622 to send his ship, the
Chudleigh, to trade and fish on this coast; his mother was
a sister of Sir Francis Gorges. He resided first at Strawberry Bank, on lands now included in Greenland, adjoining
land of Thomas Wannerton. [Suff. De.] Lawsuits in Piscataqua and Norf. courts in 1642 and 1644. He sold Dec.

1648, to Capt. Paul White, merchant, of Pemaquid, one half of all the land in Maine which had been granted by Gorges to his father 13 Dec. 1636 and later, including the island called Champernowne's. Went to Barbadoes; left power of attorney with Thomas Withers of Kittery, who leased it to Samuel Haines for 2 years. Returned to Portsmouth and afterward to the island. 50 acres of land in Portsmouth assigned him in 1652.

Opposed the claims of Massachusetts Bay to the control of Maine; was one of the commissioners of Charles II May 23, 1661; yielded to Mass. in 1668. He m. before 1675 Mary, widow of Robert Cutt. He had no children. He deeded the island where he lived 8 July, 1684, to his wife Mary; one half of it at her death to go to his dau. in law Elizabeth Cutts.

He died between Nov. 16, 1686, the date of his will, and Nov. 28, 1687, when it was probated. He beq. to wife Mary; son in law Humphrey Elliot, Elizabeth, his now wife, and Champernowne Elliot, their son; sons in law Robert and Richard Cutt; daus. in law Bridget Scriven, Mary and Sarah Cutt; and to his servant maid, Elizabeth Small. [See Sketch in "John Mason."]

See also Campion, Hill, Hilton, Lewis, Pierce, Turbat.

CHANLER,
Goodman, Portsmouth, jury man, 1659.

CHAPPELL,
William, mariner, Richmond Island, drew a bill on Trelawney in 1634. Witnessed transfer of land to Winter in 1637. Made voyages across the Atlantic. [Trel.]

CHAPMAN,
Florence, York, removed, and made Wm. Hooke her attorney for business with Wm. Dixon, 23 (6) 1647. [A.]
See Dixon, Garland.

CHASE,

Aquila, mariner, Hampton, proprietor, 1640; signed petition in 1643. [Mass. Arch. 67.] Rem. to Newbury, Mass. Sold his Hampton property 4 Oct. 1649. [See P. of M.]

Thomas, Hampton, proprietor, recd. share in common lands in 1645. Wife Elizabeth; ch.: Thomas, Joseph, James, Isaac b. 1 (2) 1650, Abraham b. 6 (6) 1652.

He died before 5 (8) 1652, when admin. of his estate was granted to his widow Elizabeth. She "entered caution" 15 (1) 1652-3 respecting 10 acres of land he had bought of Hen. Ambrose. The court allowed 48 pounds out of the estate to the five children, Thomas, Joseph, James, Isaac and Abraham, 4 (8) 1653, and the widow gave bonds for payment thereof in due time. She married second, John Garland. See also Green, Philbrick, Robie.

CHATTERTON,

Jane, "ux . . . Chatterton," was bound by Piscataqua court in 1642 to answer at next court or else go to her husband. Order repeated in 1646.

Mighill, a witness at Piscataqua in 1647.

William, a legatee and the executor of the nuncupative will of James Woodward [Portsmouth?] in 1648. "Goodman Chatterton's house" had 10 acres of land in Portsmouth assigned to it 13 Jan. 1652.

CHESLEY, CHESLIN, CHASTLY,

Philip, Dover, witness to deed of Larkham in 1642. Taxed in 1648. In court for family troubles in 1646 and 1651. Deeded his property to his wife and children, making Capt. Thos. Wiggin overseer, 28 June, 1661.

Will dated Dec. 18, 1695, beq. to eldest son Samuel and sons James, Philip and Ebenezer; rest to wife Sarah.

CHILD, CHILDS,

Robert, doctor, planter, proprietor at Nashaway (Lancaster) in 1644. He purchased the Oldham and Vines patent of land about Saco 22 (8) 1645. [A.] Joined others in petitioning the Mass. Bay govt. in 1646 for the privilege of citizenship without church-membership, etc. Made himself exceedingly obnoxious to the authorities and was arrested repeatedly and confined in his house in Boston; "being a person of quality," he was not punished as severely as others; had a brother a Major of a regiment in Kent. [W.] A stockholder in the Iron Works Company. Spent some time at Saco. Traded land with Richard Bonithon 14 July, 1647. Returned to England, and was arrested there for vilifying the Mass. govt.; was discharged on promising that he would cease to do so. [W.]

See also Nason.

CHILSON,
Walsingham, Saco, proprietor in 1659. [York De. I.] Gave house, land and goods to his son William 19 June, 1669.

CHRISTOPHERS,
Christopher, Portsmouth, deposed 18 June, 1660, ae. 26 years. [P. Files.]

CIRMIHILL, CARMIGHEL,
John, York, bought land and house 26 Dec. 1660. Sold property 15 March, 1668.
Estate settled June 23, 1678. [York De. V.]

CLARK, CLARKE,
Anthony, Richmond Island, one of Winter's fishermen, 1639-40.
Arthur, Hampton, proprietor, 1640; frm. March 13, 1640. Rem. to Salem, Mass.
Edward, Wells, took oath of allegiance July 5, 1653. Juryman for Cape Porpoise at York in 1656; d. there in 1661. Wife Barbara, ch. Samuel, Sarah (m. James Harmon), William, Edward.
Edward, Portsmouth; land assigned Oct. 19, 1659. He

was drowned shortly before June 17, 1675, when inventory of his goods was taken, brought into court at Dover March 28, 1676, and admin. granted to the widow Mary. Ch. by first wife, John and Sarah, were bound out till of age, the former to Capt. Cutt and Elias Stileman, the latter to her aunt Sarah Waterhouse. The widow and the three ch. she had by him provided for. Lived at "Docters Island."

John, Portsmouth, worked for the town and was creditor Feb. 4, 1660. He made will April 25, 1700, "aged"; beq. to wife Elizabeth, sons Jacob and Joseph. Proved July 20, 1700.

Oliver, Richmond Island; left Winter and with others "went Westward" in 1636. [Trel.]

Thomas, with Gibbons at Newichewanock in 1633.

See also Andrew, Gaile, Hook, Mitten, Reynor, Taylor.

CLAYS, CLYES, (See Cloyes in P. of M.)

John, brought suit against Champernowne in Pisc. court in 1644. John (the same?) of Falmouth, witnessed a deed to John Phillips May 3, 1658.

Jonas, of Wenham in 1643; was before Grand Jury at Dover as witness in 1648. Rem. to Wells. His wife Mary was dau. of Elizabeth, wife of Stephen Batson. (1661).

CLAYTON,

Thomas, Dover, proprietor, 1650.

CLEMENTS, CLEMENT, CLEMENTE,

Job, son of Mr. Robert, who came from Coventry, Warwick, [P. of M.] one of the pioneers of Haverhill, Mass. tanner, resided some time at Haverhill. Rem. to Dover. Juryman in Norf. court in 1648. With wife Lydia sold land in Hav. and Dov. 17 March, 1657-8. Sold a tract given him by the town of Hav. 21 Feb. 1658-9. Bought land at Dov. 21 (4) 1662.

He m. 1, 25 Dec. 1644, Margaret, dau. of Mr. Thomas Dummer alias Pyldrym, of Chicknell, co. Hants, Eng. and

Newbury, Mass.; ch.: b. at Hav. John b. 17 Nov. 1646, Job b. 17 April, 1648, Mary b. 12 Dec. 1651. He m. 2, Lydia —; m. 3, Joanna —.

Will, 4 (7) 1682, prob. Nov. 9, 1683; son Job; wife Joanna to have whatsoever she brought with her; grandchild Jane Kenney, land formerly given to her father; to the poor and the church of Dover.

See also Buckner.

CLEVE, CLEEVE, CLEAVES, CLEEVES,

Mr. George, Esquire, as designated in the patent of Gorges to him 27 Jan. 1636, came to New England about 1630. Settled at Spurwink, built a house, planted, etc. having a promise from Gorges of 200 acres of land, as he claimed. In 1632 he bought a share in the patent which Richard Tucker had purchased of Richard Bradshaw. John Winter, as agent of Robert Trelawney, ejected him from the land in 1633, and seized upon his houses. [Testimony in Maine court at Saco June 25, 1641.] He had a lawsuit in court at Saco 25 March, 1636. He visited Boston in 1643 with Mr. Rigby, "a lawyer and a parliament man, wealthy and religious," who had purchased the "Plough Patent"; they sought to obtain the help of Mass. in establishing the claims of that patent; desired to join "the consociation of the United Colonies." [W.] He petitioned the Gen. Court of Mass. 5 (3) 1645, "on behalfe of the people of Ligonia," asking protection against the claims of Mr. Vines and others, basing his claims on the Rigby patent. [Mass. Arch. 3, 179.] As agent of "Collonell Alexander Rigby, President and proprietor for the province of Laconia," he leased lands in 1651. Took oath of allegiance to Mass. govt. 13 July, 1658. As deputy president of the Assembly of Lygonia, 22 (7) 1648, he was chairman of the committee to sit at Richmond Island and report on the estate of Winter.

He deeded 20 May, 1658, to his grandchild Nathaniel Mitten, land adjoining that formerly granted to his father Michael M. Was sued by Robert Jordan in 1659, and his goods attached in a rough manner; bed and clothing taken from his sick wife, then 87 years of age.

Nathaniel Mitten was alleged by "Richard Powssley of ffalmouth" in 1687, to have been a grandson of Cleve.

See also Bradshaw, Bucknall, Jordan, Macworth, Moses, Tucker, Winter.

CLIFFORD, CLIFFER,

John, husbandman, Salisbury, Mass. proprietor in 1640; rem. to Hampton. Sold houselot in Salis. in 1642. Bought land 9 (8) 1651. His dau. Hannah had a bequest 24 May, 1657, from Susanna, wife of Thomas Leader of Boston, of 18 shillings "which is in the hands of her father."

He m. 1, Sarah —; He m. 2, 28 (7) 1658, Elizabeth Richerson; she d. Dec. 1, 1667; he m. 3, Bridget, widow of John Huggins. Ch.: John bapt. May 10, 1646, Israel, Hannah b. 15 (2) 1649, Elizabeth b. 4 (2) 1650, Elizabeth b. 31 (6) 1659, Hester b. 24 (12) 1661, [Isaac] b. 14 (12) 1663-4, Mary b. 8 (12) 1665-6, d. 30 (8) 1667.

He deposed 13 April, 1675, ae. 60 years. [Norf. Files, III.]

The time of his death is not on record. The widow Bridget made will Sept. 1, 1679, prob. Aug. 26, 1680; beq. to sons Nathaniel and John Huggins, dau. Bridget Mattoone and her dau. Mary.

See also Haborne.

CLIFTON,

William, boatswain, seaman, Portsmouth, received land of Mr. Williams at a very early date, and sold it about 1640 to Walter Abbot. [Deposition of Jane Drake.] Married a wife before 1638. [Depos. of John Jones.]

COBB,

Peter, Richmond Island, bought goods of Winter in 1639.

COCK, COCKS, see Cox.

CODOGAN, see Cadogan.

COHAM,
Thomas, witness to a deed of Francis Williams to Richard Commins in 1646. Perhaps a resident of Strawberry Bank.

COFFIN, COFFYN, COFFENS,
Isaac (Coffens) Portsmouth, "received as a tradesman" Dec. 16, 1659.

Peter, — son of Mr. Tristram, a pioneer of Massachusetts who resided at Haverhill, Newbury, Salisbury and Nantucket, believed to be of the family at Brixham, Eng. settled at our Dover in his early manhood and was a citizen of value. Signed petition to Gen. Court 10 Oct. 1665. [Mass. Arch. 106, 160.] He deposed 19 Jan. 1660, aged about 30 years, relative to the methods of the lumber business, and sales he made for Lt. Richard Cooke to Elias Stileman. [Es. Files.] Wife Abigail; ch.: Abigail b. 20 Oct. 1657, Peter b. 20 Aug. 1660, Jethro b. 16 Sept. 1663, Trustrum b. 18 Jan. 1665, Edward b. 20 Feb. 1669, Judith b. 4 Feb. 1672, Elizabeth b. 27 Jan. 1680. [Dover Hist. Coll.]

Joseph Austin, in his will, mentions "my brother Peter Coffin."

He d. 21 March, 1715, at Exeter, in his 85th year; "late judge of his majesty's superior court of judicature, and first member of his majesty's council of the province, a gentleman very serviceable both in church and state." [Boston News Letter.]

See also Heard, Starbuck.

COLCORD, COLCOTT,
Edward, yeoman, planter, Salem, 1637. Rem. to Dover. He contracted Nov. 5, 1639, to deliver clapboards "at Pascatt rivers mouth." [L.] Signed the combination in 1640. Proprietor in 1642. Lived at York in 1644. [Mass. Arch. 39, 70.] Rem. to Hampton; proprietor and commoner 23 (12) 1645. Bought a mill of James Wall in 1652. Lawsuit

with Capt. Thos. Wiggin in 1654. Suit before Gen. Court of Mass. in 1658. [Mass. Arch. 39, 20-35.] He deposed 8 April, 1673, ae. about 56 years, regarding the gift of Mr. Stephen Bachiler to his dau. Hussey before he went to England. Dea. Robert Page who came from Ormsby, Eng. calls him brother and his wife Ann sister, in a deed of land; this tract he deeded 24 June, 1673, to his children, Sarah Hobbs, Mary Fifield, and the children at home, viz. Mehitable, Samuel, Shuah and Deborah.

Wife Ann; ch.: Jonathan d. 31 (6) 1661, Hannah, Sarah, Mary b. 4 (8) 1649, Edward b. 2 (12) 1651, d. 1667, Samuel, Mehitable, Shuah, Deborah b. May 21, 1664, Abigail b. July 23, 1667.

He d. Feb. 10, 1681-2.

See also Brooks, Redman, Shrewsbury.

COLE, COALE, COOLE,

James, before the court at Saco 25 March, 1636.

John, Cape Porpoise, took oath of allegiance to Mass. govt. 5 July, 1653.

Nicholas, Senior, Wells, took oath of allegiance to Mass. govt. 5 July, 1653. He deposed 23 Dec. 1678, ae. about 52 years. [York De. III.] Sold a tract of land 25 June, 1669, reserving a "burying place for his generation." His son Nicholas sold a tract 17 Feb. 1700, which had been originally laid out to his father.

William, carpenter, Boston; had an allotment of 2 acres Feb. 20, 1637, at Mt. Wollaston. Removed to Exeter, signed the combination 5 (4) 1639. Rem. to Hampton; proprietor in 1640. Sold land 17 Oct. 1656.

His wife Eunice was accused in 1656 of witchcraft; tried, convicted, sentenced to receive corporal punishment and be imprisoned for life. She petitioned in 1662 to be set at liberty after suffering so much punishment, chiefly pleading the needs of her husband, "88" years of age, and the ruin of their small property which she had helped to collect during 20 years. [Mass. Arch. 10, 281.] Her petition was granted on condition of her departing from the jurisdiction; but she could not avail herself of the decision because she could not pay arrears or give bonds, and she remained in prison several years longer.

He d. 26 (3) 1662, "aged 81 years." Will dated 26 May, 1662, prob. 14 (2) 1663, beq. to wife Unice her clothing which was left with him; all the rest of his "free" estate he gave to Thomas Webster on condition of his keeping him comfortably during his life.

A deed was presented in court, dated 7 Nov. 1656, conveying all his estate to his wife Eunice. The court ordered the selectmen of Hampt. to take charge of the property, pay debts, and take care of the widow.

William, gent. grand jury man at Saco 25 June, 1640. Had grant of land from Gorges, adjoining that of Stephen Batson [in Cape Porpoise], 20 Sept. 1642. Witness of Gorges' deed to Wheelwright in 1643. Took oath of allegiance to Mass. govt. at Wells 5 July, 1653. Witnessed a deed in 1666, as he deposed 13 June, 1670. Deposed Aug. 1668, aged 41 years. [Bax. MSS. VI.]

See also Bonython, Dow, Powning, Royal, West.

COLLINS, COLLINGS,

Christopher, shoemaker, Scarborough, bought land of Abraham Jocelyn 10 Jan. 1659. He died, and admin. of his estate was granted to his widow Jane 26 July, 1666. His son Timothy rem. to Newbury, Mass. and sold 28 Dec. 1680, land at Blew Point (Scarborough) derived from his father Christopher. Is he not the C. C. shoemaker, who was in Boston in 1639; rem. to Braintree; gave letter of attorney 15 (10) 1645 for collection of money due to his wife, Jane Groope, from Justinian Pearce of Plymouth, co. Devon, Eng.?

See also Neale.

COMMINS, COMMINGS, CUMMINGS, COMAN, COMEMAN, COMMONS,

Richard, fisherman, mariner, Isles of Shoals, had accounts with John Winter in 1639. Partner of Thomas Turpin in buying a plantation on Pascataqua river 6 (10) 1645. Son in law of Richard Bonython, for whom he obtained land from Robert Child in 1647. Lot assigned him at Portsmouth in 1652. Took oath of allegiance to Mass. govt. 5 July, 1653. Had account with Robert Nash 27 (4) 1648. [Bax. MSS.] Signed the petition to Cromwell in 1657. He deposed 27 June, 1660, ae. about 57 years. [P. Files.] Testified in county court June 28, 1664, that he failed to appear as he ought to have done as a grand juror because "he was asked to assist Capt. Thomas Wiggin to the ordinary."

Reference to son Thomas Cummings, Court Record, 1661.

Will dated 19 June, 1678; "aged and infirm"; prob. 24 June, 1679; beq. to dau. Jane Joce and her children Richard, Samuel, Jane, Thomas, John, Margaret and Mary, Richard being the principal heir and joint executor with his mother; a parcel of land to the town to be used for the school-house.

See also Bonython, Cohan, Leach, Michmore, Turpin.

COMPTON,

John, one of the associates of Wheelwright in buying the Exeter lands of the Indians in 1638, and recipient of a grant of land there, did not remain permanently in the region but kept his home in Roxbury and was afterward a resident of Boston.

CONDOGAN, see Cadogan.

CONLEY, CUNLEY, CONLY,

Abraham, Kittery, with consent of his wife, sold land and house next to that of William Everet 24 June, 1648. Took oath of allegiance to Mass. govt. 16 Nov. 1652. Sold land 8 Dec. 1675.

Will dated March 1, 1674, prob. March 5, 1690-1, beq. to Nathan and Abraham, sons of son in law Nathan Lord; to Adrian Fry, "with whom I now live"; to neighbor John White and Robert Allen. Inventory in York De. V.

CONNELL,
Sarah, servant of Walter Abbot, gave testimony in court 16 Aug. 1655; had told "her countrymen" about the case.

COOK, COOKE,
Peyton, gent. formed partnership for clapboard making at Saco 27 Jan. 1635. [York court rec.] Traded with Winter in 1640. Clerk of Lygonia Assembly in 1648. [York De. I, 67.]
See also Wiggin.

COOPER,
William, at Pascataqua with Wanerton in 1633. [Gibbons' letter.]

CORBIN, CORBINE, CORBYN,
Robert, Casco, took oath of allegiance to Mass. Bay govt. at Spurwink July 13, 1658. He cleared and possessed a meadow from about that time; "he was slain by the Indians in the late war." [Depos. of George Ingersoll June 24, 1685.]

CORNISH,
"One Cornish, dwelling some time in Weymouth, removed to Aconienticus," was found drowned in 1644, and his wife executed for his murder. [W.]
Thomas, Exeter, with Gowen Wilson bought land of Thomas Jones in 1650. Signed petition to Gen. Court of Mass. 24 (3) 1652. Prosecuted a neighbor for slandering his wife 14 (4) 1653.
Wife Mary; ch. b. in July, 1648. [Norf. Rec.]

COTTON,
William, Strawberry Bank, juror and constable at Dover Court 1 (8) 1651. Took oath of fidelity July 11, 1659. Had lands assigned him as an inhabitant of Portsmouth Jan. 13, 1652. He deposed June 27, 1660, ae. about 46 years. [P. Files.]

He d. before Dec. 19, 1678, when the inventory of his estate was taken; the court gave the widow Elizabeth 200 li. and household goods needful; to son John a double portion; rest to ch. William, Joseph, Thomas, Benjamin and Sarah (who m. Edward Beal). William Ham beq. to "daughter Elizabeth Cotton and her children" in his will, Dec. 21, 1672. See Rev. Daniel Maud's will.

COUCH,
    Mr. *John,* York, took oath of allegiance Nov. 16, 1652.

COUSINS, COSSONS, COSENS,
    John, sailor, Casco, mentioned in records of Maine court April 4, 1637. Accounts with Winter in 1639. Testified 18 Sept. 1640, as to the name of Casco river which he had known for about 14 years. Deputy to Ligonia Assembly in 1658. [York De. I.] He deposed 26 June, 1682, ae. about 86 years. [York De. III.]
    Mr. *William,* Star Island, Isles of Shoals, grand jury man in court at Strawberry Bank (8) 1650. Sold a house he had built to Mrs. Marie Mendam 23 Dec. 1659.
    See also Carter.

COURTEOUS, see Curtis.

COVENTRY,
    Jonathan, his account was before Dover court 10 (8) 1649.

COWMAN, see Comeman.

COX, COCKS, COCK, COCKE, COXE,
    Moses, planter, Ipswich, rem. to Hampton about 1638. Margaret, wife of John Stubbin of Watertown, Mass. testified 19 (7) 1640, to purchasing of him "tried suet about the month of October last was twelve month, when he was going from Ipswich to live at Hampton first." [L.] Propri-

etor, herdsman, selectman. He m. 1, Alice —; she and her son John were drowned in the wreck of a vessel that sailed from Hampton for Boston Oct. 20, 1657. [Town rec.] He m. 2, June 16, 1658, Prudence, dau. of William Marston. Ch.: John, Mary, Sarah, Rachel, Moses b. 2 (9) 1649, Leah b. 21 or 25 (2) 1661, (m. James Perkins).

He d. May 28, 1687, ae. 93. Will dated 1 Nov. 1682, prob. July 18, 1687; "very aged"; beq. to wife Prudence, son in law James Perkins and dau. Leah, his wife; daus. Mary Godfree, Sarah Norris and Rachel Rawlings. Inventory 18 July, 1687.

William, a pioneer on the coast of Maine, in Pemaquid or its vicinity. Witnessed the deed of Summersett to John Brown of New Harbour, July 15, 1625. Witnessed Shurt's receipt to Elbridge in 1635. [A.]

William, either the above or a son, it is thought, bought a tract of land of Thomas Atkins at the mouth of the Kennebeck river, (Cox's Head,) his house being referred to in Robin Hood's deed to Thomas Webber, 29 May, 1660 [York De. III, 23,] and "lived there many years before the Indian war drove him off in the year 1677." He rem. to Salem, Mass. for refuge; his son William went back to Sagadahock about 1686, but was driven away again by the Indians. The father sold the land 26 July, 1693, his wife Mary joining in the deed. John Cock, born about the year 1661, and Thomas, born about 1664, testified in 1695 that they lived with their father John Cock, who was a "brother in law," i. e. half-brother, of William, upon that land in the right of said William. These men, John and Thomas, settled at Dorchester, and married respectively, Margaret and Mary, daughters of John Pope. [See Dorch. Pope Family.] [Es. De. IX. 142, and XI, 7. York De. VI, 140. Genealogy in Gen. Adv. I.]

CRAM, CRAME, CRAMME,

John, planter, Boston, proprietor, 1635. Rem. to Exeter; signed the combination 5 (4) 1639, and the petition in 1645. Rem. to Hampton; bought land in 1658; had deed of land

5 May, 1659, from Richard Swain, for love and brotherly affection.

He married first, Lydia — who is mentioned in the record of 1648 as having been mother of Joseph; he married second, Hester (Esther). Ch.: Benjamin, Thomas, Mary; Joseph, (drowned 24 June, 1648, ae. 15 years,) Lydia b. 27 July, 1648.

He and his wife Hester deeded land and effects 24 (12) 1665, to sons Benjamin and Thomas, who agreed to maintain them and pay to the daus. Mary and Lydia certain sums of money.

He d. 5 (1) 1682; "good old John Cram, one just in his generation." [Town rec.]

CRAWFORD, CRAWFORDE, CRAFFORD,

Stephen, Brabote Harbor, Isles of Shoals, an inhabitant who failed to attend court at Saco in 1640; was a partner of Wm. Sevey in fish business, proprietor about 1648.

He died; inventory of his estate presented in York court Oct. 15, 1647, and his widow Margaret m. 2, Thomas Willey. She was appointed admin. of the estate of her deceased dau. Susan in 1649, and guardian to her surviving dau. Sarah.

CRAWLEY, CRAWLIE, CROLY,

Thomas, Exeter, proprietor, signed the combination 5 (4) 1639. Brought suit in Norf. court in 1649 about a house, with Robert Sawers. Had a saw-mill in 1652 at "Crawley's Falls," (now Brentwood). Deposed in the Gunnison case 22 April, 1654, ae. 36 years. [Bax. MSS.] Lawsuit in 1657. Brought suit to protect his dau. Phebe from slander in June, 1660.

CROCKETT,

Thomas, husbandman, was with Ambrose Gibbons at Newichewanick in 1633. Made his home later at York; proprietor about 1641; [deposition of Nicholas Frost]. Sold house and land 21 Sept. 1647. Took oath of allegiance to

Mass. govt. 22 Nov. 1652. Testified in Gunnison case in 1654, ae. about 43 years. With wife Anne sold houses and land to Abraham Corbett, distiller, Portsmouth, 29 May, 1667.

His estate was admin. by his widow Ann 20 March, 1678-9. [York De. V.] After his death she m. Digory Jeffery; she joined with her sons Elisha and Ephraim C. 13 June, 1683, in sale of land. May 21, 1688, in consideration of money which had been paid for her deceased husband and her dau. Mary Barton, she deeded certain lands to her son Ephraim C. The latter, in his will in 1688, mentions father Thomas C. sisters Ann Roberts and Sarah Parrett, etc.

See also Sealey, Wormwood.

CROSS, CROSSE,

John, Wells, signed the Pascataqua combination in 1640. Juryman, 1647. Bound his son John to Edward Rishworth for 11 years, 12 April, 1650. Had a receipt in full from Rishworth Oct. 27, 1661. [York De. I.]

He and his son John died about Dec. 18, 1676, when inventories of both estates were taken. The son Joseph was appointed admin. of both. His son in law Francis Backus gave a receipt 14 Jan. 1677, for his wife's portion.

See also Moulton.

CROWTHER, CROWDER,

John, Strawberry Bank, in court in 1644; he deposed 24 (3) 1647, as to his being put in charge of "Wallertoone's house" at a former time. [Mass. Arch. 38 B. 48.] His wife was sent to Boston to be tried for some offence in 1648.

He died, and his estate was entrusted first to William Storer as admin. then to two other persons 8 (8) 1652, for the benefit of his creditors; land given to "Wm. Storer, marshall, for his service and venturing his life thereby."

See also Lane, Wormwood.

CUDDINGTON, CORDINGTON, CODDINGTON,

Stockdale, Roxbury. He and his wife Hannah recd. beq.

in 1643 from Elizabeth Hobbert. The wife Hannah, "an ancient woman," was buried July 20, 1644. He rem. to Hampton. Bought land 20 (10) 1648.

He d. soon after. Admin. was granted April 9, 1650, to his eldest son, John Cuddington, who, residing in Boston, sold the Hampt. land 15 (2) 1650. [Norf. Court rec.]

CURTIS, COURTIS, COURTEOUS,

Thomas, planter, York, proprietor, grand jury man in 1649; took oath of allegiance to Mass. govt. 22 Nov. 1652; signed the petition to Mass. govt. in 1654 and that to Cromwell in 1657. Sold land to Henry Lamprill, cooper, 18 March, 1683-4.

Will dated 19 April, 1680, prob. 1 Oct. 1706, beq. to sons Joseph, Dodivah and Job, daus. Abigail, Lydia, Sarah, Rebecca and Anne Curtis and Hannah Jynkins; had already given portions to sons Benjamin and Samuel C. "in a farm at Scituate."

William, Dover; the court ordered 28 June, 1650, that the town should care for him while he was lame, and pay for his cure; which he was to repay when able.

CUTT, CUTTS, CUT,

John, Portsmouth, gave promissory note to Lawrence Avery 7 July, 1650. [Court rec.] Took oath of fidelity to Mass. govt. July 2, 1657. With brother Richard sold land to bro. Robert July 25, 1658. He m. 30 July, 1662, Hannah Star; ch.: John b. 30 June, 1663, Elizabeth b. 30 Nov. 1664, d. 28 Sept. 1665, Hannah b. 29 July, 1666, Mary b. 17 Nov. 1669 (m. Samuel Penhallow), Samuel.

He died 27 March, 1681; was president of the Council at the time of his death. His will dated 6 May, 1680, codicil dated 3 Jan. 1680-1, prob. 9 April, 1681, bequeathed to sons John and Samuel, daughters Hannah and Mary, and wife Ursula; 100 li. to the town of Portsmouth toward a free school; to the church "to which I belong" 15 li. and to the poor of the town 30 li.; to the children of brother Robert

C., to cousin John Shipway and servant Bathiah Furber. Extensive lands, shipping, etc.

Richard, mariner and merchant, made a purchase of William Pomfret 24 (10) 1647. [Pisc. Court Rec.] Had houselot assigned in Portsmouth Jan. 13, 1652. Bought of Wm. Brenton of Boston, merchant, a house and land at Portsmouth, formerly in possession of Thomas Beard, after sold by Clement Campion to Thomas Burton, of London, grocer, 4 (11) 1650. [Suff. De.] Bought house and land at Kittery Aug. 29, 1650. Took oath of fidelity July 2, 1657. He was associate justice of the county court in 1664. Richard Leader calls him brother in a deed in 1656.
He made will May 10, 1675, prob. June 27, 1676; beq. to wife Eleanor; dau. Margaret Vahan (Vaughan) and her children; son William V.; dau. Bridget Daniel and her husband Thomas Daniel; bro. John and his wife and children; sister Ann and brother Shipway; their son John; the widow and children of bro. Robert Cutt; Mr. Joshua Moody and his children; cozen John Hole and his wife; the college; the church of Portsmouth. The widow in her will dated July 12, prob. July 29, 1684, makes bequest (among others) to brother John Aldersey's children £100, if any of them come or send within three years.

Robert, Kittery, witness, 1648, proprietor, 1650.
He made will June 18, 1674, giving all to wife Mary and son Richard. The widow m. (2) Mr. Francis Champernowne, who beq. to her ch. Elizabeth Elliott, Bridget Scriven, Richard, Robert, Mary and Sarah Cutt.
See also Bendall, Jackson, Paul, Webster, Windsor.

DALTON, DAULTON, DOLTON,

Philemon, linen weaver, ae. 45, with wife Hannah, ae. 35, and ch. Samuel, ae. 5 1-2, came in the Increase, April 15, 1635. A pioneer at Dedham, 1636. Rem. to Hampton; had authority to perform marriages 14 May, 1645. Rem. to Ipswich. He d. in June, 1662, Will dated Nov. 11, 1656, proved Oct. 14, 1662. Wife "Dorety" (Dorothy) son Samuel Dalton, daughter Mehitable Dalton; Hannah Dalton. The son Samuel deposed 14 (12) 1668, ae. about 30 years. [Norf. Files, 97.]

 Rev. Timothy, entered St. John's coll. Cambridge, Eng. Sept. 17, 1610, was ordained 19 June, 1614; vicar of Woolverstone, co. Suff. March 8, 1615; suspended by the bishop in April, 1636. Came hither soon after and settled at Watertown. Rem. to Dedham; adm. propr. 18 (5) 1637; frm. Sept. 7, 1637. Was one of the party sent by Ded. under permission of Gen. Court in 1638 to observe the southerly part of the patent. He contracted to saw 400 planks for a bridge, 1637. Sold his rights at Ded. in 1639. Rem. to Hampton, where he was elected "teacher" of the chh. June 2, 1639. He served with ability; opinions differ with regard to the issues which rose between him and Mr. Bachiler, "pastor" of the same chh. He gave certain lands to his kinsman Emanuel Hilliard, seaman, Jasper Blake, seaman, and to Nathaniel Bachiler, 10 (8) 1657. Mr. Henry Boad of Saco called him "cousin." Wife Ruth; ch. Samuel bapt. at Woolv. 12 March, 1617, bur. same day, Deborah bapt. 3 June, 1619, bur. 19 May, 1624, Timothie bapt. 10 Nov. 1622, Ruth bur. 28 Aug. 1624-5.

 He d. 28 (10) 1661, ae. about 84 years. [Hampt. rec.] Will dated March 8, 1657-8, proved April 8, 1662. Beq. his est. to wife; to brother Philemon and his son Samuel, and to cossen Barth. Dalton.

 The widow Ruth made, 22 March, 1663-4, to Nathaniel Bachiler, a deed of certain lands, conditioned on his providing for her in specified particulars till her death, and then paying legacies to Deborah, wife of John Smith; Elizabeth, wife of Joseph Merrie; Phebe, wife of Joseph Arnall; Joseph and George Parkers (Parkhurst;) Mary, wife of Thomas Carter of Woburn; Timothy and Benjamin Hilliard; Elizabeth Hilliard, dau. of Elizabeth Merrie; Abigail Ambross, dau. of the wife of John Severans; Mary, wife of William Fifield; Walter Roper and Hannah Willix. She

d. 12 May, 1666. In her will, dated 8 (10) 1655, inv. 24 May, 1666, she beq. to her cozens, Nathaniel Batcheler and his wife Deborah; John Smith, Jr.; Mary, wife to Mr. Thos. Carter of W.; Samuel Dalton (for his son Timothie,) and Deborah Smith.
See also Dearborn, Haborne, Hill, Perkins, Ward, Webster.

DAM, DAMME, DAME,
John, Dover, signed the combination in 1640; proprietor, 1642; taxed Oct. 19, 1648. Deacon. Signed petition of citizens to Gen. Court 10 Oct. 1665.
Wife Elizabeth; ch.: Mary b. 4 Sept. 1651, William b. 14 Oct. 1653, Susanna b. 14 Dec. 1661, Judith b. 15 Nov. 1666. [Dov. Hist. Coll.] Will May 19, 1687, recorded March 23, 1693-4. To sons John and William, daus. Elizabeth Whitehouse, Mary Cane and Judy Tibbets; gr. dau. Abigail Dam.
See also Hall.

DAVIS, DAVESS, DAVIES,
Daniel, Kittery, took oath of allegiance to Mass. govt. 22 Nov. 1652.
James, Senior, Hampton, had grant of a house lot in 1639. His son James was also proprietor in 1640. Signed petition in Howard case in 1643. One of the commissioners for trial of small cases in 1642-3. Rem. to Haverhill about 1646. Town officer. His wife Sissilla d. May 28, 1673. His dau. Judith m. Samuel Gile, and his dau. Sarah m. John Page. He or his son James deposed 14 (2) 1663, ae. about 60 years.
He d. Jan. 29, 1678, "ae. about 96 years"; will dated March 17, codicil added July 22, 1678, prob. in 1680; beq. to sons John, Ephraim, Samuel and James; dau. Sarah Page; grandchildren James, son of John, Stephen and Ephraim, sons of Ephraim, James, son of Samuel Gile. John, of Exeter, signer of petition of inhab. 1643, afterwards of Dover, clerk of market, etc. who d. in 1686, beq. a tract of land in Haverhill which his father James had bequeathed him.

John, blacksmith, Saco, 1653, later Cape Porpoise; preached without authority from church or government and was prohibited in 1680. Wife "Catterine."

John, York, had suit in Piscataqua court in 1640. With Arthur Brown sold mackerell to Winter in 1642. Took oath of allegiance to Mass. govt. 22 Nov. 1652, was appointed sergeant, and licensed to keep the ordinary. Deposed in the Gunnison case in 1653, ae. about 34 years. He m. Mary, widow of George Puddington; sold land to her son in law John Penwill 27 Feb. 1674. He deposed Oct. 1, 1678, aged about 73. [Bax. MS. VI.]

"Major John Davess, aged 70 years or thereabouts" deposed 30 May, 1683, about William Hilton.

He died before April 3, 1691, when the inventory of his estate was taken, which was rendered by his widow Mary. [York De. V.]

Nicholas, ae. 40, Sarah, ae. 48, Joseph, ae. 13, with Wm. Lock, ae. 6, cert. from Stepney parish, came in the Planter March 22, 1634. Res. at Charlestown; rem. to Woburn, 1640. Wife Sarah d. 24 (3) 1643. He m. July 12, 1643, Elizabeth Isaac. Rem. to York. Juryman Oct. 17, 1650. Took oath of allegiance to Mass. govt. 22 Nov. 1652, and was appointed constable.

Will dated 27 April, 1667, inventory rendered 12 March, 1669-70; beq. to wife Elizabeth; daughter Astine and her children, Mary and Sarah, cousins, Matthew Barnard, son of Matthew B. of Boston, and William Locke of "Owborne" [Woburn]; Mary, Elizabeth and Mehitable Dod: friends Capt. John Davis and Mr. Peter Weare overseers; wife executrix. Admin. of his est. in Plym. Col. given by Mass. Gen. Court to John Wales of Boston; inv. filed at Plym. 13 (5) 1673.

Robert, carpenter, a servant of Henry Taylor of Portsmouth, witness before grand jury in 1648. Was ordered 2 (8) 1651, to bring into court a certificate that his wife was dead; ordered 8 (8) 1652 to go to his wife in England by the first ship that sails. Sold land 4 Oct. 1660. Sold house and land at Sagamore Creek 31 Aug. 1667. [P. Files.]

Theophilus, Saco, assessed for minister's rate 7 (7) 1636, attended the court at Saco 25 March, 1636, in the capacity of "officer."

See also Andrews, Atkins, Brawne, Onion, Tristram.

DEAMAN, DEAMANT, DIAMONT, DYMENT, DEMOND, DAMON (?)

John, rope-maker, Kittery, bought house and land June 15, 1651. Took oath of allegiance to Mass. govt. 22 Nov. 1652. One of the appraisers in the Gunnison case in 1653. Selectman. Took Walter, son of John Winser, late of Hemmick, co. Devon, Eng. apprentice for 5 years from 9 Oct. next, May 3, 1660. Sold house and land on one of the Isles of Shoals 2 Nov. 1668, to Henry Maine and Andrew Deament, and another house with land Nov. 18, 1667, to his brother William Deaman.

Admin. of his estate was granted 9 July, 1667, to his son John.

DEARBORN, DEARBORNE,

Godfrey, Exeter, signed the combination 5 (4) 1639, and the petition for local court in 1645. Grand juryman, 1650. Town officer. Rem. to Hampton; bought house and land before 12 (1) 1658. [Norf. rec. I.]

He m. (1) —; he m. (2) Nov. 25, 1662, Dorothy, widow of Philemon Dalton. Ch. Thomas, Henry, Esther, Sarah, John.

He d. Feb. 4, 1685-6. Will dated Dec. 14, 1680; "aged"; beq. to wife Dorothy, ch. Thomas, Henry, John and "three daughters"; gr. ch. Ann Shatredg. Wife to have what was hers before he married her. Proved Aug. 26, 1686.

See Bachiler, Marian, Ward.

DEARING, DEERING,

George, house carpenter, came to Richmond Island in the Hercules; left the plantation July 10, 1637, claiming that his time was out. [Trel.] Rem. to Black Point. Deposed 30 June, 1645, concerning the fright that he, his wife and neighbors received from the shooting of Nash of Boston and his reckless companions. [Bax. MSS.]

Roger, who had sons Roger and Clement, d. in 1717; no evidence as to relationship with George yet found.

DENNET, DENNETT,
John, carpenter, Portsmouth, N. H.; may have come as early as 1660.

Freeman of Mass. Bay Colony May 15, 1670 (as of Portsmouth).

Wife Amy; children: John, b. Dec. 15, 1675; Amy, b. April 9, 1679, (m. John Adams); Joseph, b. July 10, 1681; Ephraim, b. Aug. 2, 1689. He d. May 1, 1709, "ae. 63 years." Alexander Dennett who settled about 1670 at Newcastle, N. H. is believed to have been a brother of John.

Will signed ("John Dennet") March 17, proved Aug. 1, 1709. Wife "Ammi," sons John, Joseph and Ephraim, dau. "Ammi" Adams; gr. dau. Margaret Adams; gr. dau. Mary Dennet "who is blind."

DERMIT,
William, was with Wanerton at Piscataqua in 1633. [Gibbons' letter to Mason.]

DIAMONT, see Deaman.

DINALL,
John, Portsmouth, took oath of fidelity in court 11 July, 1659.

DISHER,
Derman, Portsmouth, deposed 9 (9) 1659, regarding George Walton's land claim. [P. Files.]

DIXON,
William, cooper, York, had account with Florence Chapman through Wm. Hooke, 23 (6) 1647. [A.] Juryman

1649. Sold land 24 June, 1650, which he had bought of George Parker. Took oath of allegiance to Mass. govt. 22 Nov. 1652.
Will dated 13 Feb. 1665, prob. 16 June, 1666; beq. to wife Jonas, son James, dau. Susanna Frost, John Brawn, and the children of Henry Millbury.
See Chapman.

DONNELL, DONNEL, DUNNELL,
Henry, fisherman, planter, York, witnessed deed of Wm. Hooke 18 Oct. 1644; proprietor before 1648. [York De. I.] Took oath of allegiance 22 Nov. 1652. Signed the petition about Godfrey's claims in 1655. Mortg. houses, lands, fish houses, etc. in security for a contract to deliver a quantity of fish, Dec. 6, 1664. Made over to his son Joseph 29 Feb. 1671, his island called Jewell's Island, with boats, stages, flakes, and other things that pertained to the fishing business; Joseph agreeing to maintain him so long as he chose to remain on the island. [York De. VII.] He deposed 24 Sept. 1680, ae. about 78 years, regarding John Pullman's estate. [York De. V.] Wife Frances; their daughters Sarah and Margaret recd. a deed of land 2 April, 1660, from widow Ann Godfrey, "for love and affection." Margaret d. before 5 May, 1685, when inventory of her estate was presented by her brother Samuel D. He deposed 10 Nov. 1691, ae. 45 years. Elizabeth, widow of Thomas, the eldest son, recd. a tract of land from Samuel 22 March, 1703-4.
See also Godfrey, Gooch, Reading.

DOW, DOWE, DOUE,
Henry, husbandman, of Ormsby, Eng. ae. 29, with wife Joane, ae. 30, 4 ch. and servant Anne Maning, ae. 17, passed exam. to go to N. E. April 11, 1637. Settled at Watertown; frm. May 2, 1638. Wife Jone, bur. 20 (4) 1640. Rem. to Hampton; juryman, 1648; sold land 18 (3) 1649; deputy, 1655. Gave land 3 (8) 1649 to Thomas Nudd, son of his former wife by her first husband. He m. about 1642 Mar-

garet Cole, q. v. Ch. Henry, (deposed in 1669, ae. about 35,) Thomas d. at Wat. bur. July 10, 1641, Joseph b. 20 (1) 1638, Daniel b. 22 (7) 1641, Mary b. 14 (7) 1643, Thomas b. at Hampton April 28, 1653, Jeremiah b. Sept. 6, 1657, and Hannah.

He d. 21 (2) 1659. Will dated 16 (2) prob. 4 (8) 1659, beq. to wife Margaret, sons Henry, Joseph, Daniel, Thomas, Jeremiah; daus. Mary and Hannah. Hannah m. Jonas Gregory of Ipswich.

The widow m. Oct. 23, 1661, Richard Kimball, of Ipswich.

DOWNING, DOUNIN,

Andrew, Kittery, about 1652, petitioned the king in 1680, having been a "resident for 28 years and a great sufferer under the usurpation of the government of Boston."

"Daniel," whose mark is affixed to a petition to Parliament 20 Dec. 1652, may be Dennis.

Dennis, blacksmith, Kittery, 18 Dec. 1650; bought house and land "near the river of pischataqua, between ffrankes fort and watts fort," on which he was then living; juryman, 1650. Took oath of allegiance to Mass. govt. 16 Nov. 1652. He and his wife Ann in court in 1656. He and wife Patience sold land 20 June, 1679. His son Joshua petitioned Andros for confirmation of the title in 1688. [Bax. MS.]

See also Wiggin.

DOWNS,

Thomas, Dover, fined in 1657 for going in his boat on the Sabbath. Wife Katherine; ch. Elizabeth b. 17 Nov. 1663. [Dov. Hist. Coll.] Est. admin. by son Gershom, 1713.

DRAKE,

Francis, Portsmouth, had house-lot on Roger Knight's Island in 1654. Juror, 1661; propr. 1664. With wife Mary sold land in Greenland 5 Aug. 1668.

Robert, yeoman, searge-maker, Exeter, proprietor very early. Bought a house and lands in Hampton of Francis Pebodie 15 (1) 1649. Took oath of fidelity 4 (8) 1653.

Grand juryman 8 April, 1662. His sons Nathaniel and Abraham took oath of fidelity at Hampton 1 (8) 1650; sold pipe staves in 1651. [Mass. Arch. 38 B. 173.]

He died 14 (11) 1667-8. His will dated 18 May, 1663, was proved 14 (2) 1668. He bequeathed to sons Nathaniel and Abraham, and daughter Susanna; to grandchildren Abraham, Susanna, Sarah, Mary, Elizabeth and Hannah, children of Abraham, and Rachel and Jean, children of Nathaniel. Nathaniel Drake, ae. 78, and Abraham, ae. 71, deposed April 27, 1671, that they had known Isabel Bland from childhood, and that John Bland, her father, formerly lived in Colchester [Eng.?]; that his name and ancestry were Bland, not Smith.

Thomas, defendant in a lawsuit in court at Strawberry Bank in 1643, may be believed to be the husband of Jane, who deposed in the same court 27 June, 1660, stating that she and her husband lived here before Mr. Williams came to New England; that at their house Mr. W. gave 7 or 8 acres of adjacent land to Goodman Clifton, a seaman, who sold it about 1640 to Walter Abbot; that he afterward sold the same to Thomas Turpin. [P. court rec. 2, 49.]

See also Berry, Tucker, Webster, Wiggin.

DRAPER,
Nathaniel, planter, Damariscove River, gave bond for the payment of money 2 June, 1651, with John Taylor. [Suff. De. I.]

DRAYTON;
John, brought suit in Piscataqua court in 1643.

DRIVELLY,
George, party to a suit in Piscataqua court 9 June, 1641.

DREW, DRUE,
James, Portsmouth, received as an inhabitant and a lot of land assigned him Oct. 19, 1659. He m. Mary, dau. of John Jones. He d. before Dec. 30, 1674, when his estate

was granted to his widow Mary for the bringing up of the children. Sons James and Nathaniel sold land in 1695.
William, Dover, taxed Oct. 19, 1648.
Admin. on his estate was granted June 29, 1669, to widow Elizabeth. [Ch.?] Francis, John and Thomas.
See also Johnson, Locke.

DUNCAN,
Joseph, servant of Capt. Thomas Wiggin, Exeter, was drowned 24 June, 1648. [Norf. rec.]

DUNSTER, DUNSTAR, DURSTON, DUSTON, DUSTIN,
Thomas, Richmond Island, one of Winter's fishing company in 1634.
Thomas, Kittery, signed the Piscataqua combination in 1640. Lawsuit in 1643. Took oath of allegiance to Mass. govt. at Kittery 16 Nov. 1652. Constable. He deposed in Walton case 28 (4) 1660, ae. about 55 years. [P. court Files.] He and wife Elizabeth, of Portsmouth, sold house and land in Kittery 2 March, 1659-60; she, as widow, made a confirmatory deed 19 March, 1662-3. After his death the widow m. June 9, 1663 (as his 4th wife) Matthias Button of Haverhill, Mass. She d. July 16, 1690.

DURDAL,
Hugh, came in 1638 with the family of Francis Littlefield.

DURRUM,
Humphrey, Falmouth, bought 50 acres of land of Cleve 25 March, 1658.

EARLE,
William, Portsmouth, plaintiff in suit at court in Agamenticus, Oct. 12, 1652. Proprietor, 1660.

EASON, EASTON,
Nicholas, tanner, built a mill and weir at Ipswich in 1634. He also built the first house in Hampton, under the

direction of Mr. Dummer and John Spencer; was discharged from the work May 17, 1638. He rem. to Rhode Island. [See P. of M.]
See Jeffrey.

EASTOW, see Estow.

EDGE,
 Robert, York, took oath of allegiance to Mass. govt. 22 Nov. 1652. Rem. to Kittery. Sold land 23 April, 1662. [His wife] Florence and [son] Peter signed with him, by their marks.

EDGECOMBE, EDGECOMB,
 Nicholas, planter, one of Winter's fishermen from 1638 to 1641. He m. in 1642 Wilmot Randall, a servant in the family of Winter, and paid for the unexpired time of her (year's) contract. [Trel.] Took oath of allegiance to Mass. govt. at Spurwink July 13, 1658. Settled at Saco. He and his wife sold land formerly occupied by them at Scarborough 3 Oct. 1660.
 He d. before 28 March, 1681, when the widow presented the inventory of his estate. Testimony was given that he left all to his son Robert, who was to maintain the mother; "the rest of the children" are referred to. [York De. V.]

EDMUNDS,
 Henry, midshipman, Milbrook, Eng. came to Richmond Island in 1638, and worked for Winter; left after a short time.
 See Green.

ELBRIDGE,
 Thomas, merchant, of Bristol, England, one of the proprietors and some time resident at Pemaquid, mortgaged the island of Monhegan to Abraham Shurt 29 Sept. 1651. [Suff. De. I.] Lawsuits in York Court in 1659.

ELDRED,
 John, Hampton, proprietor, 1640.

ELLETT,
 Robert, Portsmouth, 1 acre of land assigned him Oct. 19, 1659.

ELLIOTT, ELLITT,
 George, sued for debt in Piscataqua court 26 June, 1654. See also Champernowne, Cutt, Fabes.

ELKINS, ELKINE, ELKINGS, ELKYN,
 Christopher, Senior, Black Point, testified 1 (5) 1654, regarding the cutting of hay at that place.
 Henry, tailor, Boston, adm. chh. 9 (9) 1634, frm. May 6, 1635. Ch. Marie bapt. 8 (2) 1638. With wife Mary and other persons who adhered to Mrs. Hutchinson and Mr. Wheelwright, he was dismissed 3 (1) 1639, to the chh. of Exeter. Signed the Exeter combination 5 (4) 1639, and a petition to the Gen. Court of Mass. 29 (3) 1645. Rem. to Hampton. His wife Mary d. 17 (1) 1658.
 He d. Nov. 19, 1668. Will dated 27 April, 1667, prob. 13 (2) 1669; "very aged"; beq. to sons Gershom and Eliezer.
 Thomas, before Gen. Court of Mass. at Boston in 1634; witnessed a deed of Cleve to Jordan at Casco in 1651.
 See also Berry, Blake, Haborne, Neale, Purchase.

ELLEN, ELLIN, ELLYNS,
 Anthony, Portsmouth, bought house and lands of William Seavey 6 June, 1648: grand juryman in 1650; constable in 1655. Testified in court in 1655.
 Inventory of his estate, taken 7 Aug. 1681, was filed Sept. 8, together with a list of the articles which his [second] wife Abigail had brought with her when she married him; it included a house and land on Great Island. He had owned

a neck of land, an island called by his name, and considerable personal property.

See also Fernald.

ELLINGHAM,

William, carpenter, millwright, proprietor, had lands granted by the town; built a sawmill. Sold one quarter of a sawmill on Sturgeons Creek 15 Oct. 1651 and other property afterward to Thomas Broughton of Mass.; engaged to work at the same a certain time. His wife Christian consented to the deed. He bought land on the river of Agamenticus and erected mills there under contract with Godfrey 7 June, 1652. Took oath of allegiance to Mass. govt. 22 Nov. 1652. Constable of Kittery in 1655. [Mass. Arch. 48, 49.] Before the court at Dover in 1668.

See Gaile.

ELSON, ELSTON,

John, "of Salem," shipwrecked in Boston bay with "two of Mr. Cradock's fishermen" 26 July, 1631. [W.] Removed to Wells; took oath of allegiance to Mass. govt. 5 July, 1653.

John Elson made will 11 March, 1683-4, witnessed by Barthl. Gedney and Simon Willard; prob. at Salem Nov. 24, 1685; beq. to wife Joanna and children John, Samuel, Ephraim, Dinah, Margaret, Hannah and Benjamin. [Es. Prob. 302, 154.]

EMERSON, EMBERSON,

Rev. Joseph, son of Thomas, a pioneer of Ipswich, Mass. became a minister; settled at York in 1648; rem. to Wells where he took the oath of allegiance to Mass. govt. 4 July, 1653; signed the petition to the Gen. Court of Mass. 30 Oct. 1654, and that to Cromwell in 1657. [Mass. Arch. 3, 219.] Was minister of Wells from 1664 to 1667. Rem. to Mendon, Mass.

He m. Elizabeth, dau. of Rev. Edward Bulkley, of Concord, Mass.; ch. Peter.

EMERY, EMEREY,

Anthony, carpenter, of Romsey, Eng. came in the James in April, 1635. Settled at Newbury, Mass. 1637. Rem. to Dover; proprietor. "Three acres and an halfe Given him by Capt. Wiggens in Ano: 37," and other lands, are specified in the town records. Signed the combination in 1640. Licensed to sell wine in 1643. Selectman in 1648. Rem. to "Cold Harbour in the province of Mayne," and sold houses in Dover, lately in his possession, 1 (1) 1651. [P. court rec.] Took oath of allegiance to Mass. govt. 16 Nov. 1652. Wife Frances joined him in a lawsuit in 1649. They made a deed of gift of land to son James 12 May, 1660; witnessed by John E. Sen. and John E. Jr.

See Estow, Grant, Spancer.

ENDLE, ENDELL,

Richard, Smuttinose Island, Isles of Shoals, partner of Stephen Ford in ownership of stage room in 1660. Michael, fisherman, of the Isles of Shoals, son in law of John Baly, had deed of land in 1662; may have been a connection of Richard.

ENGLISH,

William, cordwainer, shoemaker, sergeant, Ipswich, 1637. Rem. to Hampton; had grant of land in 1640. Returned to Ipswich, and sold, 1 (2) 1652, house lot in H. "abutting upon the green called the Ring towards the south," etc. [See P. of M.]

ESTOW, EASTOW,

William, Newbury, proprietor about 1638, as John Emery deposed at Salisbury, April 9, 1679. He was one of the first planters at Hampton, 6 (7) 1638. Deputy. Appointed in 1643 to attend to the "breeding of saltpetre." One of the commissioners of the town for minor trials, in 1649.

He d. 23 (9) 1655. Will signed 16 (8) 1655, prob. 8 (2) 1656, beq. to son in law Morris Hobbs and daughter Sarah

Hobbs, his wife; to their children John and Sarah; to son
in law Thomas Marston and dau. Mary, his wife; to the
children of Willi: Moulton. [Norf. Rec.]

EVANS, EUINS,
Griffith, before the court at Saco 25 March, 1636.
Wiliam, had land assigned him at Portsmouth Jan. 13,
1652. "Delivered his wife to the town's hands" Oct. 12,
1658; case to be decided by the selectmen.

EVERETT, AVERET,
William, Kittery, was sued in Piscataqua court in 1640.
Took oath of allegiance to Mass. govt. 16 Nov. 1652. Wife
Margaret.
He died between 25 March, 1671, date of his last deed
of land, and 23 Nov. 1674, when that sale was confirmed by
the widow, who had meantime married Isaac Nash of Dover.
Their daughter Martha, wife of Nathan Lord, joined in the
deed. [York De. IV.]

EVEREST, [Everett?]
Andrew, planter, York, had marsh land laid out in 1646.
[York De. I, 29.] Took oath of allegiance to Mass. govt.
22 Nov. 1652. Witnessed a deed in 1673. With wife Bar-
bary sold land 5 June, 1680; son Job mentioned; sold another tract 18 March, 1681-2.
See also Conley, Lord, Nash.

EVERIE,
Thomas, fined for disturbance at Portsmouth March 5,
1658-9.

FELCH, FELT,
George, mason, Charlestown, 1633, resided at Mystic
Side, 1640. He deposed 20 (11) 1654, ae. about 40 years.
He removed about 1640 to Casco Bay, settling at Great
Cove; was one of the founders of North Yarmouth, Dis-
trict of Maine. He made an agreement with his son George

on the day of the latter's marriage, (9) 1662, to pay him £40. See also deed of Jane, widow of Arthur Mackworth, gent. of Falmouth, conveying to George Felt, husband of her dau. Phillippe, land bounded by that of her dau. Purchas and that of her son James Andrews. [Norf. co. rec. IV, 75.] He removed to Malden, where he petitioned Gov. Andros in 1688 for confirmation of title to land at Casco which he bought about 1670. Giving his age as about 87 years. The town aided him and his wife, 1681-1692. Wife Elizabeth, dau. of widow Prudence Wilkinson; adm. chh. Char. 19 (11) 1639. Ch. Elizabeth, (m. (9) 1655, William Leraby,) George, Mary, these three bapt. 26 (11) 1639; Mary, (m. (2) 1660, James Nichols,) Moyses, bapt. 20 (10) 1640.

He d. in 1693; the widow d. in 1694. Genealogy.

The son Moses, of Rumney Marsh, Boston, deposed at Salem July 6, 1722, that he lived at Casco Bay in the Province of Maine about 1658, and knew Nicholas Cole, and John Puddington who dwelt in houses of their own building at a place called Merrechancake Neck . . . until driven away by the Indian enemy, said land being at Casco Bay. [Es. De. 39, 148.]

FABES, FAEBES, FABINES,

John, Senior, Isles of Shoals, signed petition for incorporation 18 (3) 1653. Elizabeth, ae. 16, who came to Boston in the Elizabeth and Ann in May, 1635, may have been his wife. Bought house, stage, mooring place and flakes for one boat of Wm. Weymouth; deed certified 29 June, 1654. Took oath of fidelity 11 July, 1659. Appointed admin. of the estate of Katherine Johns, widow, 26 June, 1660. Land laid out to him at Portsmouth in 1660.

Will signed May 14, 1696, acknowledged at New Castell same day before Robert Elliot; beq. to wife Elizabeth, and dau. Deborah Fabes. Prob. Aug. 1, 1698. Admin. on the estate of the widow Elizabeth was granted June 6, 1711, to her dau. Deborah with her husband John Holden, of Newcastle.

FELLEW,
  Abraham, Spurwink, took oath of allegiance to Mass. govt. 13 July, 1658.

FERNALD, FERNALL, FURNALD, FURNELL,
  Charles, had 50 acres of land assigned him at Portsmouth in 1852.
  John, cordwainer, Portsmouth, had lawsuit in Maine court June 5, 1637.
  Reginald, or Renald, chirurgion, physician, Portsmouth, before 1642; his son Thomas had a deed of land from Richard Vines, steward general of Gorges, 3 May, 1645. He was one of the commissioners for trial of minor cases in 1649. He signed — "Renald Fernald" — the petition of Portsmouth people for full rights, 20 Oct. 1651. [Mass. Arch. 112, 38.] Clerk of courts in 1654. He deposed in 1659 as to occurrences 17 years before. [Pisc. rec.]
  His widow Joanna made will, 23 April, 1660; it was brought into court 28 June, by Elias Stileman and Anthony Ellens, with inventory attested by Elizabeth Fernald. She beq. to daus. Sarah, Elizabeth and Mary, sons Samuel, John, William and Thomas; to John all the surgery books that were his father's; Thomas, shipwright, with wife Temperance, sold land in Kittery 4 March, 1689, to his bro. William, shipwright. Elizabeth sold land near Hinckson's Pool, 29 Oct. 1660.

FEVERILL, see Peverly,
  Thomas, [Strawberry Bank,] was in charge of cattle of Capt. Mason's at the great house in Piscataqua at an early day; testified by Ralph Gee in 1643.

FIELD, FEILD, FEILLD,
  Darby, an Irishman, resident at Marblehead in 1637. Rem. to Exeter. Signed the combination 5 (4) 1639. Travelled in Maine and went with two Indians up the Saco river valley in 1642. Was the first white man to visit and

climb "the White Hill" or one of the peaks of the White mountains. Made the journey from Saco in 18 days. His reports led Thomas Gorges and Mr. Vines to make a journey thither in August following. [W.]

Rem. to Dover. Proprietor. Sued a man in 1642 for setting the woods afire and burning up his pipe staves. Licensed to sell wine in 1644. Taxed in 1648. He became "distracted"; the court ordered that Strawberry Bank should pay a share of the expenses of his "imprisonment and keeping." "Goodie Feild' was mentioned as a proprietor in 1650

Admin. of his estate was granted 1 (8) 1651 to Ambrose Gibbins.

See Phelps, Reynes.

FIFIELD, FIFEILD,

William, came in the Hercules April 11, 1634. Settled at Hampton. He may be the "William ff . . . " who was adm. frm. of Mass. Bay June 2, 1641. Had grant of land in 1640. Signed the Howard petition in 1643. Deposed 18 Oct. 1658, ae. about 40 years, and 9 March, 1669, ae. about 55 years. [Mass. Arch. 39, and Es. Files.] Conveyed land 29 April, 1667, to son Benjamin.

Wife Mary; ch.: Benjamin, William b. 1 (2) 1651, Lydia b. 21 (11) 1654, Elizabeth b. 7 (7) 1657, Hannah b. and d. 1659, Deborah b. 6 (12) 1660, John d. 18 (1) 1665.

He d. Nov. 9, 1683.

See Colcord, Dalton, Green, Wedgewood.

FILBRICK, see Philbrick.

FISH,

Gabriel, fisherman, Boston, came to Exeter in 1638 and spent one year; returned to Boston. He gave a letter of attorney to Edward Richworth Aug. 3, 1639, to receive ten pounds from James Carrington of Thorsthorpe, co. Lincoln, Eng. Spoke boldly against King Charles and was arrested in 1639 but afterward released.

FISHCOCKE,

Edward, fisherman and pilot, Richmond Island before 1634. He went in 1635 to "the Dutch Plantation," i. e. New York, and "made covenant to stây and plant tobakko for them." Returned and worked for Winter in 1637. Was not accepted for master of the new bark Winter was having built at that time. [Trel.]

FLETCHER,

Rev. Seth, ("She:", as he sometimes signed,) Hampton, took the freeman's oath in Hampt. court 3 (8) 1654. Rem. to Wells. Witnessed a deed of John West March 15, 1658-9. Mary a witness with him in 1660. Presumably he is "Mr. Fletcher, Junior," who had for 2 years been minister at Wells, was named before Gen. Court of Mass. on a charge of "unfitnesse," May 30, 1660; but 16 of the citizens petitioned May 22, 1661, that he be allowed to go on in his ministry. The court deferred action till the court of York had acted. [Mass. Arch. 10, 92-6.]

Was he son in law of Bryan Pendleton and father of "Pendleton Fletcher" named in B. P.'s will? Did he remove to Hampton, N. Y. and Elizabeth, N. J.?

See Cutt, Pendleton.

FOGG,

Samuel, Hampton, proprietor. Bought one additional share of cow common 18 (11) 1652. Frm. 3 (8) 1654.

Wife Ann d. 9 (10) 1663; he m. (2) 28 (10) 1665, Mary, dau. of Robert, Page. Ch.: Samuel b. 25 (10) 1655, Joseph b. 25 (1) 1656-7, John b. 15 (5) 1658, Mary b. 1 (3) 1662, Seath b. 28 (9) 1666, James b. 18 (2) 1668.

He died April 15, 1672. Will dated 9 Jan. 1671; prob. 8 Oct. 1672. Beq. to wife Mary the stuff she brought into the house, etc.; to sons Samuel, Daniel, Seath, James, daughters Mary and Hannah. Father in law, Dea. Robert Page and brother Thomas Ward.

See also Shaw.

FOLLEN,
  Abraham, Spurwink, took oath of allegiance to Mass. govt. 13 July, 1658.
FOLLETT,
  John, Piscataqua, signed the combination in 1640.
  Nicholas, cooper, mariner, Oyster River, Dover, bought house and land of Thomas Johnson 6 Sept. 1652. He signed his will at "Treace in the Bay of Campeach," April 29, 1700; beq. to wife Hannah, sons Nicholas, Philip and Caleb, and gave the rest to "all my children." Probated Aug. 19, 1700. Son Benjamin ae. about 8 years; his brother Nicholas appointed guardian 6 Nov. 1705.
  William, Dover, bought part of a sawmill of Wm. Pomfret in 1651. See Footman, Hinger, Nason, Stevenson.
FOLSAM, see Fulsham.
FOOTMAN,
  Thomas, York, gave bond for payment of money to John Hurd of Boston, tailor, 29 May, 1645. Had accounts with the same 5 (2) 1648. [A.] Rem. to Dover. Taxed Oct. 19, 1648. Juryman, 1651.
  Will dated 14 Aug. 1667, prob. 30 June, 1668, beq. to wife Catherine and daughter Abigail; rest to be divided equally among his children; brother Benjamin Matthews and William Follett to assist his wife in her business. The widow m. (2) William Durgin.
FORD,
  Stephen, Smuttinose Island, Isles of Shoals, was badly frost-bitten in a storm at sea about Jan. 1651, and lost parts of his hands and arms, etc. in consequence. His neighbors raised 46 li. for his support; and the county court gave more and arranged for his maintenance. In company with Richard Endle he sued one who had trespassed on their stageroom, in 1660.
FOSS, FOST,
  John, Portsmouth, proprietor, 22 March, 1660-1.
  Will Dec. 17, 1699; proved Jan. 8, 1699-1700; wife Eliza-

beth, ch. Humphrey, William, Mary, Jemima, Elizabeth, Samuel; son in law James Warrin. See Chadbourne.

FOSTER,
   William, brother in law of Christopher Hobbs; he died before June 29, 1654, when Hobbs admin. on his estate.

FRAISEY, FRAYSEY,
   Ambrose, Piscataqua, fined in 1646 for swearing.
   William, sued in Piscataqua Court in 1641. Presented for neglecting the ordinances of God and refusing to live in an orderly course of life, in 1643. See Freythey.

FOXWELL, FOXALL,
   Richard, gentleman, Saco, assessed for minister's rate in 1636. A very early resident of Black Point; his lands adjoined those of Henry Watts. [York De. I.] Lawsuit in Maine court June 5, 1637. Took oath of allegiance to Mass. govt. 13 July, 1658. With his son John Foxwell, carpenter, he sold 300 acres of land in that "quader checker of a patentt made over by deede of gift by Capt. Ric. Bonighton unto his daughters Elizabeth and Susanna" to George Foxwell, merchant, of Exon [Exeter], England, 2 July, 1664.

FRYER, FRIER,
   Mr. Nathaniel, (incorrectly called Emmanuel sometimes) seaman, bought land in Boston in 1653; gave bonds for admission of Rich. Seward as inhabitant in 1657. Wife Christian [dau. John Scarlet]; Ch. rec. in Boston: James, b. 7 Oct. 1653, Sarah b. 20 July, 1656, Elizabeth b. 1 Nov. 1657, Nathaniel b. 9 Dec. 1660; Joshua [see Pisc. Deeds]. 2d wife Dorothy [dau. Rev. John Woodbridge]. Rem. to Portsmouth; propr. 1659; treasurer, commissioner, capt. militia. Was an active business man; administered on many estates, etc. Resided in the township of Newcastle. Made his will Feb. 10, 1704-5, proved July 2, 1715; wife Dorritey; dau. Sarah and her husband Robert Elliot; gr. ch. Abigail Elliot and Nathaniel Fryer, Jr., son in law John Hincks.
   See Babb.

FROST,

    George, witnessed the giving of possession of Cleve and Tucker's grant of land 8 June, 1637.

    Nicholas, traded at Damerill's Cove in 1632, and was fined and punished by the Gen. Court of Mass. Bay upon the complaint of Dorchester traders. Prosecuted again in 1636. [Mass. Col. rec.]

    Settled at Kittery. "A petition of Nicholas Frost of Pascattaquay, mason, to the Government & Deputy & the Assistants, neare at hand" 27 (7) 1639, was an effort to obtain justice. [L.] The bounds of his land at Sturgeon Creek meadows were set down about the year 1640. [Deposition of John White.] Selectman in 1648. Took oath of allegiance to Mass. govt. 16 Nov. 1652. He deposed 30 (4) 1658, ae. about 60 years, relative to possession of land by Thomas Crockett about 16 or 17 years before. Deposed 16 April, 1662, ae. about 70 years. [York De. II.]

    He or Nicholas, Jr. took into his service by indenture at Bristol, Eng. 25 March, 1662, Thomas Orchard; who, after arriving here, transferred himself July 10, 1663, to William Scadlocke, and to Francis Littlefield the elder before May 6, 1664. [York. De. I.]

    Nicholas, Jr. wrote from "Patoxen in Mary Land," April 28, 1673, to his brother Charles, concerning shipment of tobacco, etc.; adding that, in case of his death he desired his property to be divided between the children of Charles and those of "brother Leighton," when of age. [York De. II.] Settlement of the estate was made July 6, 1675, by his surviving brothers and sisters, namely Charles and John Frost, William Gowine alias Smyth, who had married Elizabeth, and Joseph Hammonds, who had married Katherine. The brother Charles deposed 24 March, 1680, ae. about 48 years; died in 1697, referring to brother John F. and bro. in law Joseph Hammond.

    See also Bolles, Crockett, Dixon, Howell, Pickering, Shapleigh, Taintor, White.

    Note. Henry Frost, mariner, of Ispwich, co. Suffolk, Eng.

gave a house and garden in Ipswich to his daughter Hannah, wife of Richard Stowers, of Charlestown, Mass. before 15 (8) 1647. [A.]

"Nicholas Frost of Biddeford, (Eng.) merchant," had license from bishop of Exeter April 1, 1613, to marry "Mary Bollen, of Monckleigh, gent."

FREYTHEY, FARETHYE, see Fraysey,

Alexander, "Sander," Richmond Island, left the service of Winter in 1638 and went home to England. [Trel.]

William, Richmond Island, fisherman, worked for Winter, 1636-1640. Money was paid to his mother in England on his account. He rem. to York; took oath of allegiance 16 Nov. 1652.

He and his wife Elizabeth gave a tract of land to Thomas Holms, husband of their daughter Jane, 10 June, 1671, another to son John F. 31 Oct. 1681; and still other tracts to sons Samuel and John 4 Dec. 1683.

FULLER,

Giles, proposed for a proprietor at Dedham, Mass. in 1638. Rem. to Hampton; signed petition in Howard case in 1643.

He d. in 1672 or 1673. Inventory of his estate was filed 8 April, 1673. Expenses of the "inquest" were charged. "Ric: Pettingall, ae. about 52 years, saith: I being very well acquainted with Giles ffuller of Hampton deceased & with mr. Fuller of Bastable Docter, both in old England & here in Newengland & both told mee they were of kinn & sd Giles ffuller have told mee in old England & new that Marth: ffuller Docter now of Bastable was ye nearest kinsman hee had: Sworn before ye County Court held att Hampton 14: 8 mo: 1673."

He was a son of Roger Fuller of Topcraft, co. Norfolk, Eng. yeoman. His only sister Susanna, wife of Tho. Thurton of Croydon, co. Surrey, tobacconist, applied for inheritance of his estate in London 5 April, 1677. Thurton came here to get possession of this property, and sold it after a while. [Norf. rec. Lib. III, fol. 63-9.]

William, ae. 25, with John, ae. 15, came in the Abigail in May, 1635. Settled at Ipswich; proprietor, 1635; sold house and land in 1639. Appointed gunsmith by the Gen. Court 17 May, 1637. Frm. June 2, 1641. Kept the mill in 1639. [Mass. rec.] Rem. to Concord. Rem. to Hampton. Locksmith; sold land 9 (12) 1647. Bought other land in 1650. List of his possessions March 17, 1650. [Norf. De. I.]

Wife Elizabeth d. 24 (5) 1642. He m. (2) —— who survived him. Ch. Hannah b. 8 (6) 1641.

Inventory of the estate of Wm. Fuller, late of Hampton, taken 26 May, 1693, was filed by Josias Moulton. A debt from John Fuller is mentioned.

He made will March 18, 1690-1, proved Aug. 5, 1693; wife to be maintained honorably; cousins Josiah, (son of Henry) Moulton and his wife Elizabeth; Elizabeth, wife of Daniel Dow; Mary, dau. of Samuel Fogg, dec.; Martha, wife of John Marston, Sen. of Andover; to the church of Hampton "my pewter flagon."

FULSHAM, FOULSHAM, FOLSAM, FOULCHER,

John, planter, with wife and 2 servants, came from old Hingham in 1638, and settled at Hingham, Mass. Proprietor, town officer; had liberty to erect a sawmill. Sold property in 1659 and rem. to Exeter.

He m. Mary, dau. of Edward Gilman, (who also came to Hingham and afterward rem. to Exeter.) Ch.: John, Samuel bapt. Oct. 11, 1641, Nathaniel bapt. June 2, 1644, Israel bapt. Sept. 1644, Peter bapt. April 8, 1649, Mary bapt. April 13, 1651, (m. George Marsh,) Ephraim bapt. Feb. 25, 1654-5.

He deeded to his son Peter 10 April, 1673, land and houses "in ye towne of Hingam in ye county of Norff: near Norvald comon & formerly cald by ye name of ffulsham at ye Box bushes . . . . which lately fell to mee."

He d. 27 Dec. 1681.

FURBER, FORBOWRE,
 William, husbandman, Dover, signed the combination in 1640; taxed in 1648. One of the three "wearsmen" appointed by the town 20 (2) 1644, to take charge of the fishery in the vicinity. He sold land on the north side of Kechechucke river to Thomas Noke 2 July, 1657. Constable, 1646. Signed petition to Gen. Court 10 Oct. 1665.
 Wife Elizabeth; ch. Susanna b. 5 May, 1664. [Dov. Hist. Coll.] Of Welch Cove, his estate settled Dec. 30, 1699; son William and the wives of John Dam, John Bickford and Thomas Bickford.
 See also Austin, Baker, Cutt, Hilton, Johnson, Nock.

FURNELL, see Fernald.

FURSON, FURSEN,
 Thomas, Portsmouth, defendant in a lawsuit in Piscataqua court in 1642. One of the settlers at "Bloody Point" who petitioned the Gen. Court about 1642 to be included within the bounds of Dover; which was done. Taxed in 1648; inhabitant, lands assigned 1652 and 1660.
 He m. Jane, widow of Thomas Turpin.
 See Bachiler.

GAILE, GAYLE,
 Hugh, millwright, York, sold one quarter part of a sawmill on Sturgeon creek 15 Oct. 1651. Took oath of allegiance to Mass. govt. 22 Nov. 1652.
 Sold his share in mills, built in equal partnership with Wm. Ellingham, viz. "one grist mill, one tyde mill to goe with two saws, two ffretchett mills," together with timber, land, buildings, etc. to Capt. Thomas Clarke of Boston, merchant, and Edward Rishworth of York, recorder, Oct. 19, 1653, they accepting of it " to maintayne for the Towns usse."

GARDE, GUARD,
 Roger, York, received a tract of land from Wm. Hooke 30 July, 1637; deed assigned for a debt to George Pudding-

ton 24 Jan. 1645. He was register of York court in 1640. Was mayor of York in 1644. [W.] He d. before 1666. [York Court Records.]
See also Elson, Neale, Seward.

GARLAND,
John, Richmond Island, one of Winter's fishermen in 1639.

John, Hampton, worked for Humphrey Wilson at his mill before 1655. [Mass. Arch. 38 B, 128.] Taxed in 1653. He m. (1) Oct. 26, 1652, Elizabeth Chapman; m. (2) Elizabeth Chase, dau. of Thomas Philbrick and widow of Thomas Chase. Ch. John b. 11 (1) 1655, Jacob b. 20 (10) 1656, Peter b. Nov. 25, 1659.

He d. 4 (11) 1671. Will dated 15 Nov. 1671; "about fivety years"; beq. to wife Elizabeth and sons John, Jacob and Peter.

Peter, mariner, Charlestown, proprietor, 1637; of Boston, 1638. [L.] Seems to be the man who signed the Piscataqua combination in 1640, and testified in Saco court 18 Sept. 1640, that he had known and frequented Casco river for about 14 years. Wife Joan; ch. Mary b. in 1654. at Boston.

See also Abbot, Robie.

GARNESEY,
William, York, took oath of allegiance to Mass. govt. 22 Nov. 1652.

GAWDE, GAUD,
Mark, of St. Johns, Eng. boat master in the service of Winter at Richmond's Island in 1638. Money paid to his wife in England by Trelawney. He left the plantation. [Trel.]

GEE,
Peter, fisherman, of Newton, Ferrers, England, co. Devon, residing at Isles of Shoals, signed petition for in-

corporation 18 (3) 1653. Bought land at Salisbury of Thomas Macy 18 Dec. 1657; sold it to Nathan Gold of Newbury 24 May, 1661.

Ralph, planter, Piscataqua, testified 20 July [1643] that he and certain others were left in charge of cattle upon Capt. Mason's account at the great house in Piscataqua, and stayed there a year and a quarter, receiving diet and lodging from Mr. Thomas Wanerton. [Mass. Arch. 38 B, 37.]
See Feverill.

GATCHELL, GETCHELL,

Samuel, planter, Salem, 1637. Rem. to Hampton; proprietor 23 (12) 1645. Sold house and land there 17 (3) 1648. Rem. to Salisbury; proprietor and commoner there, 1650. Wife Dorcas d. Jan. 12, 1684. Ch. Susanna (m. Joseph Norton), Priscilla, b. Feb. 26, 1648 (m. Solomon Rainsford), Samuel. The sons of the last-named rem. to North Yarmouth, Berwick, Wells, and New Meadows, Me. [Hoyt.]

He d. about 1694. Will dated April 2, 1684, prob. Oct. 6, 1697; beq. to wife Dorcas, daus. Susanna Norton and Priscilla Rainsford and son Samuel. The latter declined to admin. and widow Priscilla Rainsford of Boston took charge 18 Nov. 1697.

GIBBONS, GIBBINS,

Ambrose, came as factor or steward with Walter Neal in 1630; seems to have begun the plantation at Newichewanick (the part of Kittery which became Berwick) in 1631. Letter to him from Mason 13 July, 1632. Removed later to Dover. Had suit in court in 1641. Was chosen one of the town commissioners and first selectman 22 (2) 1648. Wife Rebecca; dau. Rebecca m. Henry Sherburne.

He made his will 11 July, 1656, "on his sick bed"; prob. May 9, 1657; copy brought from files of Gen. Court at Boston; beq. to Samuel, Elizabeth, Mary, Henry, John, Ambrose, Sarah and Rebecca, children of Henry Sherburne, to be paid them at the ages of 21 and 18.

James, planter, Biddeford, bought land in partnership with Thomas Mills 2 Aug. 1642. Took oath of allegiance to Mass. govt. 5 July, 1653. One of the Commissioners of Mass. Bay govt. He and his brother in law Robert Haywood now residing in Barbadoes, sold land in Saco 29 March, 1662; his wife Judith signed with him. Sold other land 25 May, 1687.

William, mariner, Saco. Had case in court 25 March, 1636. Testified 28 Sept. 1640, that Casco river had borne that name "for seventeene yeares gone or there aboute." [Trel.]

See also Sanders, Williams.

GIBSON, GIBSONN,

Rev. Richard, minister, came to Richmond Island in 1636 under an engagement for 3 years with Mr. Robert Trelawney, and entered at once on the duties of a parson. Went to the Bay in 1637 "to see some of his country folks." Had promised to minister to Saco people 6 months yearly, in addition to other duties. [Letter to Trelawney 11 June, 1638.]

Lawsuit in Maine court June 5, 1637. He m. about 1638 Mary, daughter of Mr. Thomas Lewis of Saco. Rem. to Portsmouth and became minister there in 1639, with a house and 60 li. a year. Was "wholly addicted to the hierarchy and discipline of England." In controversy with Mr. Larkham of Dover he "scandalized the government" of Mass. Bay. Was arrested; made confession and apology, and was discharged "in regard he was to depart the country in a few days." [W.] He went from the Isles of Shoals a little before July 20, 1647. [York Court Rec.]

GILES, GYLES, JEYLES,

Matthew, Dover, in court in 1642, taxed Oct. 19, 1648. Residing at Isles of Shoals, he signed local petition 18 (3) 1653. Returned to Oyster River and sold I. of S. property 27 June, 1659.

Wife Elizabeth was in court for uttering reviling words against some members of the church in 1664.

He d. Jan. 21, 1666-7. His estate was admin. on by Matthew Williams June 25, 1667; was divided between him and Richard Knight after paying just debts.

See Davis, Shaw.

GILL,

Arthur, shipwright, Richmond Island, 1637-9; was employed by Trelawney and Winter to build vessels. His wife came here to him; in a letter to Trelawney he refers to a daughter and a son. He removed to Dorchester, Mass. and was employed to build a large ship. [See Pioneers of Massachusetts for his further history.]

Peter, fisherman, Richmond Island, in Winter's employ, 1633-4. Returned to England. [Trel.]

GILLMAN, GILMAN, GYLLMAN,

Edward, yeoman, with his wife, 3 sons, 2 daughters and 3 servants, came to Hingham, Mass. in 1638. Proprietor; frm. March 13, 1638-9. He sold his estate in Hingham Oct. 1, 1652, having removed to Ipswich, where he was a selectman in 1649. Settled later at Exeter, where his son Edward had led the way and others had followed; both signed a petition of inhabitants 24 (3) 1652; bought one half his son Edward's house and adjacent land in Nov. 1653. Deeded certain property to wife Mary and sons John and Moses 14 (11) 1654.

Wife Mary; ch.: Mary, (m. John Fulsham,) Edward, Moses, Lydia, (m. Jan. 19, 1644-5, Daniel Cushing,) Sarah, (m. John Leavitt,) John.

He died before 10 (2) 1655, when admin. of his estate was granted to his widow, Mary, the sons and sons in law consenting. [Norf. rec. I, 45.] Genealogy claims that this family descends from the Gilman family of Caston, Eng.

See Biggs, Fuller, Goddard, Hall, Maverick, Treworgy.

GINNISON, see Jennison.

GODDARD, GOTHERD, GODWARD,

John, carpenter, Dover. He made an agreement about the year 1634, in company with James Wall and William Chadbourne, to come to Piscataqua river and settle on lands of Capt. John Mason. Resided at or near Bloody Point; was one of those who petitioned about 1642 to be included within the limits of Dover. [Mass. Arch. 437, 8.] Proprietor at Dover in 1648.

Brought suit against Francis Williams and Thomas Wonerton for false imprisonment in 1642; recovered 2 shillings and 6 pence. Sold land to William Williams 6 June, 1659. He deposed 25 June, 1662, ae. about 54 years. [P. Files.]

He died before June 25, 1667, when admin. of his estate was granted to the widow Welthen (Welthian) and son John. The widow m. (2) John Simons; division of Godard's estate was made 10 May, 1670, between herself and the children, namely, John and Benjamin Goddard; sons in law John Gilman, Arthur Bennick and James Thomas.

GODFREY, GODFREE,

Mr. Edward, gent. was son of Oliver and Elizabeth Godfrey of Barnend in the parish of Wilmington, co. Kent; born about 1588. The Council for New England made him their attorney to give possession of the Laconia grant to Gorges and Mason 17 Nov. 1629. [Mass. Arch. 3, 140.] Settled at Accomenticus or York. Claimed to have been the first person to build and settle at that place. Was one of the commissioners who held court at Saco 25 March, 1636; was the first mayor of "Gorgeana" in 1642, after its incorporation as a "city." He had many transactions in land matters with other settlers. He m. Ann Mesant, widow, housekeeper of Rev. George Burdett; received from him 18 March, 1639, a mortgage of his farm as security for the payment of her delinquent salary. [York De. II.]

He gave, 20 Jan. 1648, to his son Oliver Godfrey of Seale, co. Kent, and Mary his wife, dau. of Richard Smith, gent.

of the same county, a tract of land at Accomenticus called Point Bollogue, adjoining land of Henry Norton and Thomas Gorges; a tract adjoining Henry Dunnell's house; 2 houses on Stage Island and one third of the last divident of upland and marsh at the Neck of land. The son remained in England.

He made strong opposition to the extension of the jurisdiction of Massachusetts over Maine; see letter dated July 9, 1652. [Mass. Arch. 3, 185.] However, he took the oath of allegiance 22 Nov. 1652. Was appointed one of the three commissioners to keep court. He went to London; appealed to the Protector, Cromwell, and later to his son Richard; to Sir Edward Nicholas, secretary, 7 April, 1663; made great efforts to obtain control of Maine affairs. Was 77 years old in 1666. [Bax. MSS. I, and Me. Hist. Coll. IX.]

He died about 1667. His widow Anne deeded her farm 14 Sept. 1667, to Alice, now wife of Nicholas Shapleigh, "in consideration of natural love and affection."

William, husbandman, Watertown, frm. May 13, 1640. As guardian to his son John and administrator to Sarah, his late wife, he made Mr. Antoine Lawrence of London, linen draper, at the Boar's Head in Gracious street, his attorney 22 (4) 1648, to ask of the execs. of the will of Mrs. Key of Wooburne in Bedfordshire a legacy of 10 li. bequeathed to John. [A.]

Rem. to Hampton; bought land 3 (7) 1648; sold Watertown land in 1653. Deacon. He m. (1) Sarah —; he m. (2) Margaret —; ch.: John, Isaac b. 15 (2) 1639, Sarah b. 16 (3) 1642.

He died March 25, 1671. Will dated 2 (8) 1667, prob. 11 (2) 1671, beq. to wife Margery; sons John and Isaac Godfrey; son in law Webster; daughters Sarah and Deborah Godfrey. The widow m. Sept. 14, 1671, John Merrian [Marion]. Adopted son Nathaniel Smith mentioned in county records.

See also Cocks, Dunnell, Preble.

GODSON, GO'SONNE,
"*Mr. Ed.*" York, took oath of allegiance to Mass. govt. 22 Nov. 1652.

GOLD, see Gould.

GOOCH, GOUGE, GUICH,
John, York, a proprietor in 1640; bought land of Wm. Hooke 18 Oct. 1644; sold, 8 March, 1653, land laid out to him in 1644, and some he bought after 1646; his wife Ruth joined in the deed. Took oath of allegiance to Mass. govt. 22 Nov. 1652, and he or son John did the same at Wells 4 July, 1653. [Signature in Mass. Arch. 3, 219.] Rem. to Wells. Selectman. John, Jr. proprietor at York in 1644. He sold land Oct. 20, 1662.

Will dated 7 May, prob. 12 July, 1667; beq. to wife Ruth, sons John and James; to the latter a house at Slymbridge, Eng. which he had bought of William Hammonds; to grandchildren Elizabeth Donnell, Mary, Hannah, Phebe, Peter, Nathaniel and Ruth Weare, and Elizabeth Austin. Wife exec.; Wm. Symonds and brother Wm. Hammonds overseers. Widow and John made agreement July 13, 1667.

William, Richmond Island, one of Winter's fishermen 26 July, 1641 to 1643. [Trel.]

GOODWIN, GOODWINE,
Daniel, planter, Kittery, signed the petition to Cromwell in 1657; constable; petitioned the Gen. Court of Mass. for aid in discharging the duties of his office in the face of local opposition to that government, Dec. 10, 1662. [Mass. Arch. 3, 254.]

He gave to his sons Thomas and James 14 July, 1683, a tract "in the parish of Barwicke, town of Kittery," where he was residing. Daniel, Junior, deposed 25 March, 1686, ae. about 30 years. He deeded land to sons William and Moses 19 March, 1696-7, and to son Daniel 21 Aug. 1701; to son Thomas 13 Dec. 1711.

He m. (1) Margaret, dau. of Thomas Spencer; he m. (2) Sarah, widow of Peter Turbat.

GORGES,

Thomas, gent. Mr. cousin of Sir Ferdinando, came to Maine in 1640; was the first mayor of the borough of Gorgeana [York] and chief commissioner of the Province in 1641. He returned to England in 1643. Resided at Heavitree, Devon. Member of parliament in 1654; died Oct. 17, 1670. In his will, dated Sept. 25, 1669, prob. April 1, 1671, he mentions land he owned at "Ogungigg (Ogunquit) in the province of Maine," etc.

William, Captain, nephew of Sir Ferdinando, came here at an early day; was "gouvernour of New Somersetshire" in 1636; one of the commissioners at the court at Saco March 25, 1636.

See also Burdett, Champernowne, Cleve, Field, Godfrey, Jocelyn, Knight, Mackworth, Shapleigh, Tucker, Vines, Withers.

GOULD, GOLD,

Alexander or Sander, New Harbor, or Pemaquid, Me. with his wife Margaret, had a deed of gift of a tract of land at Broad Bay from her father John Brown of New Harbour 8 Aug. 1660. Daughters Margaret, Mary and Elizabeth. [Eastern claims.] One of these daughters married James Stilson, who petitioned Andros in 1689, giving some of these facts.

See also "Eastern Claims."

GORDON,

Alexander, Exeter.

Children: Nicolas b. 23 March, 1655-6, Elizabeth b. 23 Feb. 1664. [Norf. rec.]

His estate was administered upon Aug. 15, 1697. Widow Mary, ch. Nicholas, John, "Mrs. Smith."

GORRELL,
 Philip, Isles of Shoals, removed before 9 July, 1652, when he gave a due bill to Thomas Macy. [Norf. rec.]

GOYLE,
 Hugh, York, proprietor, 1655. [Bax. MSS.]

GREEN, GREENE,
 Henry, (probably the proprietor at Watertown, Mass. in 1642); deposed in 1652, aged about 30 years. [Arch. 38 B.]; millwright, Hampton, proprietor, 1644. He sold land 6 Oct. 1652. His dau. Mary was afflicted with a sore and placed under the care of Dr. Starr of Charlestown; then her cure was undertaken by William and Ann Edmunds of Lynn. Lawsuit over the matter in 1659. He deposed at the trial, ae. about 40 years; his nephew Giles Fifield also testified. [Es. Files, V.] He deeded land to his son Isaac 19 Nov. 1668.
 Wife Mary d. April 26, 1690; he m. (2) March 10, 1691-2, Mary (Hussey) Page, widow. Ch.: Abraham, Abigail b. 6 (8) 1650, d. 13 (3) 1669, Isaac b. 25 (—) 1651, Jacob, Elizabeth b. 11 (4) 1656, Mary, Hannah.
 "Henry Green, Esqr. Aged above 80 years, for Severall years a member of the Counsell untill by age he layed downe that place but a Justice till he died which was the 5 August, 1700." [Town rec.] Will dated 2 Aug. was proved 20 and 23 Aug. 1700; beq. to sons Abraham, Isaac and Jacob; daus. Elizabeth, wife of Joseph Cass, and the three children she had by James Chase; Mary, wife of Peter Green, and Hannah, sometime wife of John Asy.
 John, Kittery, member of a board of arbitration in 1647; proprietor, 1648; took oath of allegiance to Mass. govt. 16 Nov. 1652. With wife Julia or Julyan he deeded land in K. 20 May, 1668, to his dau. Elizabeth and her husband Thomas Abbet and to son in law John Searle 20 Dec. 1673.
 The date of his death is not found; but his widow, of

Berwick, deeded land July 10, 1683, to John Searle and his son John, and to John, son of Nicholas Jellison.

We note a deed made by John Greene of South Carolina, son of John Greene of Kittery, planter, deceased, with Humphrey Axall and Mary his wife, also of So. Car. executors of the estate of said John Greene, conveying land in Kittery, 29 Jan. 1704-5. [York De. VII.] We also note a deed made 27 March, 1708, by John Greene, mariner, Samuel G. barber, Priscilla, wife of Samuel Grise, mason, and Hannah, widow, of Boston, the widow and children of John G. mariner, late of Boston, son of Nicholas G. late of York; land at Cape Neddicke.

See also Royall.

GRANT,

Ferdinando, worked on hay for Thomas Williams of Winter Harbour in 1640; juryman same year.

James, "Scotchman," Kittery.

Peter, "Scotchman," bought land in Kittery 21 Oct. 1659, of James Emery. Other lands granted him by the town March 4, 1673-4. [York De. III.] He and his children recd. bequests from his brother James Grant of K. 12 Nov. 1679.

He made will 19 Oct. 1709, prob. 30 Oct. 1718; "aged and creasey [crazy] in body"; bequeathed to wife Johannah and seven children, William, James, Alexander, Daniel, Grisell, Mary and Hannah.

See also Agnew, Miles.

GRENAWAY, GREENEWAY, GREENAWAY,

Clement, mariner, master of a ship of Barnstable, Eng. let his servant, Peter Hogg, to Thomas Lewis of Saco, from July 5, 1635, for the work of caulking a boat; brought suit at Saco Feb. 7, 1636, for his payment. [Maine court rec.] Assessed in Saco in 1630. Sailed from Richmond Island about 15 July, 1638. [Trel.]

GREENFIELD, GRENFIELD,
   Samuel, weaver, ae. 27, of Norwich, Eng. with wife Barbara ae. 35, and servant, John Teed, ae. 19, passed exam. May 12, 1637, to go to N. E. Recd. inhabitant and propr. at Salem 14 (6) 1637. Rem. to Ipswich. His wife d. and he m. Susan, widow of Humphrey Wyth or Wise, with whom he sold land 4 March, 1638. Was one of those licensed by the Court 6 (7) 1638, to begin the plantation at Hampton. Rem. to Exeter. Signed petition to Gen. Court of Mass. Bay Sept. 7, 1643.

GULLETT,
   Peter, boat master, Richmond Island, one of Winter's fishermen; died about Christmas, 1637. [Trel.]

GUNNISON, GUNISON, GULLISON,
   Hugh, vintner, Boston, servant to Richard Bellingham, adm. chh. 22 (1) 1635. Frm. May 25, 1636. He recd. 20 li. of Mr. John Bewford of Middlesex, gent. 7 (1) 1644. [A.] Sold his house, called the King's Arms, with brew houses, etc. April 7, 1651. Rem. to Kittery, Maine. Bought land "in the great harbour of Pascataquack" of Nicholas Shapleigh 7 June, 1651. Took oath of allegiance to Mass. govt. 16 Nov. 1652. Was licensed to keep an ordinary and sell wine and strong water 24 Nov. 1652. Was sued by Nicholas Shapleigh, and resisted the marshall, on account of his manner of enforcing the writ 20 Dec. 1653. "Did give the marshall the lawe bucke [book], biding him lucke in it and act a Cording to lawe and hee would not hender hem." The testimony mentions the house where "widow Sarah Linn" was tenant of Shapleigh 3 or 4 years at the mouth of Piscataqua river; a piece of ground Gunnison had bought of S. but had not received; the brewing apparatus, still, etc. Benjamin Gillman, aged 45 years, wrote to "Brother and sister Gullison on the matter." [Mass. Arch. 60, 293.] He conveyed certain lands to his sons in law, William Sealey and William Rogers, 14 March, 1658-9, for 21 years, they agreeing to pay him ten shillings per annum.

His wife Elizabeth d. 25 (11) 1645, he m. 2, Sarah, widow of Henry Linn, who was adm. to the chh. of Boston 15 (3) 1647. Ch. Sarah b. 14 (12) 1637, Elizabeth b. 25 (2) 1640, Deborah b. (8) 1642, Hester bapt. 20 (12) 1647, Joseph b. 31 (1) 1649, Elihu b. 12 (12) 1649. He died before 26 (3) 1660, when his widow Sarah wrote a letter to Capt. Davenport, asking his offices in the settlement of her business; tells him he may ask needed money of her "father Tilly." She m. 3, Capt. John Mitchell; he died before 30 May, 1663, when she petitioned Gen. Court upon Gunnison's affairs; she deeded lands to Wm. Sealey and Wm. Rogers; this deed she confirmed, as "Sarah Morgan," 8 Sept. 1670. Meantime she had m. 4, Francis Morgan, chirurgeon, of Kittery, with whom she gave a deed of land 22 April, 1665.
See also Hill.

HABORNE, HAUBORNE, HABBORNE, RABONE, RAWBONE, ABORNE,

George, Exeter, signed the combination in 1639. Rem. to Wells; proprietor; his lands confirmed to him by the town June 30, 1648, he having possessed them 5 or 6 years. Sold in 1651 and rem. Hampton. Frm. at Hampt. court 7 (8) 1652.

He died before Oct. 3, 1654, when his nunc. will proved, giving all his estate to his wife Susanna. She m. 2, Thomas Leader. Susan, wife of Thomas Leader of Boston made will 24 May, 1657, prob. at Hampton 6 (8) 1657; beq. to her husband; to Edward Rishworth, Thomas Wheelwright, Merabah Smith, Hannah Clifford, Samuel Dalton, Robert Smith, Henry Elkins, Henry Robie and Mary Wedgewood. Inv. shows house and land in H. etc. Edward Rishworth receipted 31 (9) 1659, for his share of that est. which was given him by Susanna Habborne of Hampton.

HAINES, HAYNES,

Samuel, Dover, signed the combination in 1640; proprietor in 1642; juryman in 1646; taxed Oct. 19, 1648.

Rem. to Strawberry Bank; inhabitant, 1653; signed petition to the Gen. Court of Mass. in 1655. [Mass. Arch. 112.] He deposed 2 July, 1663, ae. about 58 years. [P. Files.]
See also Champernowne, Lewis, Withers, Young.

HAILE, HALEY, HALY, HALE,
Thomas, West Saco, Biddeford, had share of marsh; took oath of allegiance to Mass. govt. 5 July, 1653. [Bax. MSS. I.] Made deed of gift to son Thomas 21 March, 1683-4, on condition of maintenance during the remainder of his life.
See also West, Wilson.

HALL,
John, Dover, proprietor, signed the combination in 1640; proprietor and taxed in 1642 and 1648. One of the commissioners to end small controversies in 1648. Jury man, 1650. Deacon. Signed petition to Gen. Court 10 Oct. 1665.
Wife Elizabeth; child, Grace b. 16 March, 1663-4. [Dov. Hist. Coll.]
John Hall of Greenland (N. H.) made will 29 Aug. 1677, prob. Oct. 31, 1677; beq. to wife Elizabeth, son Joseph, dau. Sarah, gr. ch. Abigail Dame; to church of Dover, to be laid out for the communion table.
Ralph, Exeter, signed the combination 5 (4) 1639, and petitions in 1643 and 1647. Paid for "the dyett of the magistrates" by order of court 2 (8) 1651. Sold all lands in E. 29 Dec. 1652, to Moses Gyllman. Lieutenant; bought land of Tho: Biggs 11 Oct. 1663. Called "of Dover," he was chosen lieutenant at court July 2, 1657. With wife Mary sold land and house 19 Oct. 1664. Ch. Mary or Mercy b. at Exeter 15 Jan. 1647, d. in June, 1648; Hildea d. 16 April 1649; Sarah d. at Dover 16 July, 1663. [Dov. Hist. Coll.] He died [in 1701]. Admin. granted March 4, 1706-7,

to sons Joseph and James; division, 1708, to widow Mary and ch. John, James, Jonathan, Isaac, Benjamin, Ralph and Joseph.

See also Twambly.

HAM, HAME,

Matthew, fisherman, Isles of Shoals, 1657; constable 9 (5) 1657; juryman, 1658.

William, Strawberry Bank, grand jury man 8 (8) 1650; Jan. 13, 1652, "inhabitant," had lot. His son Matthew before court in 1657. Selectman, Portsmouth, 1656.

He died 26 Jan. 1672; his will, dated 21 Dec. 1672, prob. 27 June, 1673, beq. to grandchildren William, Thomas and John Ham; to daughter Elizabeth Cotton and her children. Matthew's son Thomas, residing in Rhode Island, sold some of the land which his grandfather had owned, 2 Aug. 1680.

HAMMOND, HAMMANS,

William, planter, Cape Porpoise, petition with others to Court at Saco Oct. 21, 1645; had in his keeping cattle belonging to John Lee in 1647. [Suff. De. I.]

Of Wells, took oath of allegiance to Mass. govt. 5 July, 1653. With wife Benedictus sold land in W. 11 May, 1661. Sold a house in Slymbridge, England, to his "brother" John Gooch, q. v. Made deed to and agreement with his son Jonathan Hammond 23 March, 1680-1.

See also Frost, Harding.

HANCOCKE, HANDCOCKE,

Henry, carpenter, worked for Winter at Richmond Island 3 years; went away in 1640. [Trel.]

HANSCOM, HANSCOMBE,

Thomas, mentioned in a proposition of Richard Claydon to come to Salem in 1629, as his brother in law. Could not come that year.

Thomas, b. about 1623, according to his deposition, came to Kittery about 1649; court case in 1651; may have been son of the man above-named. He m. May 16, 1664, Ann —, who survived him and m. (2) James Tobey. She was living in 1720. Ch.: Thomas, John, Olive, Samuel, Moses, Job,

HANSON,
Thomas, Dover, came before 1660 (?); his will proved June 27, 1666; wife Mary, sons Thomas, Tobias, Isaac, Timothy; some lands bought of William Hackett and Captain Barefoot, and others granted him by the town.

HARELL,
William, Richmond Island, fishing etc. in the employ of Winter, 1639-1641. [Trel.]

HARKER,
John, York, bought a house for Tho. Foules in 1647. [Court Rec.] He m. Dorothy, widow of Robert Mills witness of deed to Allcocke and Heard in 1650. Took oath of allegiance Nov. 22, 1652. Sold land Nov. 17, 1674. Deeded an island in York Harbor to son John July 1, 1673.

HARMAN, HARMON,
James, Cape Porpoise, m. Sarah, dau. of Edward Clark. In court 1660. Ch. Barbara, Jane and others (?). [Hist. Kpt.]

HART, HARTE,
John, was recd. as an inhabitant of Portsmouth and assigned lands Jan. 4, 1657-8. Will March 2, 1664-5; shipwright; wife to have estate for life; then to go to dau. Judith and the three ch. she had by Robert Rachell, her former husband.

HARWOOD,
Andrew, residence not stated, in court in 1643 for cutting timber within the jurisdiction of Piscataqua, and for non-attendance on religious services.

HATCH,

Charles, an apprentice of Clement Penwill or Pennywell, of Newton Ferrars, Eng. came to Richmond Island in 1633 and worked for Winter. Sept. 14, 1640, his wife acknowledged the receipt of money from Trelawney in England.

Philip, fisherman, Richmond Island, in the employ of Winter, 1638-1643
Rem. to York; bought land 23 Nov. 1648. Took oath of allegiance to Mass. govt. in 1652. He deposed 6 July, 1660, that Winter used a certain marsh about 22 years before.

He died before June 12, 1674, when Patience Hatch, his widow, gave a confirmatory deed of land.

Robin, sailor, was in 1643 one of the crew of the Margery, Ambrose Bouen, captain, in which Clement Penwill and his son Walter were also enrolled.

HAWKINS, HAUKINS,

Capt. Narias, mariner, sea-captain, came in ship with a company of men in 1634 on contract with Trelawney to fish and plant for three seasons. Wrote several letters to T. Had lawsuit at Saco March 25, 1636. Was master of ship Richmond in 1638, then of the Star, and of the Friendship in 1640. [Trel.]

See Adams, Alger.

HAYES,

Edward, Kittery, received goods before 3 Oct. 1660, at which time he gave a receipt for the same. [York De. I.]

He died about July 2, 1675, when he made a will which was probated 9 March following. He bequeathed to wife Philadelphia, sons Joseph and William, and daughters Elizabeth, Sarah and Ann. [Inventory in York De. V.]

See Jenkins.

HEARD, HERD, HIRD, HORD, HURD, HOORD, HURDE, see Harte,

John, carpenter, yeoman, Kittery, had a lawsuit in Maine court April 4, 1637. Lived at Sturgeon Creek. Took oath of allegiance to Massachusetts government 16 Nov. 1652. Town officer. His son James signed the petition to Cromwell in 1654.

He made will "weak by reason of age" 3 March, 1675-6; it was proved 21 Feb. 1676. To wife Isabel a comfortable maintenance; his daughter Susanna, widow of son James, to remain with her children at St. Crk. during her widowhood and until the children are disposed of; his lands to pass to his grandson John, son of James; certain bequests to the daus. of James, viz. Mary, Elizabeth, Katherine, Abigail and Ann. The widow of James, called now "Shuah," with her son John sold land 1 Nov. 1676. [York De. VI.] She afterward married Richard Otis; Nov. 5, 1677 an arrangement was made between them and the overseers of the will by which the estates of John and James were placed in the hands of James Chadbourne who was to take care of the widow Isabel and the grandchildren.

The grandson John made will 15 Jan. 1739, referring to his grandfather and the above mentioned bequest; was "aged and weak;" does not mention wife; bequeathed to daughters Dorcas Tucker, Shuah Bartlett, Phebe Stevens, Mary Barter and Abigail Hubbard; to Sarah and Phebe, daus. of his deceased son James Heard; to grandsons John Heard Hubbard, John Heard Bartlett, and the children of his dec. dau. Jane Coffin. Son in law Nathan Bartlett executor. The wife "Phebe" was killed by Indians, when returning from worship July 4, 1697, and John was wounded. [Pike's Journal.]

John, shipmaster, Dover, Cochecho, signed the combination in 1640. Lawsuit in Piscataqua court in 1642; "agreed." Proprietor and selectman. Bought of John Bursley 4 (5) 1649, land and houses at Exeter, but did not remove thither. Joined in petition of Dover inhabitants to Gen. Court 10 Oct. 1665. He married Elizabeth, dau. of Rev. Joseph Hull, born in England about 1628, died at Dover Nov. 30, 1706. Children, Benjamin b. Feb. 20, 1643, Mary b. 26 Jan. 1649, (m. May 6, 1668, John Ham), Abigail b. 2 Aug. 1651, (m. Jenkin Jones), Elizabeth b. 15 Sept. 1653, (m. 1, James Nute,

m. 2, William Furber), Hannah b. 25 Nov. 1655, (m. 1674, John Nason), John b. 24 Feb. 1658, Joseph b. 4 Jan. 1660, Samuel b. 4 Aug. 1663, Trustrum [Tristram] b. 4 March, 1666, Nathan [Nathaniel] b. 20 Sept. 1668.
Will dated April 2, 1687, prob. 1692.
Wife Elizabeth; ch. Benjamin, Trustrum, Samuel, Dorcas, Nathaniel, Mary Ham, Abigail Jones and Elizabeth Nute. Sarah widow of the son John, deceased, applied for a portion on behalf of her son Tristram Heard. She m. (2) William Foss.
See also Harker, Matthews, Roberts, Walton.

HEARLE,
William, Richmond Island, one of Winter's fishing company, 1638-9. Rem. to Portsmouth. With wife Beaton, sold land in Kittery 1 Feb. 1680. In his will, dated May 17, 1689, proved March 30 1691, he gave his house and lands to daughter Sarah and her husband John Cotton for life, then to their children.

HEIFERS, HEIFOR, HOFFER,
Andrew, Piscataqua, attended court at Saco June 25, 1640, admin. of his estate given to Arthur Auger July 7, 1663.
John, Richmond Island, worker for Winter 3 years, fishing, etc. 1637-9. Money was paid to his wife in England. [Trel.]

HELME, HELMES,
Christopher, Exeter, signed the combination 5 (4) 1639. The court ordered a certain sum of money to be "sent" to him in 1644. Removed to Warwick, R. I.

HEMPSON, IMPSON,
John, Richmond Island, one of Winter's fishermen, 1638-1640.

HENDRICK, HENRICK, HENDRICKS,
Daniel, planter, Hampton, proprietor, June 1640. Rem. to Haverhill, Mass.; proprietor there in 1645. Sold Hampt.

lands 8 (8) 1649; town officer. Resided at Newbury in 1652, and bought land at Haverhill. Deeded land 25 March, 1662, in trust for his seven eldest children (specified), to his bros. in law John and Robert Pike. He m. Dorothie, dau. of John Pike, Sen. She d. June 5, 1659; he m. 2, Mary Stockbridge. Children, Daniel, Hannah b. June 4, 1645, John b. May 23, 1648, Jotham b. March 21, 1649-50, Jabez b. Dec. 3, 1651, Israel b. Nov. 11, 1653, Dorothie b. May 31, 1659, Sarah b. Aug. 8, 1661, Abraham b. Aug. 2, 1663, d. Dec. 1, 1690, Deborah b. Nov. 25, 1666.

HERBERT, HARBERT, HARBUTT,
Sylvester, tailor, Piscataqua, 1660; his dau. was heir to £100 from her mother's mother, Mrs. Ramsay, of London. [York Deeds.] He bought house at Kittery in 1661. Rem. to Great Island. Admin. of estate Oct. 1, 1683.

HETHERSAY, HETHERSEE, HETHERSTILL, HEATHERSYE, HEATHERSEA,
Robert, Concord, Mass. proprietor, rem. to Charlestown; mortgaged a house in Conc. 20 (11) 1640. Called into Essex court in 1643; had lived many years away from his wife. Rem. to Exeter; signed petition of inhabitants in 1643; had lawsuit, 1648. Taxed at Dover in 1648. Bought land at York 13 Nov. 1651. Took oath of allegiance to Mass. govt. at York, 22 Nov. 1652.

HEWETT,
Nicholas, shipwright, Richmond Island, worked for Winter 10 days before 10 June, 1642. [Trel.]

HEYMAN, HEAMOND,
Pentecost, Richmond Island, one of Winter's fishermen and a servant of Stephen Sargent, 1639-1640.

HEYWARD,
John, brought suit for debt in Dover court in 1651.

HICKFORD, HECKFORD, KICKFORD,
John, son of Mr. Hickford a linen draper in Cheapside, London, came to the province of Mayne; spent some time;

returned to England soon after Sept. 6, 1639. [J. J.]
Named in records of Me. court March 6, 1636-7. Witnessed
the giving possession of Cleve and Tucker's grant 8 June,
1637. Sold a quantity of pork to Winter at Richmond Island
in 1639. [Trel.]

HICKMAN,
    Nicholas, carried a suit in Piscataqua court in 1646.

HICKS, see Hix.

HIGGINS, see Huggins.

HILL, HILLS,
    John, Dover, proprietor, 1649. Excused from training
27 June, 1661, at his request, "on account of the smallness
of his stature." He deposed the same day that he was about
35 years old. [P. Files.]
    John, residence not stated, left an undated will, giving
his estate to Capt. and Mrs. Champernowne and Mary Gunnison, probated at York 3 April, 1683.
    Peter, sailor, boat maker, Richmond Island, in the service of Winter from 1633 to 1643. He deposed 20 Nov. 1640, concerning Cleve's departure from Spurwink House. Resided at Saco. Deputy to the Ligonia Assembly Dec. 18, 1648. [Trel.] Took oath of allegiance to Mass. govt. 5 July, 1653. House at West Saco; i.e. Biddeford; had share of marsh in 1653.
    Roger, deposed [at Saco] Aug. 13, 1668, aged about 33 years. [Bax. MS. VI.]
    Valentine, merchant, Boston, admitted to the church 12 (4) 1636, admitted freeman May 13, 1640. Proprietor, town officer, deacon. Was chief owner of a large wharf property. Bought lands at Dover, and removed thither. Was chosen by the freemen to act as an assistant, with the magistrates, 5 (2) 1653. Signed petition to Gen. Court in 1654. He drew a bill of exchange 17 July, 1648, for 36 pounds, on

his "brother, Mr. John Hill, merchant, at the Angell and Starre in Cheapside," London. [A.] With wife Mary he sold, Nov. 2, 1660, a farm at Stony river, New Haven, given to her as a legacy, by Gov. Theophilus Eaton, of New Haven.

He m. 1, Frances —; she died 17 (12) 1644-5; he m. 2, Mary Eaton daughter of Gov. Eaton; she was adm. to the chh. of Boston 15 (3) 1647. Governor Eaton's will, 1656, names three children, Theophilus, Jr.; Mary, wife of Valentine Hill of Boston, late of Piscataqua, and Hannah; mentions his wife and her son Thomas Yale. Children, Hannah b. 17 (1) 1638, (m. Jan. 24, 1659, Antipas Boyce,) John b. and d. in 1640, Elizabeth b. 12 (10) 1641, d. 9 (2) 1643, Joseph and Benjamin b. and d. in 1644, Joseph bapt. 26 (5) 1646, ae. about 8 days, John bapt. 22 (6) 1647, ae. about 3 days, Samuel bapt. 10 (10) 1648, ae. about 2 days, Mary bapt. 30 (10) 1649, ae. about 1 day, Elizabeth bapt. 25 (3) 1651, Nathaniel b. Oyster River beginning of March, 1659-60.

He died before June 24, 1662, when his widow Mary received her dower. The widow m. second [Ezekiel] Knight.

"Mrs. Mary Knight was before me on the 23d of May, 1702 and acknowledged that Nathaniel Hill was the son of her first husband, Valentine Hill. John Woodman, Justs. Pac."

See also Berry, Bolles, Pormort, Purchase.

HILLIARD, HILLIER, HALLIER,

Emanuel, seaman, fisherman, Hampton, bought land and house 18 (3) 1649. Sold a house, stage, flakes, shallop, cables, etc. at Isles of Shoals 24 June, 1653.

Wife Elizabeth; children, Timothy, John b. and d. 1651, Benjamin b. 2 (9) 1652, Elizabeth b. 22 (11) 1654.

He recd. a gift of land Oct. 10, 1657, from his kinsman, Rev. Timothy Dalton.

He was lost in a vessel which sailed from Hampton for Boston Oct. 20, 1657. Admin. of his estate was granted to his widow Elizabeth 13 (2) 1658. She m. 2, Joseph Merrie, who contracted 13 (10) 1659, to pay to her children Timothy, Benjamin and Elizabeth their respective portions in due time.

HILTON,

Edward, with his brother William and Mr. David Thompson, fishmongers from London, began a plantation at Piscataqua in 1623. [Hub.] Exhaustive search of the records of the Fishmongers' Company of London, made by the compiler in 1907, failed to find any occurrence of either of these names; but a tax-roll of the city, made in 1641, [Lay Sub. 251, 22], brought to light by Mr. Gerald Fothergill, [Extracts in Reg. LXI], gives the name of Edward Hilton in the list of fishmongers, with the memorandum, "Newe England" after it. This indicates that he had certainly been in business there and had continued the shipment and sale of fish there up to a recent date. No trace of his parish or family has been found, nor the name of his first wife. He was the leader of the plantation and received the patent for the land—The Squamscott Patent, so-called, which covered what is now known as Dover, Durham, Stratham and parts of Newington and Greenland, etc. The Council for New England, "for and in consideration that Edward Hilton and his Associates hath already at his and their own proper costs and charges transported sundry servants to plant in New England at a point called by the natives Wecanacohunt otherwise Hilton's Point, lying some two leagues from the mouth of the River Pascataquack . . . where they have already built some houses and planted corne, And for that he doth further intend by God's Divine Assistance to transport thither more people and cattle . . . a work which may especially tend to the propagation of Religion and to the great Increase of Trade," . . . convey to him "all that part of the River Pascataquack called or known by the name of Wecanacohunt or Hilton's Point . . . with the south side of the River up to the ffall of the River and three miles into the Maine land by all the breadth aforesaid" etc., etc. Possession was given in the name of the Council by Capt. Thomas Wiggin and others 7 July, 1631. [Sup. Court Files, also Reg. XXIV, 264.] Part of this land was sold to individual settlers, part to the lords Say and Brook and some N. E. gentlemen. Mr. Hilton made his home after some time at Exeter; signed petition of inhabitants in 1642. Was that year appointed by the Mass. Bay govt. one of the local associate justices of the Court, sitting with the magistrates on the highest questions and acting by themselves in cases not beyond certain limits. The Gen. Court held him to be exempt from taxation on this account in 1669. He filled many important positions and was regarded highly. He m. (2) the   dau. of Mr. Alexander

Shapleigh and widow of James Treworgy, q. v. He d. before March 6, 1670-1, when admin. of his estate was granted to his sons Edward, William, Samuel and Charles; the claims of two daus. were presented by Christopher Palmer. Widow's dower to be £30 per quarter.

William, came in the *Fortune* to Plymouth in Nov. 1621. His wife and children came in the *Anne* in 1623, and lands were assigned to the family that year. Mr. Hilton wrote soon after his arrival a letter of great historical and personal value which was published by Capt. John Smith in his "New England's Trialls" in the edition of 1622. The name of the person addressed has not yet been found. He tells his "Cousin" (nephew) that he "found all our friends and planters in good health" in spite of trials they had endured; the land and productions excellent; "the companie for the most part very religious, honest people; the word of God sincerely taught us every Sabbath: so that I know not anything a contented mind can here want." Adds to the account the following wish: "I desire your friendly care to send my wife and children to me where I wish all the friends I have in England." Signs himself "Your loving kinsman William Hilton." Other letters of his are extant which show him to have been well educated and eminently intelligent and well-informed. His family stayed at Plymouth after he began the plantation at Piscataqua, and the baptizing of his babe by Rev. John Lyford, a thorn in the sides of the Puritan Pilgrims, was the occasion of the banishment of the Church of England partisans from Plymouth colony to Nantasket. But the letter above quoted from is evidence that Mr. Hilton was on the best of terms with the Pilgrims. His son William, years afterward, applying for confirmation of a deed of land near the present city of Concord, N. H., from the Indian sagamore Tahanto, affirms that his father removed from Plymouth in a short time after the arrival of his mother and the children. Mr. Hilton threw his influence on the side of the Mass. Bay govt.; was appointed a commissioner for trial of cases not above 20 shillings in 1642; freeman of the colony that year; deputy to Gen. Court in 1644. He resided near his brother in the vicinity of Dover some years; then rem. to Kittery and afterward to York. Carried on a ferry; kept public house; was one of the selectmen, etc. He d. before June 30, 1656, when his widow Frances' second husband, Richard White, admin. on his estate.

A possible clue to the connections of the Hiltons with English families may be found in the fact that a suit was brought in Pisc. Court by William Hilton, 4 (2) 1642, respecting a payment to "Mr. Richard Hilton of Northwich"; Mr. Waters found a record at Wotten-under-edge, Glouc., of the baptism of a child of this man, "coming out of New England." [See The Hilton Family, by Hassam.]

See also Bolter, Davis, Hocking, Lewis, Simmons, Treworgy, Wedgewood.

HINGER,

Mark, admin. of his estate was granted 26 June, 1660, to William Follett.

HINKSON, HINGSTON, HINKESON,

Philip, fisherman, made Arthur Gill attorney to take possession of a house and lands, fallen to him by inheritance in the parish of Halberton, co. Devon, Eng. 11 (5) 1646. [A.] Was one of Winter's fishing company at Richmond Island 1639-1643. Resided at West Saco (Biddeford) in 1653. His widow Margaret married second George Taylor of Black Point, who joined with her 20 June, 1662, in a letter of attorney to Peter Hinkson, fisherman, of co. Devon, to demand, receive and let out a tenement in Hobberton [Halberton], a legacy to Philip from John Wedge and his wife for the use of Sarah and Meribah, the two daughters of Philip and Margaret. [York De. I.]

Thomas, Portsmouth, proprietor, 1660. Dying in June, 1664, he bequeathed his estate to his wife (Martha) and child (Mary).

William, master of the ship Hercules, fished and traded on the coast of Maine and southward from 1637 to 1648. He took a cargo of fish to "Bilbow" 17 July, 1639; made many voyages to and from Plymouth, Eng. Was a legatee in the will of Robert Trelawney. Residing at Saco, 5 July, 1653, he took oath of allegiance to Mass. govt.

See Mitchell, Taylor, Walford.

HITCHCOCK,

Richard, Saco, was before the Gen. court of Mass. Aug. 5, 1634. Had a lawsuit in Maine court March 6, 1636-7.

Sold wheat to Winter in 1643. [Trel.] Took oath of allegiance to Mass. govt. 5 July, 1653. Sergeant. House at West Saco. [Bax. MSS.] Planter; had deed of his place from Vines [about 1654]. [York De. I.] Representative to Gen. court, 1660. Deposed Aug. 18, 1668, aged 60 years. [Bax. MS. VI.] Will dated 6 June, 1670, prob. 20 Sept. 1671, beq. to wife [Lucretia] and children Thomas, Jerusha, Lydia, Rebecca, Ann and Margaret.

HIX, HICKS,
   Richard, Cape Porpoise, 1660; grand jury, 1661; constable, 1669. Wife Susanna.

HOBBS, HOBES,
   Christopher, planter, Saco, took oath of allegiance to the Mass. govt. 5 July, 1653. Resided at West Saco (Biddeford). Had a share of the marsh July 12, 1653. Admin. on estate of his brother in law William Foster June 29, 1654.
   Will dated 26 Nov. 1673, prob. 28 March, 1674, beq. to son Christopher house and lands, with certain other estate unless son John should come over to take possession of it; to daughter Jane and her 4 children; to son Robert the upper plantation.
   Maurice or Morris, Newbury, Mass.; before Ipswich court in 1642; witness in 1663. Rem. to Hampton; proprietor 23 (12) 1645.
   He m. 1, Mary —; he m. 2, Sarah, dau. of William Estow. Ch. William, John, Sarah, Nehemiah, Morris b. at Hamp. 5 (11) 1641, James, Mary b. 11 (12) 1656, Bethia b. 28 (12) 1658, Hannah b. 9 (2) 1662, Abigail b. 29 (5) 1664.
   He made a deed of gift 10 Nov. 1679, to his grandchild James, son of his son James lately deceased and his wife Sarah, and to Morris and Sarah, other children of the same.
   His estate was admin. upon by sons Nehemiah and Morris Sept. 3, 1706.
   See also Bachiler, Colcord, Estow.

HOCKING, HOCKINGS,
Mr. John, went in a pinnace belonging to the Lords Say and Brook at Piscataquack to trade at the Kennebeck river. Was challenged by the men who were trading and fishing there under authority of Plymouth Colony; shot one of their men and was shot in return. Mr. George Ludlow receipted 2 Aug. 1632 to Mr. William Hilton for certain goods of Hocking's. Copy attested by Edward Rishworth June 5, 1657. [York De. I.]

HOFFER, see Heffer.

HOLE, HOOLE, HOLLE,
John, Richmond Island, one of Winter's fishermen for 3 years, 1638-1640. Removed "westward." Probably he is the settler at Kittery, constable in 1671. With wife Elizabeth sold land 26 July, 1681; rem. to the island of Barbadoes; merchant; made his wife his attorney 12 Aug. 1690. She sold land at K. 10 Jan. following. Having married a daughter of Richard Leader, he was made one of the administrators of Mr. L.'s estate in 1667.
See Cutt, Hocking, York.

HOLLICUM, HOLYCOM,
Peter, Biddeford, had share of marsh in 1653.

HOOK, HOOKE,
Mr. William, merchant, son of Humphrey Hooke of Bristol, Eng.; came to New England about 1634. [W.] Had lawsuit in Maine court 25 March, 1636. Was governor of Agamenticus and one of the patentees of the plantation in 1638. [York De. VI, 74.] Rem. to Salisbury; frm. Mass. Oct. 12, 1640. Had interests at Agamenticus still. [L.] Sold land to Samuel Bennett March 15, 1649, referring to his father Humphrey and his uncle William Hooke. His father wrote him from Bristol 5 March, 1645; had promised to pay a debt for him; assigned to him mortgages, debts, etc.

in New Eng. He settled one of his father's accounts 30 (4) 1648. [A.]

He m. Ellner, widow of Lieutenant Colonel Walter Norton; she made deed to Capt. Thomas Clarke, and he made deed to her daughter Jane, wife of Henry Simson. [York De. I and VI.]

He died before 4 (8) 1653, when his widow Elinor recd. right of admin.; she petitioned the Gen. Court 23 May, 1655, for liberty to sell lands at the Eastward belonging to her first husband, Capt. Norton; granted. She also recd. power to admin. on the estate of her late husband Wm. Hooke for herself and youngest son, but not to sell. Children, Jacob b. at Salisbury Sept. 15, 1640, William. Was not Francis who m. Mary, dau. of Samuel Maverick of East Boston, Sept. 20, 1660, also a son? Was Susanna, who m. Edward Derby in Boston, Jan. 25, 1669, a daughter?

See also Alcock, Chapman, Dixon, Dunnell, Gaile, Gooch, Simpson, Twisden.

HOOPER, HUPPER,

Thomas, residence not stated, furnished boards for fish barrels and sugar barrels, etc. to Coffin in the Piscataqua valley, Feb. 2, 1659. [Es. Files, suit of Broughton et als. 1664.]

Elisha, was credited on the books of the town of Wells as having in 1677, served "in the Indian Warrs" and credited with £00-12-06. [Me. Hist. Soc. Coll, 2d Ser. vol. VI.]

John, residence not stated, credited with making a pair of "Bootes," furnished to Mr. Winter at Richmond Island in 1642, the sum of 8 shillings being the price. [Trel.] Was he not the ancestor — father or grandfather — of John Hooper, cordwainer, of Kittery, a of Thomas of same place, residents there about 1700?

HORRELL, HORWELL,

Humphrey, Isles of Shoals, signed petition for incorporation 18 (3) 1653. [Mass. Arch. 3, 125.]

HORTON,
>Barnabas,< baker, Hampton, proprietor, 1640. Rem. to Ipswich, Mass.; sold land 12 (1) 1641; signed petition of York residents in 1654. [Mass. Arch. 3, 237.]

HOSKIN,
>John,< Richmond Island, fisherman, 1634. [Trel.]

HOW, HOWE,
>Anthony,< had lawsuit in Maine court July 4, 1637. See Shaw.

HOWARD, HAWARD,
>William,< lieutenant, Hampton, 1640; deputy, military leader and town clerk. Criticism of his course was made by a part of his townspeople in a petition to the Gen. Court 7 (1) 1643. [Mass. Arch. 67, 33-4.]
[See persons of this name in P. of M.]
See also Sawers.

HOWELL,
>Morgan,< planter, came with Vines; [Hist. Ken. Port.] Settled at Cape Porpoise, had lawsuit in Maine court March 6, 1636-7. Bought 100 acres of land of Gorges 18 July, 1643. Took oath of allegiance to Mass. govt. 5 July, 1653.
Will dated 17 Nov. 1666, prob. 1 April, 1667, beq. to "Mis" (Mrs.) Mary Bolls and her children and Mary Frost, Senior and Mary F., Jr.
>John,< Casco, about 1651; deposed 13 July, 1681, ae. about 48 years, that John Mills possessed a certain marsh "30 years since."
>Richard,< before Dover court in 1655.

HUGGINS, HIGGINS, HUGGIN, HUGINS, HUCKINS,
>John,< Hampton, proprietor, June, 1640, mortg. house and land 22 (1) 1643-4, as security for the delivery of pipe staves. [Ips. town rec.] Wife Bridget deposed 6 (8) 1659, ae. about 44 years. [Es. Files.] Children, Susanna, Mary b. 29 (3) 1650, Bridget b. 26 (10) 1651, John, Martha b. 11 (9) 1654, Anna b. 15 (1) 1658, Nathaniel b. July 15, 1660.

He died 7 (4) 1670. Will dated May 31, prob. 11 Oct. 1670; aged about 61 years; beq. wife Bridget and son John; younger children to have christian education. Sons John and Nathaniel made a deed of agreement and partition 7 Oct. 1680. The widow m. 2, John Clifford.

Robert, Dover, signed combination in 1640; proprietor, 1642.

HULL (incorrectly called Hill in passenger list),
Edward, sued for debt in Dover court in 1651.
Rev. Joseph, of Somerset, a minister, ae. 40, came in the ship from Weymouth, Eng. March 20, 1634-5, with wife Agnes, ae. 25, (sic.) children Joane, ae. 15, Joseph, ae. 13, Tristram, ae. 11, Elizabeth, ae. 7, Temperance, ae. 9, Grissell, ae. 5, and Dorothy, ae. 3, and servants Judith French, ae. 20, John Wood, ae. 20, and Robert Dabyn, ae. 28. Twenty-one other families came at the same time, who were allowed by the General Court, 5 (8) 1635, to "sit down at Wessaguscus after called Weymouth." Freeman Sept. 2, 1635. After a brief stay at Wey. he rem. to Hingham; was one of the commissioners to assist the magistrates 6 (7) 1638; deputy. "Gave his farewell sermon" [presumably to the church of Hull] May 5, 1639. [Hob.] Rem. to Barnstable; meeting of church at his house Nov. 3, 1639. Accepted the call of the people of Yarmouth to be their pastor; was excommunicated by the church of Bar. May 1, 1641, for so doing contrary to their advice but was received to fellowship again after due apology Aug 10, 1643. Rem. to York, Me. and was settled as minister in 1643. [W.] Witnessed a deed of Thomas Gorges in 1643; he and Roger Garde measured land of Mr. Godfrey 5 May, 1644; his wife Agnes also witnessed a deed in 1645.

Children recorded here; "daughter" [Joanna], m. about 28 Nov. 1639, John Bursley; Benjamin bapt. at Hingham March 24, 1639, Naomi bapt. at Bar. March 23, 1639-40, Ruth bapt. at Bar. May 9, 1641.

See also Williams.

HUMBER,
 Mr. Humphrey, before Hampton court 3 (8) 1654.

HUMPHREY, HUMPHREYS,
 Jeremiah, in the employ of Rev. Robert Jordan at Richmond Island in 1648. [Trel.]
 See Wiggin.

HUNKINS, HUNKINGE, HUMPKINS,
 Archelaus, Arcullus, Hercules, Isles of Shoals, 1649; appointed on grand jury in 1650, but paid a fine rather than attend: lot of land assigned him in 1652. Mark Hunkins [his son] had sons Mark and Archelaus. Signed petition to Gen. Court 18 (3) 1653. Appointed one of the commissioners for settling minor cases there. Rem. to the main land of Portsmouth.
 Will dated 21 Aug. 1659, inventory taken Sept. 6, 1659, of Portsmouth property, and that of Isles of Shoals property taken later; beq. one third to his wife for her life, then to pass to his "eares"; the other two thirds to dau. Ann Hunkins and her children.
 John, Dover, had an account with Hercules. [Es. Prob.] Wife Agnes; children John b. in 1651, d. in England in 1666, Hercules b. 11 July, 1656. 2d wife Richard survived him.
 He made will 25 Aug. proved June 7, 1681. Wife to have all she brought, 100 li. in movables and a home in lieu of dower; ch. John, Peter William, Mark, Agnes and Elizabeth. The widow "Richard" m. George Snell of Portsmouth; in her will, Sept. 24, 1691, proved April 23, 1695, she mentions "my sister Margery Vittery of Kingsward (Kingswear) co. Devon, Eng. and my son George Littlejohn of Halwel, co. Devon."

HUNNIWELL, HUNNEWELL, HONEWELL,
 Roger, West Saco, 1653. [Bax. MSS. 1, 87.]
 John Honewell of Middletown, Conn., brickmaker, sold land at Winter Harbor in the province of Maine, commonly

called Honewell's Neck, 18 Dec. 1692.
See William Honywell of Plymouth, N. E. 1633-1641, [P. of M]. See also Ambrose Hunnewell of Sagadahock, [Reg. LIV, 140].
See also Jordan.

HUNT,
Richard, one of the "Shrewsbury Men" who held the Dover and Squamscott patent; signed the combination in 1640; was witness to a deed of Rev. Thomas Larkham in 1642.

HUTCHINSON, HUTCHINS,
John, carpenter, ae. 30, came in the Bevis in May, 1638, to Boston.

John, residence not stated, contracted 2 (10) 1659, with Brian Pendleton, John and Richard Cutt, Henry Sherburne and William Seavey, committee of Portsmouth, to build a new meeting house 40 feet square and 16 feet high, a flat roof and a substantial turrett with a gallery about it, etc.; and to repair the old meeting house and fit it up for a house for the minister. [Court rec. II, 34.]

Samuel, brother of Rev. John Wheelwright's wife, came to Exeter with the family. Had a part in negotiation for land at Wells for that settlement in 1641. Seems not to have *lived* in Maine or New Hampshire.
See Wheelwright.

HUPPER, see Hooper.

HUSSEY,
Christopher, yeoman, resident of Saugus (afterward called Lynn), Mass., 1632; frm. May 14, 1634. Rem. to Newbury; proprietor, 1637. Rem. to Hampton, of which he was one of the first planters Sept. 6, 1638. Commissioner to end all business under 20 shillings, May 22, 1639; lot-layer Oct. 31, 1639. Signed petition in Howard case in 1643. Captain, deacon, deputy, etc.

He m. 1, Theodate, dau. of Rev. Stephen Bachiler, who gave to them all his cattle, goods and debts on his return to England; [deposition of Colcord;] she d. (8) 1649. He m. 2, 9 (10) 1658, Ann [widow of Jeffrey] Mingay; she d. June 24, 1680. Children, Stephen, Mary bapt. at Newbury April 2, 1638, Theodate bapt. at Hamp. Aug. 23, 1640, d. (8) 1649, John, Huldah.

He was one of the early proprietors of the island of Nantucket; he, "now resident in Hampton," deeded all his lands and rights in the island of N. to sons Stephen and John 23 Oct. 1671 and 6 Dec. 1681.

He died 6 March, 1685-6, ae. about 90; buried 8 March. Will *signed* 28 Feb. 1684, codicil dated at Salisbury Oct. 28, 1685, was proved 7 (8) 1686; beq. to his "2 sons" Stephen and John Hussey; daughter Mary, now wife of Thomas Page; son John Smith and daughter Huldah, his wife.

Mary, widow, Hampton, proprietor, 1638-1640. She sold to John Woodin for three pounds, 25 (2) 1648, a joint possession in 16 acres of land, part of it adjoining land of Christopher Hussie.

She died 16 (4) 1660.

See also Green, Shrewsbury.

INGERSOLL,

George, Falmouth, bought 55 acres of land adjoining that of Thomas Skilling March 25, 1658.

He deposed 24 June, 1685, ae. about 67 years, concerning the clearing of land by Richard Corben 28 years before.

Note. Richard, from Bedfordshire, Eng. sent over with his family by the Mass. Bay Co. in 1629, to Salem, had son George. [P. of M.]

INIOUN, see Onion.

JACKSON,

John, cooper, Strawberry Bank, brought suit in Piscataqua court 30 (7) 1651, against Henrie Duglasse for 18 weeks of his son, to the value of 8 li. sterling. Juryman, 1652. Bought house and land of Ambrose Lane 2 June, 1651. Took oath of fidelity July 2, 1657. With wife Joane deeded land to son Thomas J., cooper, of same place, 25 June, 1660, and to son John 7 Nov. 1666; Thomas was one of the witnesses to the latter deed.

He died before July 12, 1660, when admin. on his estate was granted to John Cutt. June 25, 1667, the estate was granted to the widow Joane and son Richard; after her death division was to be made to the sons Richard, Thomas and John.

Richard, Portsmouth, constable, took oath of allegiance July 11, 1659. See son of John, above.

See also Bailey, Jocelyn.

JAMES,

William, with others brought suit for wages in court at Kittery Oct. 16, 1647. Sold house and land in 1651. Trouble with Wormwood family, witness in Dover court 8 (8) 1650.

See Lawson.

JEFFREY, JEFFRIES, GEOFFERIE, GEOFFREY,

Gregory, Cape Porpoise, had a grant of land from Cleve Nov. 1, 1651. Took oath of allegiance to Mass. govt. 5 July, 1653. Had lawsuit in Portsmouth court in 1660.

Will dated Jan. 14, 1661-2, prob. 7 March, 1661-2, beq. to wife Mary; son John to have a portion at 17 years of age; to the church of Saco; to kinsman Charles Potum. The widow m. 2, John Lux; beq. her estate to son John Jeffrey and her children Mary and Joseph Lux; placed the estate in Mr. Lux's hands Sept. 8, 1664. Recorded 7 Feb. 1665.

Mr. William, gent. called by Winthrop "an old planter" was deputed with Rev. William Blackstone to put J. Oldham in possession of his grant. [Suff. Deeds I, XIII.] Brought a letter from Morton to Winthrop Aug. 4, 1634. Was associated with Nicholas Easton in building the first house at

Hampton in 1638, but does not appear again in records here. Settled at Weymouth (Mass.). Freeman May 18, 1631. Signed a bond for Jeremy Gould in 1641. [L.]
Ch. Mary, b. 20 (1) 1642.
See also Bush, Crockett, Lewis, Mussell.

JENKIN, JENKINS, JINCKINS, GINKENS,
Joseph, residence not stated, had lawsuits in Piscataqua court in 1642. [See P. of M.]

Reginald, yeoman, one of the fishermen at Richmond Island in 1637; settled at Kittery; took oath of allegiance to Mass. govt. 16 Nov. 1652. Deeded to his daughter Philadelphia Hayes of K., widow, 7 March, 1675-6, land and house, lately in possession of her husband, Edward H. deceased. He deposed 23 June, 1683, ae. about 75 years, as to his buying land of John Newgrove between 40 and 50 years before. [York De. IV.] Deeded salt marsh to son Jabez 10 Feb. 1678. The latter, ae. about 27 years, and Stephen, ae. about 28 years, deposed 29 May, 1682, in a land case.

JENNER, GINNER,
Rev. Thomas, Roxbury, Mass. frm. Dec. 8, 1636. Rem. to Weymouth; proprietor, with son Thomas in 1636. Was called to be pastor of the church, and he and his people were brought into harmony by a gathering of elders 9 (11) 1637. [W.] Deputy, arbiter in a case before Gen. Court in 1640. Rem. to Saco, Me. [Mass. Hist. Col. 4-7.] Sold wheat to Winter, 1643. [Trel.] Wrote letter to Gov. Winthrop in 1641.

28 (10) 1649, his son Thomas, of Charlestown, sold land at Weymouth which had been his father's, and "Mrs. Jenner" consented to the deed. Esther, [the wife or a daughter?] was adm. to the church of Char. 9 (5) 1648. Gov. Edward Winslow wrote from London April 17, 1651, referring to his having purchased Mr. Jenner's library on behalf of a Society, and paid £50 on account to Mr. J., then in Norfolk co., Eng. [Hazard Coll. II, 178-180.]

Patrick, Dover, bought land and house of Valentine Hill 11 May, 1659.

JEWELL,
George, mariner, Richmond Island, had a "stage," and carried on fishing in 1632. Had suit in Maine court April 30, 1637. He was drowned in Boston Harbor in 1637. [W.]
Samuel, York; his wife Mary had a deed of land from Wm. Hooke 24 July, 1650. She witnessed his deed to Allcocke, 1650.
Residing at Isles of Shoals, he signed the petition of the people for improved privileges 18 (3) 1653.

JEYLES, see Giles.

JOCELYN, JOCELEIN, JOSELIN, JOSELYN, JOSSELYN, JOSLIN,
Abraham, Scarborough, with wife Rebecca, sold land 27 Oct. 1659; deed witnessed by Henry and Margaret J. Rem. to Boston, and with wife Betteris, sold land at Scar. which had been in his possession "for divers years past," 8 June, 1660.
See Thomas J. husbandman, of Hingham, Mass. and his son Abraham. [P. of M.]
Henry, gent. lieutenant, son of Sir Thomas, knight, came early to the coast of Maine. Was one of those authorized by the Council for New England 1 Nov. 1631, to give possession of a grant of land to Capt. Thomas Cammock; which was done in July, next year. [Trel.] Sir Ferdinando Gorges appointed him "servant and steward general," and one of the commissioners for the government of the colony. In this capacity he attended court at Saco 25 March, 1636. He took oath of allegiance to Mass. Bay govt. at Spurwink 13 July, 1658.
He was one of the commissioners appointed by Charles II in 1661, to have charge of the province.

His wife Margaret joined him in a deed of land to Ellner Jackson and her son John, planters, 20 May, 1663.

John, gent. son of Sir Thomas, came with his father in the Nicholas, arriving at Black Point July 14, 1638; resided there a while, studying the land and people. Returned to England, and came again in 1663, for another visit. Wrote "Two Voyages to New England" and "New England's Rarities," in which he presented many of his observations in a racy style. The "Relation" published at London in 1673, is given in Mass. Hist. Soc. Coll. third series, vol. 3.

Sir Thomas, knight.

He was appointed by Gorges deputy governor of all his possessions in New England, and came to Black Point July 14, 1638. He was then 78 years old. [Trel.] He returned before Sept. 3, 1639.

See also Cammock, Collins, Purchase, Roberts, Smith, Wall.

JOHNS,

Catherine, widow, her estate admin. by John Fabyan June 26, 1660.

JOHNSON,

Edmund, ae. 23, came in the James to Boston in July, 1635, settled at Hampton; proprietor, 1640 and 1646. Lawsuit 1648.

He died 1 (1) 1650. Inventory 4 (1) 1650-1. Admin. of his estate was granted 8 (2) 1651 to his widow Mary. She m. July 11, 1651, Thomas Coleman, who secured 7 (8) 1653, to the children their portions of their father's estate; to Peter, the eldest, 32 pounds; to John 16 pounds, to James 16 pounds, and to Dorcas 16 pounds, to be paid the sons at 21 years of age and to the daughter at 18 or marriage. He was to pay the cost of educating the children . . . to read and write.

Edward, Mr. licensed by Gov. Winthrop to go forth on

trading to Merrimack; of which Dep. gov. Dudley complained in Aug. 1632. [W.] Had accounts with the court July 1, 1634.

Edward, gent. bought land for the use of John Treworgy 5 May, 1636, located on North side of Piscataqua river. [York De. I.] Took oath of allegiance to Mass. govt. at Kittery 16 Nov. 1652. Petitioned Gen. Court with others in 1654. Was one of the province commissioners in 1667. [York De. V.] With wife Priscilla and son Benjamin sold land 24 Aug. 1669, to John Card, cooper. He and his wife gave to John Harmon, husband of their daughter Deborah, a tract of land in consideration of life care for themselves, 18 Aug. 1680. He deposed 29 June, 1682, ae. about 89 years, that about 42 or 43 years agone "Mis Ann Messant alias Godfrey lived with Mr. Geo. Burdett, then minister of Agamenticus, now called Yorke, in the Province of Mayne," and received certain lands in lieu of money she had lent him. Mrs. Priscilla J., ae. about 65 years, confirmed the testimony. [York De. III.]

James, husbandman, was at Kittery in 1636 according to his deposition about Capt. Mason's will, made 31 May, 1652, his age being about 50 years. Resided at "Little Harbour, Piscataqua river;" one of the residents of Bloody Point who petitioned in 1642 that they might be included in Dover. [Mass. Arch. 3, 438.] Surety in court in 1642. Allowed to keep the ordinary at Dover and to maintain a ferry to Strawberry Bank and Hiltons, by Hampton Court, 24 (2) 1649. Sold his house at Long Beach to James Rawlins; acknowledged the deed in court 2 (8) 1651. Took oath of fidelity July 2, 1657. Major in 1659. Took James Barkeley apprentice. With wife Mary sold house and lands 6 Nov. 1660.

He died before June 8, 1678, when inventory of his estate was taken at Great Island; goods in possession of widow Mary. After her death the only surviving children Mary, wife of James Odiorn and Hannah, wife of Thomas Jackson, made division of the estate, Nov. 16, 1694.

Thomas, planter, Dover, had suit in court in 1641; taxed

Oct. 19, 1648. Sold house and land to Nicholas Follett in 1652.

He died before June 26, 1661, when admin. of his estate was granted to Wm. Furber and Wm. Follett. The court ordered 30 June, 1663, that his child should live with goodman Layton till she is ten years of age, and then choose a guardian. She died soon; and as no heir made claim for the estate, 27 June, 1665, the court ordered it given to the selectmen of Oyster River, "according unto the Law title eschates."

See also Abbot, Barkeley, Bradbury, Lewis, Sinkler, Swadden, Wanerton, Wiggin.

JONES,

Alexander, seaman, Isles of Shoals, had suits in Dover court in 1651. Mortg. land and privileges for three boats on Great Island 11 June, 1661. With wife Hannah sold land 18 Feb. 1668.

John, blacksmith, Strawberry Bank, was in charge of "Wallertoone's" [Wanerton's?] house before 24 (3) 1647, as he testified. [Mass. Arch. 38 B, 48.] Deposed about former acts of the Royal Commission 7 Oct. 1665, aged about 50 years. [Mass. Arch. 106, 155.] May be the J. J. aged 20, who came to Boston in the Susan and Ellen in April, 1635. He was sued 8 (5) 1650, by Jeremy Sheres, for detaining his apprentice, Francis Jones. He and wife Ann sold land in 1658 and 1661.

He took oath of fidelity 11 July, 1659. They deposed in 1660, relative to Wm. Clifton's land which was spoken of in their house in the year 1637.

His will dated 2 Sept. prob. 17 Sept. 1667, beq. to wife Anne, children Francis, Nathaniel, James and John Jones, and Mary Drew.

Rice, [Richard], Isles of Shoals, signed petition in 1653.

Thomas, butcher, from Elsing, co. Norfolk, Eng. came in the Mary and Ann in 1637, ae. 25 years. Settled at Newbury; proprietor in 1637. Rem. to Exeter; sold land in 1639.

Had grant of house lot at Hampton Dec. 24, 1639. Herdsman, 1640. Signed petition of Exeter inhabitants in 1643 and 1647. Child Susanna bapt. at Hampt. Oct. 29, 1639. Rem. to Charlestown, and sold land in Newbury 6 July, 1650. Deposed in 1654, ae. 45. He died Oct. 24, 1666. Will dated Sept. 24, prob. [Mdx. co.] Dec. 18, 1666, beq. to wife Abigail and dau. Susanna Goose; son in law William Goose mentioned in inventory. The widow m. second Thomas Chadwell and was received to Char. church June 14, 1668, with memorandum to this effect. She made will 8 June, prob. 19 June, 1683; bequeathed to her husband; to sister Ann Pearson of Piscatag; to grandson Joseph Goose and his sister Susanna Crosse; to sister Wheeler's daughters; refers to Joseph Goose's agreement dated July 28, 1882.

Thomas, Kittery, had suit in Maine court 25 March, 1636. Was in the service of Alexander Shapleigh about 1639, as he testified 2 May, 1679, ae. about 70 years. [York De. VI.] Residing "further northward," he took oath of allegiance at Kittery 16 Nov. 1652.

Thomas, Portsmouth, deposed in Walton case in court 28 (4) 1660, ae. about 24 years; perhaps son of the above.

William, Bloody Point, signed the combination in 1640; was one of those residents who petitioned about 1642 to be included in the limits of Dover. [Mass. Arch. 3, 438.] Was put under bonds in 1644 to "goe to his wife in Old England."

See also Bursley, Clifton, Cornish, Johnson, Webster.

JOPE,

Samson, Richmond Island, one of the fishermen in 1637. Went back to England and, in 1639, was recommended to be sent over to finish the ship that Winter was having built. Referred to in Winter's account in 1642.

JORDAN,

Rev. Robert, gent. minister, is believed to be the person who was matriculated at Baliol College, Oxford university,

June 15, 1632, described as "son of Edward Jordan, of Worcester, pleb. aged 18."

He came to New England about 1637; stayed with his kinsman Mr. Purchase until May, 1641, when he came to Richmond Island, where he settled as minister. The plantation at Pemaquid desired at that time to have him all or half of the time. In the controversy between Winter and Cleve respecting land titles he naturally took the side of Winter. Letters of much interest from him are in the Trelawney Papers. He took oath of allegiance to Mass. govt. at his house at Spurwink 13 July, 1658. He deposed 1 July, 1660, ae. 49 years. [York De. I.]

He was appointed one of the commissioners of Charles II in 1661. He rem. to Great Island in Portsmouth; he and his wife Sarah of Cape Elizabeth made a deed of gift 29 Feb. 1675 to their son Robert.

He m. about Jan. 1643-4, Sarah, daughter of John Winter. Children, John, Robert, Dominicus, Jedidiah, Samuel and Jeremiah. All these and their mother are mentioned in the will of the minister, dated 28 Jan. 1678, proved July 7, 1679. [Me. Wills, 57, and York De. III.]

The widow and son Robert sold land at Scarborough to Richard Hunniwell 20 Jan. 1684. [Bax. MSS.]

See also Bowden, Bucknall, Humphreys, Mackworth, Purchase, Spencer, Thorpe, Tristram.

JOSE, JOCE, JOYSE,

Christopher, mariner, Portsmouth, Isles of Shoals, in court in 1651; witness to a deed of land at the Shoals in 1653. Proprietor, 1660. Bought land in Portsmouth of Elias Stileman in 1662. With wife Jane, 10 Oct. 1664, he sold land granted him by the town. Children, Richard b. 10 Nov. 1660, Thomas b. 27 June, 1662, Joanna b. 13 March, 1664, Margaret b. 10 Oct. 1666, John b. 27 May, 1668, Jane b. 18 July, 1670, Samuel b. 6 May, 1672, Mary b. 8 July, 1674. [Dov. Hist. Coll.] He carried on the fishing business and merchandise.

His wife was a dau. of Richard Cumins who gave his estate to her and her children.

Will dated 14 Sept. 1676, prob. 25 June, 1678, beq. to children Richard, Thomas, Joanna, Margaret, Mary, John, Samuel and Jane; to "cousin" Thomas Jose; and to wife Jane; 3 pounds to the church in Portsmouth and 3 pounds to the "Colledge."

The widow Jane made her will Oct. 31, 1689, bequeathing to eldest son Richard his father's cloak, a copper kettle, a gold ring and a silver porringer; to daughter Johanna Sivert a negro woman and a gold ring; to dau. Margaret White a silver platter, silver whistle and chain, brass kettle, silken quilt, gold ring and a cow, and 20 li. in money; to son John seal ring, silver tumbler and spoons, 2 cows and 20 li.; to daus. Jane and Mary her clothes and ten pounds in money, to each a gold ring, a twenty shilling piece of gold and 20 li. with 10 li. apiece as a gift from their grandfather; to son Samuel a featherbed, a seal ring and 20 li.; to Mary also a silver tankard; something to grandson Thomas Joce; mentions shop, goods, etc.

JOSSELYN, see Jocelyn.

JOY,

Richard, carpenter, in the employ of Winter at Richmond Island, worked on a ship that was launched 14 June, 1641. His "boy" did good service.

Walter, Kittery, had allotment of land in 1650. [York De. 1.]

See Curtis, Jynkins, Spencer.

KENT,

Oliver, Dover, taxed in 1648. Lawsuit in 1655. He died, and admin. on his estate was granted to his widow Dorothy and John Bickford June 28, 1670.

See Wakefield.

KICKEFORD, see Hickford.

KID,
   James, before Dover court 2 July, 1657.

KIMBALL, KEMBLE,
   Thomas, wheelwright, Hampton, was son of Richard and Ursula K. of Ipswich, Mass. [P. of M.] Came from England with his parents in 1634. Resided in Dover in the year 1657, as he deposed at Portsmouth, 28 June, 1678, being then "about 57 years of age" Rem. to Hampton. Bought land 15 Oct. 1658.
   Wife Mary; children, Elizabeth b. and d. 1658, Richard b. Nov. 20, 1659.
   Genealogy.
   See Dow.

KING,
   Richard, Portsmouth, bought Thomas William's rights in "Champering island" 13 Aug. 1649. Admin. of his estate was granted to Brian Pendleton Oct. 4, 1653.
   Thomas, carpenter, in the service of Nicholas Langworthy of Stonehouse, Eng. came to Richmond Island and worked for Winter in 1634. Rem. to Hampton. Proprietor, June, 1640. One of the committee to build a pound in 1642. Rem. to Exeter; sold Hamp. property 29 Sept. 1644. Signed Exeter petitions in 1643 and 1647. Laid claim 25 (1) 1650, to house and land in Hamp. he had bought of Robert Hithersa. Was authorized to keep the ordinary and sell wine and beer 8 (2) 1651.
   He made will 11 March, 1666-7, prob. 9 (2) 1667; beq. to wife Miriam; to neighbor and country man Jonathan Thing; cousin Henry Moulton; cousin Christian Dolhortt [Dolloff] and cousin Rachel, his present wife; to servant William Willy; to John Moulton.

KNIGHT, KNITE, KNIT,
   Francis, Mr., Pemaquid, had a receipt of all dues from Robert Nash of Boston 7 (10) 1648. Gave bond to John Bushnell of Boston 1 Feb. 1648. [A.]

Ezekiel, Wells, proprietor, with wife Ann sold dwelling house and lands 20 Aug. 1645 [York De. I.] Took oath of allegiance 4 July, 1653. [Mass. Arch. 3, 219.] One of the town commissioners for small cases; selectmen. [See Hill.]

Richard, miller, Hampton; proprietor, June, 1640; contracted in Aug. following to keep a mill at the landing place. Lawsuit in Strawberry Bank court in 1642. Fined for not appearing. Sold house, mill and lands 5 (3) 1645. [Suff. De. 1.]

Robert, Mr., merchant, York, before 1643, [see testimony and letter in Mass. Arch. 38 B. 48-55.] Took oath of allegiance to Mass. govt. 22 Nov. 1652. Had letter of credit from Wrath Bathorne to his brother, Mr. Roger Bathorne, dated at Malago, 9 April, 1647, for his occasions in New England or Newfoundland. [A.] He deposed 7 Dec. 1658, ae. about 71 years, and again 6 July, 1671, ae. 86, as to what he heard Mr. Tho. Gorges say before he "went for England," —which is known to have been in 1643. [York De. I.] Gave land to his grandson John Redman, Jr. 18 Feb. 1666. His daughter Joanna m. Rowland Young; he gave land to grandson R. Y. Jr. 12 Aug. 1673, deed witnessed by the boy's sister Mary, who deposed as Mary Mowlton 24 June, 1678.

He died between 23 June, the date of his will, and 24 Aug. 1676, when it was proved; beq. his "small estate" to his son Richard Knight, living in Boston. [Me. Wills, 56, and York De. III.]

Roger, who was with Wanerton at Pascataqua in 1633, afterward lived at Strawberry Bank; brought suit in court in 1644. Received for work on the "Great house" a parcel of marsh land at S. B. 20 Jan. 1643, from Thomas Wannerton, agent for the patentees. [Pisc. court rec.] With wife Ann sold land 7 May, 1653.

Thomas, Dover, witness to deed of Obediah Bruen in 1642.

Walter, Piscataqua, ordered by the court 8 (8) 1652, to go to his wife in England by the first ship.

See also Abbot, Giles, Hill, Littlefield, Nicholds, Pierce, Shurt.

KNIL (Neal?),
Charles, with Gibbons at Newichewanick (Kittery or Berwick) 1633.

KNOLLES, KNOLLYS,
Rev. Hansard, came to New England in 1638. Took the side of Mrs. Hutchinson in the controversy of that day, and was allowed or compelled to remove to Piscataqua. Wrote to England letters of criticism upon the authorities of Mass. Bay. Was called to account for them at Boston, and apologized publicly 20 (12) 1639. Signed the Piscataqua combination in 1640. Contended with Larkham and his adherents at Dover. Was proved guilty of criminal conduct. [W.] A protest was entered against him and Edward and Timothy Tomlins 28 (7) 1641, for taking possession of a part of Long Island, by the claimant, James Forett. [Suff. De. I.]
See also Leavitt.

LAHAM,
Richard, one of the signers to the Piscataqua combination in 1640.

LAHORN,
Henry, one of the signers to the Piscataqua combination, 1640.

LAKESLAW, LAKESTAY,
John, Richmond Island, in Winter's employ, 1641-3.

LAMPREY, LAMPRILL,
Henry, cooper, Hampton.
He deposed in 1666, ae. about 50 years. Deeded to the three eldest children that were with him, viz. Henry, Daniel

and Elizabeth, all his movable goods, 26 Sept. 1668. Sold land to son Daniel 10 July, 1673.

Wife Julian, (Juliana, Jillian, Gillian); children, Henry, Daniel, Elizabeth, Benjamin b. 29 (9) 1660, Mary d. 7 (4) 1663. The wife died 10 (3) 1670.

He died Aug. 7, 1700. [Dow.]

See also Bachiler, Curtis.

LANDER, LANDERS, LAUNDER,

John, sailor, Richmond Island, came with Capt. Narias Hawkins about 1635; worked for Winter.

John, Pascataquack, made equal division with John Billine, 10 Jan. 1639, of house, land, shallop, swine, etc.; made a similar division in almost identical language 10 Jan. 1649. [York De. I, 10 and 15.]

LANE,

Ambrose, merchant, from Teignmouth, co. Devon, Eng. came to Strawberry Bank at an early date. Acquired considerable property. Returned to England and left his estate in the hands of Sampson Lane, who deeded it back to him by way of mortgage 22 (1) 1649; a house and land; sawmill in building at Sagamore's creek; a ship of 100 tons in building; 200 tons of Isle of May salt, and a house now in possession of John Crowther, all as security for the payment of 1000 li. Sold land to John Jackson in 1651, Ambrose Lane, Jr. being one of the witnesses; signed petition in 1652.

He died; his widow Christian appointed Thomas Jago of Dartmouth, Devon, her attorney, and he, 17 June, 1656, made Nicholas Shapleigh, Abraham Browne and William Seavey, merchants, local agents; they sold his land to Henry Sherburne 9 March, 1659. [Pisc. court rec. and Suff. De.]

Sampson, (Samson), merchant, 1649, being captain of a ship, and claiming to be a subject of the king of Spain, was before the Gen. Court of Mass. in 1651, for taking vessels which belonged to La Tour, a subject of France, in

violation of certain agreements, etc. [Mass. Arch. 60, 169-171.]
See also Moses, Moulton, Reyner, Savage.

LANGDON,
Tobias, Portsmouth, had one acre of land granted him in 1658. His accounts with John Odiorne about fishing the past winter and spring, were presented in court in 1660. Made an adjustment 7 June, 1662, with Henry Sherburne, [his wife's father,] about her marriage portion, by exchange of certain lands.

Admin. of his estate was granted 27 June, 1665, to his widow Elizabeth; the eldest son was to have a double portion at 21 years of age; the other children to have single shares at 18.

LANGSTAFFE,
Henry, Bloody Point, Dover, propr., 1642; juror, 1646. Portsmouth, 1669.

LAPTHORNE,
Stephen, Richmond Island, in service of Winter in 1637; his wife and children in England were maintained from his wages. He went back in the Star in 1640.

LARKHAM,
Rev. Thomas, came to Piscataqua about 1641; a man of good parts and very wealthy. Gathered a church in opposition to that of which Mr. Burdett was pastor and carried on a contest with him, resorting even to arms and violence. Triumphed partly through Burdett's faults. [W.] Signed the combination in 1640. While "pastor of the church at Northam," i. e. Dover, he bought Obediah Bruen's share in the plantation; this he sold Nov. 13, 1642. [Mass. Arch.]

He returned to England, not, however, escaping scandalous charges, which we should be glad to believe untrue. [W.] See also Ballew, Gibson, Hunt, Knowles, Maud.

LAWSON, LAWTON,

Christopher, cooper, Exeter, signed the combination 5 (4) 1639. Rem. to Boston, proprietor about 1643, but carried on business at Piscataqua. Signed Exeter petition in 1646. Had right of fishing from the town. His wife Elizabeth gave power of attorney 20 (8) 1646 to Barnabas Fower for collection of legacies from Henry and Thomas James of Filton, co. Gloucester, Eng. [A.] Proprietor at Haverhill in 1649. His wife deserted him and returned to Eng.; he petitioned for a divorce from her 11 Oct. 1670.

He deposed in 1671, ae. about 55 years. Children, Thomas b. 4 (3) 1643, Mary b. 27 (8) 1645.

Admin. of his estate was granted 20 Nov. 1682, to Edward Thyng.

LAYTON, LATON, LEIGHTON, LIGHTON, ALLAITON,

Thomas, Dover, signed the combination, in 1641. His land mentioned in list made in 1642. Constable, selectman. Signed with his mark petition to Gen. Court 10 Oct. 1665.

He made a deed of gift 16 Feb. 1670, to son Thomas Layton, Jr.; "Thomas Lighton" proprietor at Biddeford in 1653.

He died 22 Jan. 1671. [Dov. Hist. Coll.] Will dated 21 Sept. 1671, "aged sixty seven yeares or thereabouts," was prob. 25 June, 1672. Beq. to present wife Joanna, only son and heir Thomas, and daughters Mary, wife of Thomas Roberts, Jr., Elizabeth, wife of Philip Cromwell, and Sarah, unmarried. His Indian servant John, to be set free and provided with five pounds in money on the death of Joanna.

William, mariner, Kittery, bought house and lands of Isaac Nash 20 June, 1656. Signed petition of Dover people to Gen. Court 10 Oct. 1665.

John, Biddeford, 1653. Of Saco, signed petition to

Cromwell in 1657; his will speaks of sister Elizabeth; children of Thomas or William?

See also Frost, Johnson, Nutter.

LEACH,

James, weaver, Great Island, Portsmouth, grand jury man, 1654-5. Took oath of allegiance and was sworn constable June 27, 1656. On behalf of Jane Leach, formerly wife of Walter Michemor, he sued Richard Cummings 26 July, 1660, for a share of the profits of a fishing voyage about 11 years since. Sold land to Richard Ely, of the same place, merchant, 24 April, 1663. Made will Jan. 14, 1696-7, proved June 30, 1697. Wife Jane, sons John and James Leach; "dafters."

See also Bachiler.

LEADER,

Richard, gent. merchant, Lynn, agent for the Iron Works Co. in Sept. 1645. He had formerly been employed about mines in Ireland. Covenanted with the Adventurers in Iron Works in 1644 to take charge of their affairs 7 years at £100 per annum, with house, ground for horses and cows and passage for himself, wife, 2 children and 3 servants. [Mass. Hist. Coll. 4-6.] [Suff. De. I. 62.] Rem. to Kittery; took oath of allegiance to Mass. govt. 16 Nov. 1652. Complaint against his intrusion in 1651, made by 23 inhabitants in a petition to Parliament Dec. 20, 1652. [Bax. MSS.] Proprietor at Boston, Aug. 24, 1653. [W.] Sold the slitting mill in Lynn to Capt. Wm. Hathorne in 1650. Sold lands in Boston in 1655. He gave bonds with George Leader 5 Dec. 1655, that the latter should go to England within 18 months, and render full account to John Beex & Co. of all his doings in court about sawmills at Piscataqua river, etc. Sold his land to John and Richard Cutt, in consideration of 30 pounds paid "by my brother Richard Cutt," 30 Oct. 1656. Admin. of his estate was granted June 30, 1668, to John Hole and Samuel —, they having married the daughters of said Leader.

See also Clifford, Haborne, Lord, Nason, Smith.

LEUDECUS, LEWDECUS,
   David, Dover, "edgling," contracted for feathers with Griffin Montague 9 Aug. 1659; bill assigned to Richard Otis 3 July, 1660, by Elizabeth L. The estate of Mrs. Ludecas "of Dover" was admin. on June 28, 1664, by James Middleton.

LEE, LEA,
   John, Senior, Saco, sold wheat to Winter of Richmond Island in 1643; had some cattle at Cape Porpoise, in the hands of certain persons, and mortgaged them 18 Dec. 1647. [Suff. De. I.]
   See Spurrell, Tristram.

LEGAT, LEGATE,
   John, Hampton, proprietor, June, 1640; clerk of the writs; [Mass. Arch. 112, 8.] Sold lands in Hamp. 30 Oct. 1642, to Anthony Taylor, for a bill under the hand of Edmond Littlefield. Schoolmaster, May 21, 1649. Commissioner for minor trials, sworn 24 (2) 1649. [Norf. court rec.] Also of Exeter; sold cattle in 1648 to Christopher Lawson. Sold houses and lands 29 (5) 1650, part of which had been given him by the town and part of which he had bought. [Suff. De.]
   He m. Ann, widow of Thomas Wilson between 1642 and 1644. Admin. of his estate was granted April 11, 1665, to John Huggins.
   See also Booth, Needham, Stone.

LEMON,
   William, Kittery, died and gave his estate to Mr. Antipas Maverick, who was made administrator 26 June, 1660.

LEAVITT,* LEVITE, LIVET, LEVITT,
   Thomas, Exeter, signed the combination 5 (4) 1639. Rem. to Hampton; signed the anti-Howard petition March 7, 1643. Wife Elizabeth; Ch. James b. 10 (9) 1652 [Norf.

---

* Note. Samuel Leavitt, son of John and Sarah (Gilman) Leavitt, of Hingham, Mass. came early to Exeter, and had descendants through son James et als.

Rec.] He m. (2) Isabella, "dau. of Joshua and Joanna Bland, of Martha's Vineyard," wid. of Francis Austin. [Hist. Exe. and Hampt.] He d. Nov. 28, 1696, ae. above 80. His widow d. Feb. 19, 1699. His will dated July 9, 1692, gave his property to his wife and children Aretas, John, Hezron, James, Isabella Towle, Jemima Knowles and Keziah Tucker; proved May 25, 1697. The widow made her will Feb. 8, 1699, proved July 9, 1700, giving her property to the above-named daughters and son John and her grandchild Sarah Knowles.

LEVERICH, LEVERIDGE,
Rev. William, "a godly minister," came in the James to Salem Oct. 10, 1633. Went with Captain Thomas Wiggin, who was returning from a visit to England, to Dover, where he was first minister. It would appear that there was no church organized there, however, for he was admitted to the church of Boston 9 (6) 1635, and admitted freeman 7 Feb. 1636-7. Not long after he removed to Sandwich, Plymouth colony; there he had a good term of ministerial service; but joined in a colonization movement at Oyster Bay, Long Island, about the year 1658.

LEWIS, LUIS, LEWES,
George, Casco, deposed in court in 1640, respecting the price of beaver; "Had refused to work for Mr. Arthur Mackworth unless he could have beaver at 6 s. per pound." Deposed in the Nash case July 2, 1645. Took oath of allegiance to Mass. govt. at Spurwink 13 July, 1658. His eldest son John had land adjoining his in 1657. [York De. I.]

Morgan, party to a lawsuit in Piscataqua court in 1640.

Philip, Strawberry Bank, brought suit and recovered land lying near Capt. Champernowne's farm, by the creek next Winacott river, 3 (8) 1648. Bought part of a sawmill at Dover of Wm. Pomfret in 1651. He deposed Feb. 2, 1663, ae. about 40 years. [P. Files.]

Philip Lewis of Greenland signed his will 1 Nov. 1700;

beq. to son Abraham; to John, James, Philip and Hannah, children of his son Jotham; to son John Johnson and dau. Hannah, his wife; they to care for his wife; cousins John Tucke and James Philbrook overseers. Some land at Hampton; part of a sawmill, owned with Samuel Haines, etc. Prob. 8 July, 1701.

Thomas, gent. "having been at the charges to transport himself and others to take a view of New England," etc. he, in partnership with Richard Bonython, received a patent 12 Feb. 1629, of "that part of the main land called Swackadock," between Cape Elizabeth and Cape Porpus; William Blackstone, clerk, William Jeffries and Edward Hilton, gents. gave possession for the Council June 28, 1631, in presence of Thomas Wiggin, Henry Watts and [George Vahun]. [Mass. Arch. 3, 149. Bax. MSS.] Lewis and Bonython undertook to transport 50 persons to the plantation within 7 years, etc. He was one of the commissioners who held court at Saco 25 March, 1636, where he was then residing.

His daughter married Rev. Richard Gibson about 1639.

"*Old goodman Lewis,*" took oath of allegiance at Kittery 22 Nov. 1652.

See also Cass, Gibson, Greenaway, Moses, Watts, Wilson.

LIBBY, LIBBEE, LEBBY, LYBY, LYBBY, LEBBY, LIBY,

John, Richmond Island, was in the fishing company of John Winter from 15 Dec. 1636, to Feb. 13, 1639. Worked for him again 6 weeks in 1643. Some money was paid for him to Mr. John Sparke by Mr. Trelawney. He settled at Scarborough; bought land of Jocelyn 1 Jan. 1663. He suffered in the Indian war of 1676. He deposed July 10, 1677, ae. about 75 years, that he came to this country 47 years before; that his 4 sons had kept himself, his wife and 8 small children from want; but that the enemy had burned their houses and destroyed cattle and corn; that one of his four sons had lately been killed at Black Point, another wounded, had since died, and the other two were at B. P. He asked that the latter might be discharged from the garrison, having served there the extraordinary period of nine months. Signed "John Liby." The petition was granted, and Henry and Anthony released.

In his will, unsigned and undated, he beq. 5 shillings apiece to each of his children; 50 shillings each to the younger sons, Matthew and Daniel. The wife to have all the estate at her disposing, to maintain the children. Inventory taken 9 Feb. 1682; attested 5 May, 1683. [York De. V.]
Genealogy.

LINN, LINNE, LYNNE,

Henry, Boston, proprietor, punished by order of court 28 Sept. 1630. Whipped and banished in Sept. 1631, for writing letters "full of slander against the government and churches." [W.] He returned to Boston. Rem. to York in 1645; his house referred to in a deed of Barnard. "He went to Virginia, carrying most of his property, and there died, leaving widow and 4 children, and little estate." Vines and his council ordered that his tobacco be sold, debts paid, and the balance placed in the widow's hands for the benefit of the children. She came back to Boston for a short time. Papers recorded 28 (3) 1647, in Aspinwall's Note Book.

The wife Sarah was a daughter of William and Alice Tilley of Boston. She m. 2, Hugh Gunnison, 3, John Mitchell, and 4, Francis Morgan, of Kittery, chirurgeon. She being admins. of the estate of Capt. John Mitchell, her late husband, sold land formerly owned by [her previous husband] Hugh Gunnison, 22 April, 1665.

Children, recorded at Boston: Sarah b. 20 (6) 1636, Elizabeth b. 27 (1) 1638, Ephraim b. 16 (11) 1639, Rebbecca b. 15 (12) 1645; all baptized 23 (3) 1647. See Gunnison and Tilley.

See also Sanders.

LIPPENCOTT,

Bartholomew, had lawsuit in Piscataqua court in 1644.

LISTEN, LISSON,
   Nicholas, Salem, Mass. 1637, proprietor at Marblehead. Named in the account of George Pollard in 1646. Bought house at Exeter of George Barlow 20 (3) 1649. Brought suit in 1651 about a house he had sold. [Norf. rec.] Signed petition to Gen. Court 24 (3) 1652. Had land granted to him, which he sold to James Wall, who sold it again 11 May, 1654.
   Admin. on his estate was granted Dec. 8, 1714, to Alexander Magoun and Nicholas Gordon; division of the real estate made to daus. Hannah, Elizabeth and Mary or their legal representatives Oct. 13, 1743.

LIMAN, (LYMAN?)
   John, "from further Northward," took oath of allegiance at Kittery 16 Nov. 1652.

LITTLEFIELD, LITTLEFEILD, LETLEFEILD,
   Edmund, Exeter, signed the combination 5 (4) 1639. His wife Annis, ae. 38, with 6 children, and servants John Knight, and Hugh Durdal, came in the Bevis in May, 1638. It may be presumed that he either came at that time, (though not named in the passenger list,) or had come before. He rem. to Wells, Me.; had a grant of land from Thomas Gorges 14 July, 1643. Took oath of allegiance to Mass. govt. 5 July, 1653, as also did his sons Francis, Senior, Anthony, Francis, Junior, and Thomas.
   He made will Dec. 11, 1661, bequeathing his estate to wife Annis, sons Francis, Anthony, Thomas, Francis, Junior, and John; to daughters Elizabeth Wakefield, Mary Barrett and Hannah Littlefield. Inventory rendered 24 (10) 1661. The widow and sons Thomas and the two Francises made an agreement concerning the estate 17 Dec. following. [York De. I.]
   The widow made will 12 Dec. 1677, giving her estate to her daus. Elizabeth Wakefield, Mary Barrett, Hannah Cloyce and Meribah; to sons Peter Cloyce and John and Thomas

Littlefield; to grandchild Katherine W. [Inventory in York Deeds V.]

See also Frost, Legate, Wakefield, Wardwell.

LOCKE,

John, carpenter, Portsmouth, had grant of house lot in 1656. With wife Elizabeth he sold house and land to James Drewe, mariner, 23 March, 1660-1. Rem. to Hampton about 1666.

He m. about 1652 Elizabeth, daughter of William Berry. [Hist. Hamp.] Children, John, Elizabeth, Nathaniel, Alice, Edward, Trifena, Rebecca, Mary, William b. April 17, 1677, James, Joseph.

He was killed by the Indians Aug. 26, 1696. Estate settled 1708.

See Bolles and Davis.

LONGLEE,

Thomas, Portsmouth, lot assigned him, one acre, 24 Feb. 1657-8.

LOPES,

John, servant of John Winter at Richmond Island, 1636-9.

LORD, LORDE, LAWDE,

Nathan, Kittery, signed (with mark) petition to Parliament concerning Mr. Leader 20 Dec. 1652. [Bax. MSS.] He m. Martha, daughter of William Everett, born about 1640, as she deposed 23 June, 1682. She joined him in a deed of land June 22, 1678, to Thomas Abbet and Jonathan Nayson. His son Nathan deposed 25 March, 1686, ae. about 29 years. Abraham Conley calls him "son in law" in will, dated March 1, 1674. This may mean step-son; or Lord may have married a daughter of Conley for his first wife.

See also Nash, Phillips.

LLOYD, LOYD, LYDE,
    Edward, Piscataqua, Portsmouth, bills of exchange and receipts of his in court records 29 Aug. 1660; received town lands 4 Feb. 1660-1.
    He m. at Boston Dec. 4, 1660, Mary, daughter of Rev. John Wheelwright. Child Edward received from Mr. Wheelwright a bequest of property in Mumby, Langham and Minge, Lincolnshire, Eng.
    He died before June 30, 1663, when admin. on his estate was granted to Richard Stileman and others. 21 Oct. 1667, the widow, having contracted to marry Theodore Atkinson of Boston, received from him an ante-nuptial portion. [Norf. rec. II.]

LUCAS, LUKES,
    William, Richmond Island, worked for Winter 2 years before June 22, 1640. Money had been paid to his "dame" and "sister" in England. One "Widow Lucas," of Milbrooke, Eng. had a servant, William Allen, who was indentured to the plantation at about that time; this may have been the "dame" of William L.

LUX, LUXE,
    Nicholas, Kittery, aid to the marshall, deposed 21 Dec. 1653. [Bax. MSS.]
    William, Portsmouth, jury man at Dover court in 1657; constable for the lower part of Portsmouth. Took oath of fidelity July 2, 1657. Was appointed "water bayley in place of Robert Mussell, resigned, 30 June, 1668. Admin. of his estate was granted June 17, 1684, to his widow Audrey.
    She made her will 9 June, 1688, prob. 1 Feb. 1691-2, beq. to her son in law, Andrew Cranch, of Great Island, and his children John and Elizabeth; to dau. Abishag, wife of Thomas Marshall, of Great Id.
    See also Jeffrey.

LYFORD, LEYFORD, LEYFER,
    Andrew, witness to James Woodward's will 27 (4) 1647.

McCORMACK, MECKERMECKE, ACKORMUCK, COR-MICK, OCCORMACKE,

Dennis, "the Irishman," his service was sold in 1654 to John Pickering; the court at Dover ordered, July 2, 1657, that he serve the full five years for which Pickering had bought him; but 11 July, 1659, the court ordered Pickering to pay him 3 li. sterling, and dismiss him. A lot of land was assigned him at Portsmouth as an inhabitant, in 1660.

MACWORTH,

Arthur, gent. received from Gorges through Vines 30 March, II Charles, [1635] a tract of land which had "long been in his possession." [York De.] Mentioned in records of court at Saco April 4, 1637. Witnessed the giving of possession of land to Winter June 30, 1637; and, as Gorges' agent, gave possession to Cleve of a tract "from Cleve's house to the falls of Casco river," at about the same time.

He m. 2, Jane, widow of Samuel Andrews.

He died "before the submission of Scarborough and Falmouth to Massachusetts authority," as Rev. Robert Jordan testified Aug. 17, 1660; and it was his declared will that "his wife Jane should dispose of his estate equally between her former husband's children & the children between them." [Me. Wills, 44.]

The widow, "of Cascoe alias Falmouth," deeded land 29 April, 1667, to her son in law Abraham Adams, "for some time married to her daughter Sarah Mackworth"; he was of Boston, "dish-turner" and "cooper," and his heirs sold this land in 1703. [York De. VII.] Nathaniel Wharfe had m. Rebecca, the eldest daughter; they deeded their right in certain lands to their brother in law Francis Neale 20 June, 1666.

She conveyed to George Felt [Junior], husband of her daughter Phillippe, a tract of land bounded by that of her daughter Purchas and that of her son James Andrews. [Norf. court rec. IV, 75.] She removed to Boston. Made

will 20 May, 1676; beq. to sons in law Abraham Addams and William Rogers; to daus. Rebecca Rogers and the children she had by Nathaniel Wharfe; to daus. Sarah Addams and — Purchas; "to my four daughters."
See also Lewis.

MADDIVER,

Michael, Myhell, planter, Richmond Island, 1641-2; settled at Black Point. Took oath of allegiance to Mass. govt. 13 July, 1658.

He bought a plantation at "Papuding in Falmouth" of Walter Gendull; this he conveyed 14 July, 1669, to his son Joel. [See Carter.] See also Baddiver. Agnes Carter alias Maddiver, ae. about 82 years, 26 June, 1682, was probably wife first of Richard Carter and second of Michael Maddiver. [York De.]

MADDOCK,

Henry, Saco, took oath of allegiance to Mass. govt. 5 July, 1653.

MAINE, MAYNE,

John, of Mayne's Point, Casco before 1648; removed to York. He, ae. 70 years, and his wife Elizabeth, ae. 60, testified 3 Jan. 1664, as to the planting of a tract of land adjoining his land at Casco, near Mayne's Point, 35 or 36 years.

He bought, about 1657, a house and 60 acres of land "neare the middle of Casco Bay"; was driven away by the Indians; two sons were slain; house burnt; wife and rest of family hardly escaped with their lives. [Petition to Andros, 1687. Bax. MSS.]

See also Carter, Deaman.

MANNERING,

Philip, had suits in Piscataqua court in 1642 and 1649.

MANSFIELD,
"The widow" mentioned in Portsmouth records in 1652.

MARIAN, MARRIAN, MARION, MERIAN,
John, Sen. Hampton, bought land of widow Judith Parker 23 (3) 1645; proprietor. He deeded land and housing 1 Jan. 1671, "to Henry Dearborne and my daughter Elizabeth, his wife," and their two eldest male children; and to Isaac Godfrey, husband of his dau. Hannah. Deeded other lands to the sons in law 3 June, 1681, in consideration of their agreement to provide for himself and his wife for the rest of their lives.
He m. 1, Sarah —, who d. 26 (11) 1670; he m. 2, 14 (7) 1671, Margery, widow of William Godfrey; she d. 2 May, 1687, ae. about 78 years. [Dov. Hist. Coll.]
Compare John Marian, shoemaker, of Watertown, Mass. a son of Isaac M., of Stebbin, co. Essex, Eng. [P. of M.]
See also Bolter.

MARSHALL,
Christopher, Boston, admitted to the church, "singleman," 28 (6) 1634; freeman May 6, 1635. Child Anna bapt. 13 (3) 1638. Was dismissed to the church of Pascataqua 6 (11) 1638.
See Hilton, Lux.

MARSILL, [MARSHALL?]
Richard, one of the men of the ship Margery, fishing at Richmond Island under command of Capt. Clement Penwill, in 1643.

MARSTON, MASTON, MASTINE, MARSON,
Robert, Hampton, proprietor, June, 1640.
He died about 1644, when his "heir, Syment," sold his lots. [Town record.]
Thomas, Hampton, signed petition in Howard case in 1643. [Mass. Arch. 67, 33.] Juryman at Hamp. court in

1648. He deposed 9 March, 1669, ae. about 52 years. He deeded land to his son James 18 June, 1681.

Wife Mary, daughter of Wm. Estow; children, John b. 10 (—) 1650, Bethia d. 2 (4) 1655, Ephraim b. 8 (8) 1655, James b. 19 (9) 1656, Caleb d. 31 (8) 1671.

Thomas M. d. Sept. 28, 1690, and inventory of his estate was rendered 6 (8) following by William M., John Smith and Henry Dow.

N. B. It is difficult to separate entries relating to Thomas, the citizen in 1643, and Thomas, son of William, Senior.

William, Senior, Hampton, with William, Junior, signed the anti-Howard petition March 7, 1643.

He d. June 30, 1672. Will dated 25 June, prob. 8 Oct. 1672; beq. to eldest son Thomas; sons William and John; daughters Prudence Cox and Trifana Marston; wife Sabina executrix.

[Compare with William M. of Salem, Mass. in P. of M.]

See also Brown, Estow, Page, Ward.

MARTIN, MARTEN, MARTYN,

Francis, Mr. Richmond Island, 1640; "hath never a servant and cannot work himselfe;" Winter settled him at Casco; but he wrote to Trelawney concerning him in 1640 and 1642: "He is old and his [2] children are not brought up to work, so I know not what shift he will make to live; . . . therefore advise with his cousin John Martin;" etc. Winthrop describes the sad experiences of a Mary M. in vol. 2 of his History; she may be one of these unfortunately-bred children.

John, Dover; lawsuit brought against him and his wife Hester in 1647, which was decided in their favor. Proprietor in 1648. Grand jury man in 1650.

His will was proved June 30, 1664.

Wife Sarah, ch. Sarah, Mary, Mehitabel, Hannah and Abraham; servant William Peirce; brother "Larefet;" (was this John Larriford whose estate was admin. March 26, 1672)

See Atwell, Peabody, Roberts, Tare.

Richard, Richmond Island, one of Winter's fishermen from 1636 or 1637 to 1643.

Settled at Falmouth; took oath of allegiance at Spurwink, 13 July, 1658.

His will dated 11 Jan. prob. 20 Feb. 1672-3, beq. to wife Dorothy, son in law Robert Corben and his wife Lydia, Samuel White and Benjamin Attwell. The widow deeded land to her son in law Robert Corbine who had married her daughter Lydia, 10 Dec. 1673, conditioned on life care and maintenance.

Richard, Dover; also proprietor at Portsmouth, 1660. Wife Sarah; ch. Mary, b. June 7, 1655, Sarah, b. July 3, 1657, Richard, b. Jan. 10, 1659, Hannah, b. Jan. 2, 1664, Michael, b. Feb. 3, 1666, John b. June 9, 1668, Elias, b. April 18, 1670. [Dov. Hist. Coll.], Michael Mann, whose will is in N. H. Deeds 5, 77, dated Dec. 6, 1687, proved Sept. 14, 1691, desires "my unkle Richard Martyn" to be overseer of the will.

Richard Martyn made will Jan. 27, 1692-3, proved April 17, 1694; wife Mary; reference to her former husband's estate; sons Michael, Nathaniel, daus. Cutt, Kennard and Joce; my sister Martyn and her children Edward and Susannah.

Robin, Richmond Island, worked for Winter in 1640.

MATTHEW, MATTHEWS,

Francis, Exeter, signed the combination 5 (4) 1639. Gave bonds for Elizabeth Giles in 1644. Bought land in June, 1640. He removed to the part of Dover now Durham. [Hist. Ex.] Sons, Walter and Benjamin, dau. Martha, m. (1) — Snell; m. (2) — Brown. He d. before July 23, 1653, when his widow Thomasine entered caution about land at Great Island which her husband had formerly bought of John Hurde of Sturgeon Creeke. She deeded land to her grandson, William, son of Godfrey Brooking, 16 Oct. 1689. After her death the surviving son Benjamin (ae. about 40 years) admin. on the estate and recd. remuneration for his care of his mother for many years, Nov. 6, 1705.

Nicholas, Richmond Island, in the employ of Winter, 1638-1640.

See also Footman.

MATTOONE, MATTOUN,
 Hubert, (Hubertus, Hughbert), Kittery, took oath of allegiance to Mass. govt. 16 Nov. 1652. Voter at a town meeting in Portsmouth April 6, 1657.
 Robert, Portsmouth, juryman in 1657; constable for the upper part of the town; took oath of allegiance July 2, 1657. See Clifford and Higgins.

MAUD, MAUDE, MAWDE, MAWD,
 Rev. Daniel, came in the ship James from Bristol, Eng. in May, 1635, in company with Rev. Richard Mather. Settled first at Boston, Mass. Admitted to the church 20 (7) 1635; frm. May 25, 1636; chosen schoolmaster Aug. 12, 1636. Appointed clerk of the writs 10 Dec. 1641. Was dismissed 17 (1) 1644-5, to the church of Dover, whither he had removed. Was settled as their minister after the departure of Mr. Larkham. The town voted 1 (6) 1648 to build him a house.
 He m. Marie [Mary] Bonner, servant to Rev. John Cotton; she had been admitted to Boston church 3 (6) 1634, and was dismissed to the chh. of Dover 18 (6) 1644, being described as "now wife to Mr. Daniel Mawd, teacher of the church there."
 He made his will 17 (11) 1654, proved Jan. 26, 1655-6. Bequeathed to "my wife's 4 children twenty markes when they come to capablenesse"; to Mr. Roberts; to his wife "a cloth gowne wch was my wifes"; "There is a booke of Mr. Norton's, wch is intitled the Orthodox Evangelist wch I would have my sister Cotton to have — and an other booke I borrowed of my bro: Cotton* wch is to come to his son Seaborne"; "favorite or best hat to Elizabeth Cotton, som other to Joseph and one to Sarah." "Susan Halston & his brothere & sister & sistere in law who have no need of supplyes fro me, I desire to be heartily remembered to them; they are all in years." See William Cotton.

---

* Rev. John Cotton, of Boston.

MAVERICK, MAVERICKE,

Antipas, merchant, of the Isles of Shoals, bought 10 acres of land of Edward Small 23 June, 1647. Of Kittery, he took oath of allegiance to Mass. govt. 16 Nov. 1652. Settled accounts with his brother Moses Maverick of Marblehead 13 Aug. 1675. Rem. to Exeter; sold land in Kittery 16 June, 1678.

He died 2 July, 1678; admin. granted July 15 foll'g to Edward Gilman and Abigail his wife, dau. of deceased. His brother Moses gave a receipt in full to the estate. [York De. III.] Stephen Paul of Kittery, shipwright, and Katherine his wife, and Edward Gilman of Exeter, yeoman, and Abigail his wife, sold land 7 June, 1682, "which was our deceased fathers Antipas Mavericke."

See also Wheelwright.

MAXWELL, MAXELL,

Alexander, planter, York, was in the employ of George Leader with whom he had differences, etc., 1654. Bought 70 acres of land up the river of York adjoining to a parcel of Arthur Bragdons, and 10 acres of meadow on the northwest branch, of Thomas Moulton, 23 Jan. 1657. He made a deed of gift to his brother in law, John Frost, 2 Nov. 1678, of certain land in York. With wife Annis sold land 24 March, 1680-1.

Will dated 15 May, 1707, bequeathed to wife Sarah; to Mr. Moody, and to the church.

MEDD, MEADES, MEADER, MEDER,

John, Exeter, signed petition of inhabitants Sept. 7, 1643. [Mass. Arch. 112, 8.] Oyster River, juryman in 1659 and 1660.

Wife Abigail; children, Elizabeth b. 26 March, 1665, Sarah b. 11 Jan. 1668, Nathaniel b. 14 June, 1671. [Dov. Hist. Coll.]

MELCHER,

Edward, Portsmouth, 1657; propr. 1660. Wife Elizabeth.

Will Aug. 5, 1695, proved Aug. 24; land to be divided between his three children Nathaniel, Samuel and Mary; sister in law Sara Acreman; wife to live with daughter Mary; son in law Samuel Jackson.

MELLIN,
William, Richmond Island, from 1638 till 1642.

MERIDA, see Ameridith.

MENDAM, MENDUM,
Robert, Kittery, bought house and land 21 Sept. 1647. Took oath of allegiance to Mass. govt. 16 Nov. 1652. Constable. Testified in the Gunnison case April 22, 1654, ae. 50 years. [Bax. MSS.]

Will dated 1 May, prob. 18 May, 1682, beq. to son Jonathan and his sons Robert, Jonathan and David; to grandson Robert Michamore. Inventory in York De. V.

See Cousins, Raynes.

MECHEMORE, MICHEMORE,
Walter, Isles of Shoals, partner of Richard Commins about 1649. His widow m. James Leach.

See also Carter, Mendam.

MERRY, MERRIE,
Joseph, carpenter, Haverhill, sold house and land in Hav. 22 Dec. 1644. Removed to Hampton. Sold house near Falls river 4 (3) 1655.

First wife Mary —; second wife Elizabeth, widow of Emanuel Hilliard; contract of marriage made 13 (10) 1659. Children, Joseph b. 19 (10) 1654, Hannah b. 29 (9) 1660, Abigail b. 18 (5) 1662, Barsheba b. 16 (4) 1665, Samuel b. 16 (9) 1669.

See Hilliard.

MESSER,
Thomas, Sheepscot, lived on the side of the Cove, next north west of the salt water falls of the river, before 1660,

when his daughter Lydia was born; she m. — Stanwood about 1677 and removed; was of Gloucester, Mass. in 1742, as she deposed. [Eastern claims.]

MILES, MILLES, MILE, see also Mills,

Joseph, Kittery, brought suit at Dover in 1649. Took oath of allegiance to Mass. govt. at Kittery 16 Nov. 1652. Deposed in the Gunnison case in 1654, ae. about 35 years.

Robert, mentioned in records of Maine court held at Saco March 6, 1636-7. His son James, of Lynn, Mass. sold land at Kittery to James Grant 4 May, 1666.

MILLS, MYLLS, see also Miles,

Edward, Richmond Island, in Winter's fishing company 3 years, 1638-1640. [Trel.]

John, Black Point, testified Sept. 8, 1640, that he had known Casco river 13 or 14 years, — [probably on fishing voyages in the earlier years.] Came as a servant to the plantation at Richmond Island in 1633; had a grant of 60 acres of land at the mouh of Black Point river from Capt. Gorges; was one of the witnesses of Winter's possession of an adjoining tract by virtue of a deed from Vines 12 July, 1638.

He died before 29 June, 1675. [Deposition, York De. IV.]

Robert, Saco, 1637; wife Dorothy; 4 small children; he d. before 1647 and the widow m. John Harker.

Thomas, fisherman, Saco, bought land 2 Aug. 1642; rem. to Wells; took oath of allegiance to Mass. govt. 5 July, 1653. Deeded land in 1681 to sons in law John and Nathaniel Cloyce.

See also Gibbons, Howell, Watts.

MIDDLETON,

James, before Dover Court in 1659. See Leudecus.

MILLER,

Joseph, Portsmouth, 1642; worked for John Godard 1647-1666; deposed 2 April, 1660, ae. about 29 years. [P. Files.]

Joseph, Dover, called to court at Strawberry Bank in 1642; lawsuits in 1646. Sold all his lands 20 Sept. 1647, to John Goddard.

MINGAY, MINGEY, MINGY,

Jeffrey, Dedham, proprietor, 11 (6) 1637. Sold (8) 1639. Frm. May 13, 1640. Removed to Hampton. Propritor June, 1640; signed Howard petition in 1643. Bought land 21 Oct. 1648. One of the commissioners to try small cases in 1649.

He died June 4, 1658. Nunc. will prob. 5 (8) 1658; beq. all to his wife and Eliakim Wardwell. The widow m. 2, Christopher Hussey.

MITCHELL, MICHELL,

Paul, sailor, Sheviock, co. Cornwall, Eng. came to Richmond Island and fished with Winter's company, 1639-1640. Returned to England, but came again on a fishing voyage in the Hercules, Capt. Wm. Hingston, having made an indenture for 2 years. [Trel.] Remained here. Settled at Saco. Was drowned in 1654.

John, Captain m. about 1660 Sarah, widow of Henry Linn; and Hugh Gunnison; died before April 22, 1665. The widow married Francis Morgan. [See all these names.]

MITTEN, MITTIN, MITTON,

Michael, gent. Casco, possessed an island in Casco Bay in 1637 of Cleave. Pet. of daus. Elizabeth Clarke and Ann Graves to Andros, 1687. [Bax. MSS.] Deposed in the case of Cleve vs. Winter in 1640. Sold fowl to Winter same year.

Took oath of allegiance to Mass. govt. 13 July, 1658.

For accounts of his character see Winthrop, vol. 2.

His widow Elizabeth gave land 1 March, 1662, to Thaddeus Clarke who had married her daughter Elizabeth. She afterward married—Harvy, and as his widow sold land in 1681. [York De. III.] She gave land 8 May, 1667, to Thomas Brackett of Casco who had married her daughter Mary Mitton. Nathaniel Mitten, called a grandson of Cleve.

MOFFAT, MUFFETT,
Robert, inhabitant April 6, 1657.

MOODY,
Rev. *Joshua,* son of Mr. William of Newbury, minister at Portsmouth, "Mr. Moody to have his maintenance for this year by way of subscriptions," by vote of the town of Portsmouth 14 Feb. 1658. He made his will Sept. 18, 1693; it was proved July 12, 1697. To be buried by his first wife and the deceased children he had by her; gave to present wife Ann what she brought with her and other estate at Ipswich; daughter in law Lydia Jacobs; son Samuel Moodey; daus. Martha Russell, Hannah and Sarah.
See Bradbury, Cutt, Pickering.

MOORE, MAWER, MOUER,
Richard, Cape Porpoise, leased land of Cleve 20 May, 1647. Sold land 1 July, 1652. Removed to Wells; took oath of allegiance to Mass. govt. 5 July, 1653.

William, Mr. fisherman, Boston, had a lot granted him at Mt. Wollaston [Braintree], Feb. 19, 1638, for 9 heads. Probably the resident of Salem in 1638. Received lands at Exeter in 1639; removed to Exeter, and a few years later was at York. Took oath of allegiance to Mass. govt. at Y. 22 Nov. 1652. Proprietor; bought more land of Henry Roby in 1653. Residing at Ipswich, 22 Jan. 1660, he sold land on the east side of Exeter river to his daughter Mary, wife of Robert Powell.

William More of Ipswich made will 14 Aug. 1660, prob. 26 Sept. 1671; beq. to daughter Mary Powell; dau. Ruth Roby and her eldest daughter; eldest son William and son Thomas; daughter Elizabeth More. Inventory showed some land at Exeter. William, of York, (who may be supposed to be this son), made will March 31, 1691, prob. 2 June, 1691; beq. to wife Dorothy, sons John, Robert, William and Thomas, daughters Elizabeth Trafton, Sarah Welcom, Elianor, Ann and Mary Moore.

MONTAGUE, MOUNTAGUE,

Griffin, carpenter, Muddy River, Boston, 1635. [Col. rec.] Sold the time of his apprentice, John Bundy, to William Brewster of Plymouth 6 March, 1636-7. Rem. to Exeter; proprietor, 1639. Rem. to Cape Porpoise. Took oath of fidelity to Mass. govt. July 5, 1653. Contracted 9 Aug. 1659, to furnish 150 pounds of Geese and duck feathers to David Leudecus, "edgling," of Dover; bill assigned by Elizabeth Lewdecus to Richard Otis 3 July, 1660. Mrs. Anne Looman, of Weymouth, Mass. bequeathed something to her grandchild John Montague that dwells at the Eastward, 21 (8) 1659.

He died about March, 1672; will dated 7 July, 1671, prob. 1 April, 1672, beq. to wife Margaret; desired to be buried by the side of deceased son John. Samuel Snow of Boston, executor of the will of the widow, sold land at Cape Porpoise 8 Sept. 1682.

MONKE or MONLO,

George, Starre Island, Isles of Shoals, was appointed constable for a year and a half at Dover court 8 (8) 1649. Bondsman for Thomas Wedge in 1650.

MORGAN,

Francis, chirurgeon, Kittery. He m. Sarah (Tilley) (Linn) (Gunnison) Mitchell, q. v.; Dr. Morgan and his wife joined in a deed of land that had belonged to Gunnison April 22, 1665, and she herself confirmed the title to another piece of property 8 Sept. 1670. Dr. Morgan made a written contract Nov. 10, 1671, with William West (deposing that his age was 51) to use his utmost care to cure West of "an uncerated fistula on his throat." Sold land to Nicholas Shapleigh Aug. 25, 1673. Mrs. Sarah Morgan deposed June 29, 1670, aged about 51 years. [Bax. MS. VI.]

Robert, of Pemaquid, was one of the men of whom Thomas Purchase complained 31 May, 1641, for taking furs

which he claimed he was keeping for an Indian sachem.
[L.]

MORRAY,
James, Oyster River, was killed by the falling of a tree; inquest held 11 Nov. 1659. [P. Files.]

MORRIS, MORIS,
Richard, Mr. Boston, member of the church with his wife in 1630; juror Nov. 9, 1630; frm. May 18, 1631. Chosen lieutenant to Capt. Underhill 4 March, 1633-4. Resided sometime at Roxbury; deputy, 1633-4. Lieutenant of Boston Castle in 1635-6. He signed the remonstrance of the friends of Mrs. Hutchinson, and removed with the Wheelwright party to Exeter; was dismissed to that church 6 (11) 1638. Signed the combination 5 (4) 1639. Was of Dover in 1639, shipping clapboards. Wrote a letter in Latin to some one in authority in connection with the restoration of Capt. Underhill, in 1640. [L.] Wife Lenora was dism. to Exeter church 3 (1) 1639-40.

Was he the Richard Morris who resided at Portsmouth, R. I. in 1643 and 1655?

William, Dover or vicinity, took oath of fidelity at court July 2, 1657.

MORSE, MOSSE,
Daniel, Hampton, proprietor, June, 1640.

MORTON,
Thomas, of Clifford's Inn, gent. in company with Capt. Wollaston, arrived in N. E. in 1622, with 30 servants. Settled at Mount Wollaston, afterward included in Braintree. His dissipations and riotous dealings with both whites and Indians were utterly disgusting to the settlers at Plymouth and Boston, and endangered the peace and welfare of the whole region. He was remonstrated with to no effect; then punished in 1630 for wordy attacks on the government and

people of Mass. Bay, for injuries done to the Indians and for selling weapons to them, etc. Wrote a hostile book, "The New English Canaan." Was sent to Eng.; lay a long time in Exeter jail. Came to Boston in 1644; was tried; freed on acct. of his age and poverty, and allowed to go out of the jurisdiction. Rem. to Agamenticus, and d. about 1646. [W. and B.]

MOSES, MOYSES,

John, Strawberry Bank, after an apprenticeship of 7 years to Cleve and Tucker of Casco Bay, received from them 6 April, 1646, 100 acres of land at Casco Bay, adjoining that of George Lewis. He and his wife Alice carried suit for slander against certain persons in Dover court 3 (4) 1648; acknowledgment to be made openly at Dover and Strawberry Bank. Juryman in 1651. Bought land of Ambrose Lane 15 April, 1651. Lands assigned him 1652 and 1660. With wife Ann sold land 12 Sept. 1667, and conveyed other land 6 Jan. 1679, to son Aaron, who was to pay a portion to his sister Sarah.

MOULTON, MOLTON,

John, of Ormsby, Eng. husbandman, ae. 38, with wife Anne, ae. 38, children Henry, Mercy (or Mary), Anne, Jane and Bridget, and servants Adam Goodens, ae. 20, and Alice Eden, ae. 18, passed examination April 11, 1637, to go to New England. Settled at Newbury; frm. May 22, 1638. Was one of the founders of Hampton named in Col. rec. 6 (7) 1638. Lot-layer; deputy in 1639. Appointed with John Cross in 1640 to take an inventory and appraisal of all the cattle of Hamp. for the Gen. Court. Children recorded Hampt. John, Ruth bapt. March 7, 1641.

He died in 1650; will dated 23 Jan. 1649, prob. 1 (8) 1650, beq. to wife Ann, children Henry, John, Ann, Jane, Bridget, Mary and son Samborne (husband of Mary).

The widow died 12 (2) 1668.

Thomas, yeoman, Newbury, proprietor, 1638. Removed to Hampton. Deposed in 1655, ae. about 50 years. [Arch. 38 B.] Bought land at York of John Allcocke 22 March, 1655, having removed thither; sold it 20 Jan. 1657, to Alex. Maxwell. [York De. I.] Sold Hampton lands in 1654, giving deed 11 July, 1662. Made deed of gift 5 June, 1684, to sons Jeremiah and Joseph, wife Martha joining in it.

Children, by wife Martha, Thomas bapt. Nov. 24, 1639, Daniel bapt. Feb. 13, 1640-1; by wife "Mary" (sic copia), Mary b. 25 (11) 1651, Hannah b. 19 (4) 1655. [Norf. Court rec.]

Compare Thomas M. master of Ralph Glover's boat in 1630. [Mass. rec.]

William, Hampton, took freeman's oath at Salisbury court 3 (8) 1654.

His children received bequests from William Estow.

Wife Margerite; children recorded, Hannah b. 15 (12) 1651. Sarah b. 17 (10) 1656. Ruth b. 7 (3) 1659, Robert b. 8 (9) 1661, William b. 25 (3) 1664, Mary d. 27 (5) 1664.

He died 18 (2) 1664. Will dated 8 March, 1663-4, prob. 11 (8) 1664, beq. to wife Margerite, children Joseph, Benjamin, Robert, Hannah, Mary, Sarah, Ruth and the child unborn. Father in law Robert Page and brother in law Henry Dow executors.

See also Fuller, King, Wall, Wedgewood, Young.

MUNJOY, MONJOY,

George, mariner, ship-carpenter, came from Falmouth, in Casco, province of Maine, to Boston; was adm. chh. 5 (3) 1647; frm. May 26, 1647. He sold, Aug. 18, 1667, property left him by his father John M. of Abbotsham, co. Devon, Eng. to William Tytherley, of Bythefoard, co. Dev. mariner, now res. in Boston; his sister Mary, wife of John Sanders of Braintree, N. E. joined in the deed; reference made to their sister Martha M. of Abbotsham. [Suff. De.] He m. Mary, dau. of Dea. John Philips, q. v. Ch. rec. at Bo.: John b. 17 April, 1653, George b. 21 April, 1656, *John* bapt. 27

(2) 1656, Josiah b. April 4, 1658, Philip bapt. 1 (4) 1662, Mary bapt. 1 (5) 1665, Hephzibah bapt. 9 (9) 1673, (m. Oct. 1, 1691, Nathaniel Alden,) Pelatiah and Gershom bapt. 20 (4) 1675. [Were any of these ch. of George, Jr.?]
George Munjoy deposed in Maine court 9 July, 1674, ae. about 47. Inventory of his estate in various places, taken 24 Sept. 1685, is recorded in York Deeds V. His widow Mary sold her lands to Thomas Danforth president of the Province of Maine, 10 June, 1681. [Bax. MSS.]

MUNNS,
Mark, ae. 30 years, testified in the Gunnison case 12 May, 1654. [Bax. MSS. I.]

MUSSELL, MUSTELL,
Robert, fisherman, Portsmouth, land owner, appointed by the court 8 (8) 1652, to be "water baylife, to look after the ships that shalbe ridinge in the great harbour," to see that they discharge no ballast into the river, etc. Resigned the office 30 June, 1668. Took oath of fidelity July 2, 1657. Had land recorded in the town book July 21, 1660, "which he had possessed about 15 or 16 years, — 4 acres on Great Island." Deeded to his daughter Alderey, wife of Wm. Lux, his houses and lands on Great Island 10 Aug. 1667.
Will dated 1 March, 1663, prob. 30 June, 1674, beq. to daughter Auderey Lux and her two daughters; to dau. Mary Jeffrey, son Richard Roe, and to the minister of Kittery, Mr. Belcher.
John and Frances Crunch, Thomas and Elizabeth Cossen, Thomas Marshall, Jr.; Christopher and Mary Frederick and Thomas and Elizabeth Pearce, all of Newcastle, N. H. only surviving heirs of Robert Mussell, sold land in Kittery, formerly his property, April 10, 1718.

NANNEY,
Robert, ae. 22, was one of those "sent away," [perhaps meaning fitted out,] by Robert Cordell, goldsmith, Lombard

street, London, who came in the Increase April 14, 1635. Came early to the Piscataqua, signed the combination in 1640; had a lawsuit in 1642. Married Katherine, daughter of Rev. John Wheelwright. Rem. to Boston, Mass. [See P. of M.] Appears to have resided in Massachusetts.

NASH,

Isaac, shipwright, Dover, with wife Margery sold land and house in Kittery, formerly belonging to William Everett, dec., whose wife he had married, 20 Jan. 1656. They sold another tract of land, the title to which was confirmed by her daughter Martha, wife of Nathan Lord, 23 Nov. 1674.

Robert, Boston, traded along Maine coast; testimony given before Cleve and Tucker at Casco in 1645 about his doings at Stratton's Island the previous month. [Bax. MSS.]

See also Comins, Dearing, Knight.

NASON, NAYSON,

Richard, yeoman, Kittery, took oath of allegiance to Mass. govt. 16 Nov. 1652. Sold land 20 Feb. 1654, to George Leader for John Beex & Co. as chosen deputy to Gen. court 24 March, 1656. [Mass. Arch. 48, 49.] Deeded land with consent of wife Abigail to sons Benjamin and Baker Nason, 20 Sept. 1694.

He made will 14 July, 1694, "under the infirmities of old age;" gave to wife Abigail whatever belonged to her former husband Nicholas Follett, and other estate; residue to be divided between his own children and children in law, John, Joseph, Benjamin and Baker Nason, Sarah Child, Mary Witham, Nicholas Follett and Sarah Meader; Benjamin N., Nicholas F. and John M. executors. Recorded 15 March, 1696-7.

See also Locke.

NEALE,

Captain Walter, gent. came in 1630 to Piscataqua, as governor of Gorges and Mason's province. Was deputed by the

Council for New England 1 Dec. 1631, to give possession of a grant of land to the representatives of Robert Trelawney and Moses Goodyear. Was governor of the Lower Piscataqua until the year 1633. [Hub.] Resided at Little Harbor with servants in 1649. Deposition of Capt. John Littlebury in 1649. [Bax. MSS.]
"Returned to England," it is said.
What connection, if any, exists between the above and the two following?
Francis, Spurwink, took oath of allegiance to Mass. govt. July 13, 1658.
He m. a dau. of Arthur Mackworth, whose daughter Rebecca, wife of Nathl. Wharfe, calls him brother in law in deed of lands at Casco 20 June, 1666. [Norf. Court rec. IV.]
He petitioned Andros [1689] to have his land surveyed, deposing that he was "for upward of thirtie yeares Since an inhabitant in Casco alias ffalmouth untill such time as he with severall others lost his all in this world and was forced from thence by ye Barbarous Indians." [Bax. MSS.]
Francis Neale of Salem made will 1 Aug. 1695; beq. to son Samuel N. granddaughter Sarah N., wife's sisters Mrs. John Blanoe and Phillippe Felt, Thomas Elkins, a former servant, John Blanoe, Sen. and Thomas Cloutman; the rest to Bartholomew Gedney "who hath been as a father to me in a strange place when I was driven out by the enemy." The will was not probated but the son Samuel was appointed administrator. Sara, widow of Francis N. Jr. and "Mother Collins" are mentioned in his accounts.

Walter, Dover, juryman 28 (4) 1659.
Wife Mary; children, Samuel b. 14 June, 1661, Mary b. 31 March, 1668; "she herself died first Friday in April following, 1668." [Dov. Hist. Coll.]
See also Bailey, Hilton, Knil, Mackworth, Purchase, Williams.

NEEDHAM,
Nicholas, Braintree, proprietor, 1636. Rem. to Exeter;

signed the combination 5 (4) 1639. Was chosen to the unique office of "ruler of the town"; resigned the place Oct. 20, 1642. Presided over meetings of the inhabitants, signed grants of land, etc. in that capacity. Made a parcel of "boults" in Piscataqua Great Bay for Henry Roby; testimony of John Legat in Salem, recorded in Norf. court rec. 4 (8) 1653. See Wheelwright.

NEWELL,
Walter, Kittery, signed the petition to Cromwell in 1657.

NEWET, NUTE,
James, Dover, signed the combination in 1640; had lawsuit in 1642; was taxed Oct. 19, 1648. With wife Sarah deeded lands to sons James and Abraham in 1671.

NEWGROVE, NEWGROWE, see Yougrofe.

NEWMAN,
George, had lawsuit in Maine court July 3, 1637.
Matthew, witnessed John Brown's deed at Pemaquid 15 July, 1625.

NICHOLS, NICHOLDS,
James, Piscataqua, administration of his estate was granted 1 (8) 1651 to Walter Knight. See Felch.

NILES, NYLE,
Richard, Richmond Island, one of the fishermen, 1638-1642.

NOCK,
Thomas, Dover, bought land of William Furber 2 July, 1657. Constable, 1661. Signed petition to the General Court 10 Oct. 1665. [Mass. Arch. 106, 160.]
Wife Rebecca; ch. Thomas, Silvanus, Rebecca, Elizabeth b. 21 Nov. 1663, d. 12 May, 1669; Henry, b. 8 Feb. 1666.
He d. 29 Oct. 1666; admin. granted to the widow and others June 25, 1667. The widow m. Philip Binmore, and

gave bonds 20 Feb. 1676-7, for the guardianship of her son Henry Nock. The son Thomas d. in 1677; in his will dated 15 Feb. 1676, prob. 31 Oct. 1677, he beq. to mother Rebecca, sister Rebecca, brothers Silvanus and Henrie and uncle Jeremy Tibbetts. Rebecca (Nock) Binmore d. before April 2, 1680, when her estate was settled.

NORMAN,

Matthew, planter, of Pemaquid, als. Aldworth towne in N. E. gave bond in March, 1640-1, with Robert Shute of Winnegansett to Matthew Merchant, late of Bristol, haberdasher, for payment of a debt for commodities bought of Merchant in Bristol. [L.]

William, Strawberry Bank, m. Margerie Randall and was before the Court for it in 1650, charged with having a wife in England; he admitted it, but seems to have continued the American connection though not a good husband. See Court Records.

NORTON,

Francis, Charlestown, was agent of Mrs. Ann Mason, in care of her estate at Piscataqua in 1638. Remained but a short time. See P. of M.

Mr. Henry, York, gave bonds in Gen. Court at Boston 4 March, 1634-5. Provost marshall in 1645. Received land of Wm. Hooke July 20, 1650. Took oath of allegiance to Mass. govt. 22 Nov. 1652, and was again appointed marshall.

He d. at a time not on record. Inventory filed April 3, 1679, "some time after his decease." [York De. V.]

See Gatchell, Godfrey, Sanders, Simpson.

NUDD,

Thomas, son of — Nudd and Jane his widow who m. as her second husband Henry Dow. Thomas came to this country with Mr. Dow, having passed examination as passenger in England 11 April, 1637. He lived first at Watertown, but rem. to Hampton about 1648, where his father in law gave him a tract of land in 1649.

Wife Sarah —; children, John b. and d. 1661, Sarah b. 23 (12) 1662, d. 4 Oct. 1664, James b. 24 (9) 1665, d. 20 (8) 1668, Thomas b. and d. 1668-9, Samuel b. Sept. 13, 1670, Mary b. April 1, 1673, d. Nov. 8, 1683, Hannah b. 23 Oct. 1678.

NUTTACHE,
Capt. York, took oath of allegiance to Mass. govt. 22 Nov. 1652.

NUTTER,
Hatevil, Hate Evil, planter, Dover, a resident in 1635. [Mass. Arch. 112, 46.] Had lawsuit in 1640. Proprietor in 1642. He and his company made an agreement with the selectmen of the town in 1647, to set up a sawmill. Ruling elder of the church. Signed petition to Gen. Court 10 Oct. 1665.

He made a deed of gift to his sons Anthony and John 10 April, 1669, of land granted to him by the town in 1643, etc. and one to his daughter Elizabeth and her husband, Thomas Layton, Jr. 13 Feb. 1670.

He made will 28 Dec. 1674, aged about 71 years; beq. to present wife Anne; son Anthony, daughters Mary Winget (Wingate) and Abigail Roberts. Proved 30 June, 1675.

See Philips, White.

OAKMAN,
Samuel, Spurwink, took oath of allegiance to Mass. govt. 13 July, 1658.

Administration on his estate was granted June 30, 1680, to his widow Mary. [York De. V.]

OCCORMACKE, see McCormick.

ODIORNE,
John, of Boston, removed to Portsmouth; lawsuit at York, 1656; had land assigned him in 1660; sold a cable, a

main sail for a shallop and a stage he had built at Smuttinose Island 29 June, 1660.
See Langdon.

OLIVER,
   Benedick, Isles of Shoals, deposed 18 June, 1660, ae. 31 years. [P. Files.]

OKERS,
   Rowland, Richmond Island, one of the fishermen in 1634. [Trel.]

ONION, ONYON, INIOUN,
   Thomas, yeoman, Portsmouth, purchased Robert Davis' lot at Sagamore Creek before Jan. 4, 1657-8. With Robert Purinton sold land 1 Aug. 1672. Wife Margaret.

OTIS, OATES,
   Richard, blacksmith, Dover, lawsuit, 1652; juror, 1659. He contracted 16 Oct. 1679, to deliver pipe staves to Wm. Vaughan of Portsmouth in payment for 2 chaldrons of sea coal. Contracted with George Broughton of Berwick to deliver boards to James Chadbourne 1 Sept. 1685.
   Wife Rose; children, Richard, Stephen, Nicholas, Rebecca, Rose, Solomon b. and d. 1663, Experience b. 7 Nov. 1666. He m. second Susanna or Shuah, widow of James Heard.
   He was killed by the Indians in 1689. Many *legends* about the family. [See Reg. V, 177, etc.]

PAGE,
   Robert, husbandman, ae. 33, with wife Lucy, ae. 30, and children Francis, Margaret and Susanna, and servants William Moulton, ae. 20, and Anne Wad, ae. 15, of Ormsby, Eng. passed exam. April 11, 1637, to go to N. E. Settled at Salem. Wife Lucy adm. chh. 1639. He was adm. frm. May 18, 1642. Rem. to Hampton; proprietor June, 1640; selectman, deputy,

deacon, yeoman. His wife Luce d. 12 (9) 1665. He secured the claims of his brother Edward Colcord and his wife Ann to certain lands in 1654 and 1679. Ch. Rebecca and Samuel bapt. at Sal. 1 (7) 1639. He d. Sept. 22, 1679. Will dated 9 Sept. prob. 29 Nov. 1679, beq. to sons Francis and Thomas; daus. Mary Fogg, Margaret Sanborne, Rebecca Marston, and Hannah, wife of Henry Dow; gr. ch. Seth, James, and Hannah Fogg; Joseph, Benjamin, Robert, Hannah, Sarah, William, and Ruth Moulton; Jonathan Samborne; Rebecca, Hannah, Samuel, Lucie and Meriah Marston; Joseph, Samuel, Symon and Jabez Dow; Robert, Samuel, John, Mary and Lucie Page; "to grandson Robert Page that chest that I brought outt of old England"; (some of these gr. ch. called by their marriage names in the will.)

Thomas, tailor, ae. 29, with wife Elizabeth, ae. 28, and children Thomas, ae. 2, and Katharine, ae. 1, and servants Edward Spurks, ae. 22, and Kat: Taylor, ae. 24, cert. from All Saints, Stayning, (London,) came in the Increase in April, 1635.

Thomas, gent. Saco, (Maine,) had suit in Maine court May 2, 1637; gave bond for payment of money 22 (1) 1640-1. [L.] Grand juryman in 1640. Gave bond for John Winter in 1641.

See Green, Hussey, Shrewsbury.

PALMER,

William, yeoman, Newbury, proprietor; was one of the first persons licensed by the Gen. Court of Mass. to begin a plantation at Hampton, 6 (7) 1638. Frm. March 13, 1638-9. Comissioner for minor trials; lot layer. Contracted with the town in 1640 that his son Stephen should take care of the herd of calves. Son Edward had land grant in 1641. He conveyed all his property in Hampton and Newbury, March 10, 1645, to John Sherman of Watertown and Martha, his daughter, Sherman's wife, in lieu of an inheritance in Great Ormesby, Eng. which belonged to her.

He m. Grace, widow successively of John Sherman and Thomas Rogers; she survived him and m. [fourth], Roger Porter of Watertown; she died June 3, 1662, ae. about 70 years; beq. to her daughters Elizabeth, wife of Daniel Smith, and Martha, wife of John Sherman, and their children, and to her brother, John Coolidge. John and Martha Sherman sold their share in his estate in 1661 to his youngest son Joseph Palmer.

[See Reg. LI, 309, etc.]

William, planter, Kittery, resident about 1642 [deposition, York De. II]; suit in court at Strawberry Bank, 10 (9) 1642. Bought house at Str. Ba. and sold it 4 Sept. 1651 to Thaddeus Riddan. Took oath of allegiance at K. 16 Nov. 1652. Deeded land 24 Aug. 1669 to his daughter Sarah and her husband William and their children. George Palmer, ae. about 43 years, deposed 28 Aug. 1663 about an execution levied "by Wiliam Palmer, constable of Kittery."

William, mariner, Great Island, died intestate; admin. of his estate was given 6 Aug. 1685, to his widow Abishag. Query, is this the above?

See Bachiler, Hilton, Riddan.

PARKER,

George, carpenter, ae. 23, came in the Susan and Ellen to Boston in April, 1635. Seems to be the "carpenter," of York, who sold land 23 Nov. 1648. Took oath of allegiance to Mass. govt. 22 Nov. 1652. Proprietor. He and his wife Hannah made deed of gift to son in law Peter Bass 10 April, 1683.

James, one of the witnesses to possession of Lewis and Bonython's land in Maine June 28, 1631.

Rev. James, Weymouth, a godly man and a scholar, many years a deputy of the Court, was called to Pascataqua to be their minister in 1642. Had good success. [W.] Residing at Strawberry Bank, he sold houses and lands at Weymouth 26 (9) 1644. Frm. May 29, 1644. He removed to

Barbadoes where he and his family were reported in 1647 by Mr. Vines.

Basil, see Thomas Brooks.

John, York, his land referred to in the bounds of an adjoining tract in 1651. Took oath of allegiance to Mass. govt. 22 Nov. 1652.

John, fisherman, Damerills Cove, testified in 1645 to the loss of time to his fishing company which arose from the performances of Nash and others at Stratton's island. [Bax. MSS.]

John, "of Kennebecke, aged about fivety yeares," testified to the signing of an Indian deed of lands which he had occupied "upwards of 26 yeares," and received confirmatory deed 21 July, 1684. [York De. IV.] Sold land to Capt. Sylvanus Davis 1 June, 1661, his wife Margery joining; confirmed the deed 13 Nov. 1684. Sold an adjoining tract "in Kennebecke river" 3 June, 1661, to his sister Mary Webber. With wife Margery gave land in Kennebeck to Wiliam Baker, house carpenter, and his wife Sarah, their daughter.

John Parker, Jr. bought land of the Indians in 1650, what is now Phippsburg, Me. [Varney's Gazetteer of Maine.]

Samuel, admin. on his estate granted to Em. Hilliard June 25, 1656.

Widow Judith, Hampton, proprietor, 1640. Removed to Charlestown; sold a house and land at Hamp. 23 (3) 1645 to John Marian, payment to be made at either of her dwellings in any of the towns in the bay, namely Charlestown, Watertown, Roxbury or Dorchester.

See Dixon, Shrewsbury.

PARTRIDGE,

John, Portsmouth, propr. 1660; juror, 1667; leather-sealer, 1668. Wife Mary. Will, Aug. 28, prob. Sept. 5, 1722; "very aged"; daus. Hannah Almery, Mary Elliot, Sarah Hunking, Joanna Roberts, and Ruth Tarrett; gr. son, Jonathan Partridge.

PAUL, PAULL,

Daniel, shipwright, mariner, from Ipswich, co. Suffolk, Eng. and of Boston, N. E. Aug. 26, 1640, gave letter of attorney for the sale of lands in Ipswich and delivery of money to wife Elizabeth. [L.] of Kittery, bought land 21 March, 1648. Took oath of allegiance to Mass. govt. 16 Nov. 1652. Gave land to his son Stephen 18 July, 19 Charles II, on occasion of his marriage to Katherine, daughter of Antipas Mavericke. With wife Elizabeth sold, Oct. 15, 1659, to Richard Cutt, his dwelling house in Kittery with lands, cattle, etc.

See Maverick, Tibbets.

PEABODY, PEABODIE, PAYBODY, PEBODIE,

Francis, husbandman, ae. 21 years, certified from the parish of St. Albons, co. Hertford, England, came in the Planter April 2, 1635. Settled at Ipswich; proprietor, 1636. Removed to Hampton, proprietor, June, 1640 freeman 18 May, 1642; one of the commissioners to try cases of limited amount in 1649. Sold house and land in March, 1649-50. Rem. to Topsfield, Mass. Lieutenant. He deposed 24 (4) 1662, ae. about 50 years. He m. Mary, daughter of Reginald Foster; she d. April 9, 1705.

Children, John, Joseph, William, Isaac, Sarah, Hephsibah, Lydia, Mary, Ruth b. 22 May, 1658, Damaris b. and d. 1660, Samuel b. 4 June, 1662, d. 13 Sept. 1667, Jacob b. 28 July, 1664, Hannah b. 8 May, 1668, Nathaniel b. 29 July, 1669.

He died Feb. 19, 1697-8. Will dated 20 Jan. 1695-6, prob. Aug. 7, 1698, bequeathed to wife Mary; sons John, Joseph, William, Isaac and Nathaniel; to Jacob, Kezia and Mercy, children of deceased son Jacob; son in law Daniel Wood; grand son Samson How; daughters Lydia Perley, Mary Death, Sarah How and Hephsibah Ray.

See also Drake.

PEARCE, PIERCE, PEIRCE,

Richard, carpenter, Muscongus, bought of "Capt. John Summerset" [Samoset], Indian sagamore, a tract of land at

Round Pond and Pemaquid river, 9 Jan. 1641. He is called "brother in law" by John Brown, Jr. of Pemaquid and Framingham.

His children, Richard, born about 1647, John, born about 1652, George, born about 1662, and Elizabeth, (married Richard Fullford,) removed to Salem, Mass. The sons testified to the above Nov. 29, 1717, and made an agreement together with their deceased sister Elizabeth's daughter, Elizabeth, wife of Samuel Martin.

[Ess. De. 37, 257, and Gen. Adv. I, 95.]

See also Bachiler, Pierce.

PENEWELL, PENWILL, PENNYWELL, PENNELL, see Hatch,

Walter, Senior, Saco, inhabitant, 1647; land in Biddeford, 1653; bought land Sept. 29, 1659.

M. Mary, dau. of Robert Booth. Ch.: Walter, John, Mary, Deborah, Sarah and Susanna. [Hist. K. Port.]

An inventory of his estate was presented in court 21 May, 1683, by his widow Mary. His son Walter P., weaver, sold some of the land 13 July, 1687. Joseph P., mariner, of York, sold one sixteenth part of the ship True Dealing, of York, of 55 tons burden, to Abraham Brown of Boston, 1 Jan. 1670; the inventory of his estate was presented March 6, 1682, by Walter P.; this may be evidence that Joseph was also a son of Walter, Senior.

See also Booth, Hatch, Marsill, Purrington.

PENDLETON, PENDILTON,

Capt. Brian or Bryan, Watertown, frm. Sept. 3, 1634. Town officer, deputy, member artillery company. Rem. to Sudbury, being one of those to whom the court gave the right to begin the plantation 6 Sept. 1638; proprietor and selectman, 1639. Appointed by the Court to train the company 13 May, 1640.

Rem. to Portsmouth; had lots assigned in 1652; deputy, May 13, 1658; major, councillor. Rem. to Saco and Cape

Porpoise, Me.; returned to Portsmouth. Signed petition of Isles of Shoals people for better defences, etc. 18 (3) 1653. Associate judge of county court in 1664. He deposed 2 (5) 1669, ae. about 70 years. [Norf. De. II.] A letter of his from Winter Harbor, dated 13 Aug. 1676, describes Indian troubles; [Reg. I, 53.] "A man of great estate, & very precise independent," so he was described in a paper written about 1668 from a royalist point of view. [Bax. MSS.]
Wife Eleanor joined him in a deed of Watertown land March 20, 1648.

He made will Aug. 9, 1677, schedule proved April 5, 1681; beq. to wife Eleanor, son James and his children, and to grandson Pendleton Fletcher. [Me. Wills, 59, and York De. V.; Reg. III, 122.]

Joseph, Portsmouth, had land grant in 1652.

See also Cadogan, Hutchinson, Spencer.

PEPERELL,

William, of [Iplappen] in Devonshire, asigned to John Sparks of Dartmouth, 7 (9) 1648, all his wages due from Wm. [Stimson], Mr. of the Eagle of Colchester, viz. 36 s. a month for 8 mos. from 20 Feb. to 14 Oct. last past. [A.]

This suggests a famous man who came later to N. H.

See Bray.

PERCYVAL,

Richard, one of the Shrewsbury (Eng.) men who received a patent from the crown for lands at Dover and vicinity. He sold his share May 4, 1640, to Obediah Bruen.

PERKINS,

Abraham, son of John, the eldest son of John, Senior, of Ipswich, Mass. received a bequest from his grandfather in 1654. He was a proprietor at Hampton and freeman May 13, 1640. Kept an ordinary in 1651. [Norf. rec.]

Wife Mary; children, Mary bapt. Dec. 15, 1639, Abraham b. Sept. 2, 1639, (slain by the Indians 13 June, 1677; estate admin. 9 Oct. 1677); Luke b. 1641, Humphrey b. Jan. 23,

1642, James b. April 11, 1644, Timothy b. July, 1646, James b. Oct. 5, 1647, Jonathan b. 30 (3) 1650, David b. 28 (12) 1653, Abigail b. 12 (2) 1655, Timothy b. 29 (4) 1657, Sarah b. 26 (5) 1659, Humphrey b. 17 (3) 1661.

He died Aug. 31, 1683; will dated Aug. 22, proved Sept. 18, 1683; wife, sons Jonathan, Humphrey, James, David and Luke, dau. Sarah; gr. ch. John Perkins and Mary Fifield. The widow Mary died May 29, 1706.

Isaac, son of Isaac of Ipswich, Hampton, proprietor 23 (12) 1645. Bought farm of Rev. Timothy Dalton in 1652. Gave land as a marriage portion to his son Jacob on his marriage with Mary, daughter of Thomas Philbrick, 19 March, 1668-9. Conveyed his estate to son Ebenezer 6 Jan. 1680, in consideration of his caring for himself and his wife Susanna the rest of their lives.

Children, Lydia, Isaac, (drowned 10 (7) 1661), Jacob bapt. May 24, 1640, Rebecca, Caleb, Benjamin b. 12 (12) 1649, d. 23 (9) 1670, Susanna b. 21 (6) 1652, Hannah b. 24 (2) 1656, Mary b. 23 (5) 1658, Ebenezer b. 9 Dec. 1659, Joseph b. 9 (2) 1661, (drowned 10 (7) 1661,) Daniel d. 1 (6) 1662.

He died in Nov. 1685.

See Bradbury, Cocks.

PETTIE, PETTIT,

Thomas, Boston, having served Oliver Mellowes three and a half years, received a grant of a house plot from the town 8 (11) 1637. He removed to Exeter; signed the combination 5 (4) 1639. Signed petitions to Gen. Court of Mass. in 1645 and 1647. Allowance was made to him in 1650 for attending Hampton court as constable.

Wife Christian; children, Hannah b. at the "beginning of February," 1647; Thomas, Jr. had a grant of land in 1649.

PEVERLY, see Feverill,

Thomas, Portsmouth, land owner in 1652; juror at Dover court; took oath of fidelity July 2, 1657.

Will dated 19 April, proved June 30, 1670, bequeathed to

wife Jane and children John, Thomas, Lazarus, Samuel, Jeremiah, Sarah Peverly, dau. Holmes and Martha Noble.

PHILBRICK, FILBRICK,

Thomas, Watertown, Mass. proprietor, 1636. He sold house and land Jan. 23, 1645, and removed to Hampton where his son John had been a proprietor since 1640. Covenanted to furnish the town with powder, bullets and match; lawsuit about the matter in 1650.

Wife Elizabeth d. 19 (12) 1663. Children, James, John, Thomas, (deposed 11 (2) 1667, ae. about 42 years,) Elizabeth, (m. Thomas Chase,) Mary, (m. Edward Tuck,) Martha, (m. John Cass).

Will dated March 12, 1663-4, "very aged"; prob. 8 (8) 1667; mentions children James, Thomas, Elizabeth, Hannah, Mary, Martha; grandchildren John and Hannah Philbrick, James Chase, (son of daughter Elizabeth Garland), and Martha Cass, daughter of daughter Martha. [See Reg. VII, 358, and XXXVIII, 279.]

PHILLIPS, PHILIPS,

John, Dover, proprietor, signed the Piscataqua combination in 1640.

He was drowned. Inventory taken March 20, 1641-2 by George Smith and John Dam. Hatevil Nutter and Edward Starbuck were appointed 28 (5) 1642 by Dover court to sell the goods, pay debts, and return the overplus, if any. Inventory and list of debts filed 18 July, 1643.

John, millwright, bought land at Casco bay and the river of Presumpsca of Cleve 1 Aug. 1650. Took oath of allegiance at Spurwink 13 July, 1658. Estate settled 9 March, 1679-80. [York De. V.]

William, vintner, inn-holder, lieutenant, major, Charlestown, admitted to the church with wife Mary 23 (7) 1639. Frm. May 13, 1640. Removed to Boston. He made William Phillips, of Bedlam, shoemaker, his attorney for collection of accounts in England, 10 (12) 1648. [A.] Daniel Field of Tring, Eng. in a letter to Seth Sweetser, May 10, 1642, sent love to Wm. Phillips and his wife. The latter died 1 (3) 1646. He m. 2, Susannah, widow of Christopher Stanley; she d. 16 (4) 1655. leaving a will dated 10 (7) 1650, prob. Aug. 2, 1655. Beq. to dau. in law Mary Feild, daus. Martha Thurston and Rebecca Lord, Elizabeth and Phebe Phillips and Sarah; sons William and Nathaniel P.; Elizabeth and William Aspinwall; any of her brothers' or sister's' children that may come over; Richard and George Bennitt, who were her servants; rest to her husband. [Reg. V, 447.] He m. 3, Bridget, widow of John Sanford. He mortgaged his house in Boston, called the Ship Tavern, for the payment of certain sums to her children March 10, 1657. He was one of the commissioners of the Mass. Bay Colony for Maine in 1653.

He bought of Beex & Co. of London, 11 March, 1658-9, the patent of land on the southwest of Saco river, formerly granted to Vines. Removed to Saco. Carried on a large amount of business in land, mills, mines, &c. Wife Bridget joined him in deed of a tract 10 Nov. 1662. They also deeded to his son Nathaniel 22 June, 1664, "in lieu of a legacy left to Nathaniel by my last deseased wife Susanna, one sixteenth of a silver mine about 40 miles above Saco Falls, which I bought of an Indian known by the name of Captain Sunday, in partnership with my sun Alden." Two sixteenths of this he deeded 30 March, 1663, to his "sons Zachary Gillim and Ephraim Turner of Boston." Deeded one fourth part of a sawmill, etc. at Saco Falls, to son in law John Alden of Boston, mariner, with Elizabeth, his wife, Nov. 28, 1662.

Having returned to Boston, he sold the tract between Kennebunke and Batson's rivers to Edward Spragg in Bishopsgate in London, packer, Robert Lord of London, mariner, John Alden, and Samuel and Nathaniel Phillips, his sons, 12 June, 1676. He further deeded a tract 8 miles square, on the West side of Kennebunke river & 8 miles from the sea, etc. to his children and those of his "now wife," namely: Samuel (eldest son), William, (youngest son); Mary Feild (eldest daughter), Martha Thirston (second daughter), Rebecca Lord (third daughter), Elizabeth Alden (fourth daughter), Zacchary Gillum (son in law), Sarah Turner (youngest daughter), Elephell Stratton (daughter of my wife Bridget), Peleg, John and Elisha Stantford (her sons), and Robert Lord of London, mariner (his son in law). Other persons included in the purchase were John Woodmansey of Boston, merchant, Theodore Atkinson, felt-maker, John Santford, writing schoolmaster, and William Hudson, vintner; dated June 15, 1676.

Children recorded in Boston: Elizabeth, (m. 6 (5) 1655, Abiel Everill, m. 2, April 1, 1660, John Alden), Phebe bapt. 16 (2) 1640, (m. July 26, 1659, Zechariah Gillam), Nathaniel bapt. 19 (2) 1641, Mary b. 17 (12) 1643, John d. Aug. 1657.

Will dated in Feb. 1682-3, proved 29 Sept. 1683, beq. to wife Bridget; sons Samuel and William; the latter having been 4 years in captivity among the Spaniards, his portion might be used for his redemption; to daughters Mary Feild and Elizabeth Alden.

See also Clayes, Munjoy.

PICKARD,
Edmund, mariner, Smuttinose Island, had lawsuit for possession of stage-room in 1660.

He returned to England, and from "Northam neare Biddiford in the county of Devon," sold vessels, flakes, stage-room, etc. at said island, 13 July, 1661.

PIERCE, PEIRCE, PERSE, see also Pearce,
John, fisherman, York, probably the "John Peirce of Noddles Island, planter," to whom Capt. Champernowne sold 100 acres on his island at Kittery, which he reserved from the sale to White 14 Dec. 1648. [York De. I.] Signed petition of inhabitants in 1653. [Bax. MSS.] Bought house and field of Edward Rishworth 9 Dec. 1653, "which was formerly ould Robert Knight's." Sold the same 26 Dec. 1660. With wife Phebe sold land 19 June, 1670, to Makem Makentyre, (who refers to him as "father Pearce" in his will in 1712.)

He m. a second wife Ellner; she died in 1675. Her will, dated 27 Aug. prob. 24 Jan. 1675, beq. to son Joseph and daughters Sarah and Mary; the inventory refers to her deceased husband John. [York De. V.]

PICKERING, PICKRIN,

John, Piscataqua, gave bonds in 1635 for Nicholas Frost's appearance at Boston court; discharged 5 April, 1636. Was ordered by Pisc. court in 1642 to "deliver the Old Combinatio at Strawberry Bank" to the next court. July 5, 1654, he bought the remaining 5 years service of "an Irish servante man" who had been brought over " as a captive" by Mr. George Dill. See Meckermecke. He took oath of fidelity 11 July, 1659. He deposed 27 June, 1660, ae. about 60 years. [P. Files.] He conveyed to his son John for 15 pounds a year during his life, and other considerations, his water grist mill and other buildings and lands 7 Nov. 1665.

He died 18 Jan. 1668. [Dov. Hist. Coll.] He made will dated 11 (11) 1668, bequeathing to son Thomas and daughters Rebecca, Abigail, Mary and Sarah; it was brought into court 29 June, 1669, but not allowed; admin. was granted to his son John, and children Rebecca, Abigail and Thomas placed under the guardianship of Mr. Joshua Moody.

See Ugroufe.

PHIPPS, PHIPS,

James, gunsmith, from Bristol, England, resided at a point which now bears his name, near the present town of Wiscasset, Maine. He had a wife who bore him 26 children, of whom 21 were sons; of these the only one celebrated is William, born Feb. 2, 1650.

William learned the trade of ship carpenter; became master of a ship; sailed to England and the West Indies; discovered an immense amount of treasure in the form of gold and silver in a wrecked ship. Carried it to England, receiving not only a part of the wealth but the honor of knighthood. Returned to New England. Became commander of an expedition against Canada; was afterward appointed governor of the province of Massachusetts, and had a remarkable history.

So runs the account as given by Rev. Cotton Mather.

See deposition of Peter, son of John White, partner of Phipps in land holding at "Negwusset" (now in Woolwich, Me.) in York Deeds XI, 15.

James Phipps died . . . and his widow m. second John White, with whom she sold land to her son William Oct. 4, 1679. [Deposition of Dame Mary Phipps, executrix and heir to Sr. Wm. Phipps, Kn't deceased." |Me. Gen. Reg. VIII, 202.]

PINKHAM, PINCOMBE,

Richard, Dover, signed the combination in 1640. Proprietor, 1642. Was appointed to beat the drum on the Lord's day and take care of the meeting house in 1648. Brought a suit in court in 1649. Before the court in 1652.

He made deed of gift of his property in 22 June, 1671, to his son John in consideration of John's agreement to maintain him the rest of his life.

PLAISTED, PLAYSTEED,

Roger, gent. Quamphegon, York, witnessed deed of Richard Nason in 1654. Received a due bill from John Auger 15 Oct. 1655. With wife Olive sold land next to the Salmon Falls mills, 18 April, 1671.

His widow Olive and son James, admins. of his estate, gave a receipt 17 Aug. 1676. The sons William and James, admins. gave a quitclaim deed 4 Aug. 1679. Daniel Simpson of York, husband of Frances, daughter of Roger Plaisted, Jr. eldest son of Lieut. Roger P. sold her share or claim to the estate 2 July, 1701.

See also Angier.

PLIMPTON, PLUMPTON,

Henry, Dover, estate settled 8 (8) 1652.

POMFRET, POMFRETT,
William, planter, Dover, signed the combination in 1640. Town clerk, selectman, 1648. One of the commissioners to end small causes; lieutenant; in list of jury men in 1646. Returned to Gen. Court in 1653 the names of assistants chosen. [Mass. Arch. 38 B, 8.] Sold house and lands 10 (1) 1651; sold two thirds of a sawmill at Bellemie's banke, given to him by the town, 16 (5) 1651.
He died 7 Aug. 1680. [Dov. Hist. Coll.]
See Cutt, Follett, Lewis.

PORMORT, PORMONT,
Philemon, was married at Alford, co. Linc. Eng. Oct. 11, 1627, to Susanna, dau. of William Bellingham, came to New England. Chosen schoolmaster at Boston, Mass.; admitted to the church with wife Susann 28 (6) 1634; frm. May 6, 1635. "Intreated to become schole-master" 13 (2) 1635. Proprietor. Sympathizing with Mrs. Hutchinson and Mr. Wheelwright, he removed to Exeter; was dism. from the chh. 6 (11) 1638. Signed Exeter combination 5 (4) 1639. Returned to Boston and was in the employ of Valentine Hill 9 (8) 1645. [A.] Removed to Wells, Me. Was dismissed from the church there at his own request before 1653. [Bax. MSS. I.]

He or some of his family removed to Great Island (Portsmouth).

His wife Susan died 29 (10) 1642; he m. 2, Elizabeth —. Children, Lazarus b. 28 (12) 1635, Anna b. 5 (2) 1638, Pedajah b. 3 (4) 1640, Borshuah bapt. 4 (5) 1647, Mary, (m. 24 (9) 1652, Nathaniel Adams, Jr.), Elizabeth, (m. in 1656 Samuel Norden), Martha, bapt. 19 June, 1653.

POTTLE,
John, Portsmouth, proprietor, 1660.

POWELL,
Michael, fisherman, York, had grant of land at Cape Neddicke for the fishing trade, in partnership with John Ball

and others, 3 July, 1649. Compare with M. P. merchant, of Dedham and Boston, Mass. [P. of M.]
See also Moore.

POWNING, POUNING, POUNDING,
  Henry, Kittery, one of the creditors of John Phillips of Dover in 1641; removed to Dover, then to Boston, where he was received to the church from that of Dover 15 (8) 1648; freeman, Mass. May 29, 1653. Wife Elizabeth; children recorded in Bo.: Elizabeth bapt. 3 (12) 1649, Mary bapt. 5 (8) 1651, Henry b. 28 April, 1654, Hannah b. 8 April, 1656, d. 6 (5) 1657, Hannah b. and d. 1658, Sarah b. 3 Aug. 1659, Daniel b. 27 Aug. 1660, Anna or Hannah b. Feb. 29, bapt. 6 (1) 1664.
  He d. before July 27, 1665, when the inventory of his estate was presented by the widow Elizabeth; land at Kittery mentioned. [Reg. XVI, 228].
  Land was laid out to him at Cole's Harbor by the selectmen 3 March, 1651; this was sold 13 Oct. 1684, by Elizabeth, widow of the said H. P., shopkeeper, of Boston, deceased, with Jonathan Bridgham and Elizabeth, his wife, Mary, Sarah and Daniel P. children of the said Henry. [York De. IV.]

PREBLE,
  Abraham, Scituate, witnessed a deed in 1639; took oath of fidelity, date not specified. Removed to York, Me.; bought land of Edward Godfrey 20 Dec. 1642. Recd. 20 acres of land from Wm. Hoole 19 July, 1645. Witnessed grant of mill privileges to Ed. Rishworth in 1651. Took oath of allegiance to Mass. govt. 22 Nov. 1652. Was appointed one of the commissioners to hold court at York.
  He m. at Scituate Judith, daughter of Nathaniel Tilden. Child, Nathaniel bapt. at Second church of Sci. April 9, 1648.
  [Adm. of est. in Mr. Baxter's records Vol. 1.]
  [See wills of Prebles, residing at several points in Kent, Eng. in Reg. L, 118; see Genealogy.]

PUDDINGTON, see Purington.

PURCHASE, PURCHAS,

Mr. Thomas, gent. (seems to have been a brother of Oliver, an early settler of Dorchester, Mass. who came from Dorchester, Eng.); came to Maine about the year 1625; see Indian deed in York De. IV, 14. Resided at Pejepscot, now Brunswick, or in that vicinity. Was friendly to Sir Christopher Gardiner, and aided him in 1631. [Thomas Wiggin's letter in Mass. Hist. Coll. VIII, 320.]* He yielded to Gov. Winthrop and the Mass. Bay Co. 22 (5) 1639, jurisdiction over a tract of land "at Pagiscott, on both sides of the Androscoggin river, 4 miles square toward the sea," reserving his own property as specified and that of other inbabitants not particularly named. He sued certain men for taking from his premises at Pag. some moose skins that belonged to Abacodusset, an Indian sagamore, May 31, 1641. He removed to Lynn. Sold three eighths of the ship Blessing to Valentine Hill 29 (8) 1644. [A.] Rev. Robert Jordan was a kinsman. He m. 1, Mary —, who came to New England with Sir Chr. Gardiner; she died at Boston 7 (11) 1655. He m. 2, Elizabeth; children, Elizabeth, (m. John Blaney), Jane, (m. Oliver Elkins), Thomas, (m. Elizabeth, dau. of Samuel and Jane Andrews), and d. before 10 Jan. 1683, [York De. IV,] and two others. See Neale.

He died May 11, 1678, ae. 101 years. Will dated 2 May, 1677, prob. 25 (5) 1678, beq. to widow Elizabeth and five children. Had lost most of his estate at the Eastward. Widow and son Thomas execs. Friends Mr. Henry Jocelin, cousin Oliver Purchase of Hammersmith and Edward Alline, of Boston, overseers.

The son Thomas was lost at sea with Mr. Habbackuck Turner and others; administration of his estate granted Nov. 25, 1684, to his widow Elizabeth; John Blaney and John Williams, cooper, both of Salem, sureties. [Es. files.]

See Neale, Felch, Mackworth.

---

* He was one of the commissioners who held court at Saco 25 March, 1636.

PURINGTON, PURRINGTON, PUDDINGTON,
George, York, bought land 15 April, 1640. Had deed of land for debt 24 Jan. 1645. Witnessed a deed 3 July, 1647. He died before 1662, for his widow Mary married 2, John Davis, and sold, with him, 15 March, 1661-2, a tract of land to John Gard, of Boston, merchant. They also sold land to her son in law John Penwill, mariner, 27 Feb. 1674-5. Will dated 25 June, 1647, recorded 18 Jan. 1665-6, beq. to wife Mary, sons John and Elias, and daughters Mary, Frances and Rebecca; conditional bequest to brother Robert P. whom he appointed one of the overseers.

Robert, York, had lawsuit about pipe staves in Piscataqua court Sept. 24, [1641]. Constable for the lower part of Strawberry Bank in 1649. Had 10 acres of land in Portsmouth assigned to him as an inhabitant Jan. 13, 1652. He deeded to his sons Robert and John his lands and houses "on the plaine southward from the meeting house of Portsmouth" 11 Feb. 1655; "A P," "his wife," joined her mark to his in the signature.
See also Davis, Onion.

PURSTON,
Thomas, "from further Northward" took oath of allegiance at Kittery 16 Nov. 1652. [Is it not clerical error for Durston?]

RABONE, see Haborne.

RAGGS, RAGG,
Jeffrey, Dover, in court in 1642; taxed in 1648.

RAINES, see Raynes.

RAND, RANDE, RANN,
Francis, Piscataqua, with his wife witnessed in a case before the grand jury in 1648. Constable for the upper part

of Strawberry Bank, appointed 5 (5) 1649; in office in 1651. Lands, 1660. Wife Christian, sued for slander in 1655.

He took the oath of fidelity July 2, 1657.

His will, dated Dec. 31, 1689, proved Feb. 19, 1691-2 gave his estate to his sons Thomas and Samuel after his and his wife's decease on conditions specified; to sons John and Nathaniel, daus. Sarah Herrick and Mary Barns.

RANDALL,

Richard, Saco, 1659; son Richard rem. to Cape Porpoise. [Hist. K. Port.]

Wilmot, a maid servant, Richmond Island, in the service of Winter from 26 July, 1641; Nicholas Edgecombe married her in 1642, and paid 5 li. to W. "for yeldinge up of her tyme." [Trel.]

RASHLEY, RASHLEYGHE,

Rev. Thomas, was admitted to the church of Boston, Mass. as a "studyent" 8 (1) 1640. Child John bapt. 18 (3) 1645, ae. about 6 weeks. He was "chaplain" at Cape Ann in 1643. [Lechford, P. D.] Removed to Exeter; proprietor in 1643; minister. [Mass. Hist. Coll. 4-7.]

RAWLINS, RAWLENS, ROLLINS,

James, planter, Newbury, Mass. frm. May 14, 1634; proprietor; fined 5 Aug. 1634, for charging too high a price for the labor of one of his servants whom he had let out to another man. Resident in 1638. Removed to Dover; signed the combination in 1640; proprietor taxed in 1648. Signed petition to Mass govt. in 1654. Bought house in 1651; sold land 14 July, 1657.

Made will Dec. 16, 1687, proved July 25, 1691; wife Hannah, eldest son Ichabod, other sons, Benjamin and Joseph; remainder to be divided between "all my children, sons and daughters."

RAYNES, RAINES, RAYNER,

Francis, captain, Dover, proprietor, sold land to Darby Feild; litigation over succeeding transfers of the land in court 10 (8) 1649. Of York, took oath of allegiance to

Mass. govt. 22 Nov. 1652, and was then appointed ensign. Witnessed deed of Allcocke 31 Dec. 1652. Sold land in Braveboate Harbor 17 March, 1660. With wife Eliner gave house and farm (after their deaths) to their son Nathaniel, and after his death to his eldest son Francis; deed dated 8 July, 1684.

His will dated 21 Aug. 1693, recorded 15 Oct. 1706, beq. to wife Elinor; son Nathaniel and his sons Francis, John and Nathan; Francis, son of Joseph Hodsdon; grandchild Elizabeth H.; daughter, wife to John Woodman; to Samuel Matthews, his wife and children, David Mendum and John Diamond's children.

See also Tompson.

READ, READE, REED, REEDE, etc.,
 Robert, Boston, frm. April 17, 1644. Land gr. in Bo. 1637, having been a res. in 1635. Sealer of leather. Rem. to Exeter, N. H.

Signed the combination 5 (4) 1639; took freeman's oath at Pisc. court 17 (2) 1644.

Rem. to Hampton.

Wife Hannah d. 24 (4) 1655. Second wife Susanna survived him and m. John Presson. Ch. Hannah, (m. John Souter,) Mary, Rebecca b. and bapt. at Bo. 29 (7) 1646, Deborah bapt. 28 (11) 1648, ae. about 3 days, Sarah bapt. 1 (7) 1650, Samuel bapt. 3 (2) 1653, d. 31 (1) 1654. Samuel b. Feb. 28, 1654.

He was lost in a vessel which sailed from Hampton for Boston Oct. 20, 1657. [See Whittier's poem, "The Wreck of Rivermouth."] His goods and lands were appraised at 84 pounds, 29 (8) 1657 and 5 (1) 1657-8.

The daughter Hannah, with her husband John Souter, brazier, of Boston, the dau. Mary, and the dau. Sarah by her guardian, John Souter, sold their shares in house and land in Boston owned by their father Robert Read, late of Hampton, deceased, 6 Jan. 1662-3, and Susannah, wife of John Presson of Boston and relict of said Robert Read, conveyed her right the following day; recorded 11 June, 1668. See also Walford, West.

READING, REDDING,
Thomas, Plymouth (town or colony,) volunteer for the Pequot war in 1637. He m. 20 July, 1639, Ellene Penny. Placed his male child, about 5 years old, in care of Gowen White 4 June, 1645, to be brought up to the age of 21 years. Removed to East Saco, Me.; took oath of allegiance to Mass. govt. 5 July, 1653. [Bax. MSS.]
His widow Ellner, of Casco Bay, sold land 10 March, 1673-4, to James Andrews of Falmouth, who had paid a mortgage given by her late husband Thomas R. in the year 1672. John Redding of Weymouth, Joseph Donell of Casco Bay and Ruth, his wife, and John Taylor of Boston sold their rights in another tract which the widow sold in 1680. [York Deeds.]

REDMAN, RIDMAN, READMAN,
John, blacksmith, Dover, built a house on land of the Dover and Squamscott patentees, and was afterward sued by them therefor Sept. 3, 1641. Removed to Hampton. Testified in Colcord and Wall case in 1658. Took freeman's oath at Salisbury 24 (2) 1649. Mortgaged house and land at Hamp. 2 Dec. 1651. With Richard Knight of Boston, weaver, sold land at Smutty Nose Island, Isles of Shoals, 30 Nov. 1668. Sold land 6 July, 1671. Deposed about March, 1659-60, ae. about 42 years; [Es. Files]; and 14 (8) 1673, ae. 56. [Norf. Files.] Gave marriage portion to his son John on his wedding Martha, daughter of John Cass, 18 Feb. 1666; and Robert Knight of York also gave land the same day to "my grand child," John, Jr.; sold land to son John Aug. 20, 1681.
Wife Margerite died 30 (3) 1658; he m. 2, Sabina, widow of Wm. Marston, who died Nov. 10, 1689. Children, John, Mary b. 15 (10) 1649, Joseph b. 20 (2) 1651, Sam: b. 12 (2) 1658.
He died Feb. 16, 1700, "ae. about 85."

REEVES,

William, Kittery, testified in the Gunnison case 21 Dec. 1653, ae. about 38 years; was a sailor in John Treworgy's bark, the Bachelor, about 16 or 17 years before. [Bax. MSS. I.] Probably the person who came to Boston in the Elizabeth and Ann in April, 1635, ae. 22; was before the Gen. Court of Mass. 4 (10) 1638, and before Es. court in 1640.

REMICK, REMETH, RAMAY,

Christian, planter, Kittery, took oath of allegiance to Mass. govt. 16 Nov. 1652. Gave land to his son Isaac 16 Oct. 1686, and 20 June, 1691, sons Jacob and Joshua witnessing the deeds; they also witnessed that of same date in which Abraham, another son, surrendered any claim he might have.

He made a conditional deed to his son Joshua 18 Oct. 1693, and another, dated "the one and thirtieth day of April," 1703, wife Hannah joining.

REYNER, REYNOR, RAYNER, RAYNOR, RAINER, etc.,

Rev. John, b. at Gildersome, co. York, came in 1635 or 1636 to Plymouth. Was chosen teacher; lands granted him Feb. 6, 1636. Frm. 6 March, 1637-8. Wrote a letter on Moral Laws in 1642. [B.] Was called to be pastor at Dover, N. H. and rem. thither. Signed petition of inhabitants to Gen. Court 10 Oct. 1665. [Mass. Arch. 106, 160.] He m. 1st a dau. of — Boyes; he m. 2, Frances Clarke, who had been a maid servant in the family of Rev. John Wilson, and was dism. to the chh. of Plym. 18 (7) 1642. Ch. Jachin, Anna, (m. Job Lane,) John, Elizabeth, Dorothy, Abigail, Judith, a dau. b. 26 Dec. 1647, Joseph b. 15 Aug. 1650, d. 3 Nov. 1652.

Mr. John Reynor, teacher of Dover church, d. 21 (2) 1669. He made his will 19 April, probated 30 June, 1669. He bequeathed to his wife land in Gildersome in the parish of Batly in the county of York, England, etc.; to the 5 ch. of present wife, John, Elizabeth, Dorothie, Abigail and Judith;

to son Jachim, of Rowly, and daughter Hannah, wife to Job Lane, of Billerica, "a cup I had with their mother," etc. The will was brought into court 29 June, 1669, and inventory presented by his widow Frances. [See Lane Family Papers in Reg. XI, and B.]

REYNOLDS, RENNOLLS, REIGNALLS, REYNALLS, RENNELS,

John, fisherman, witness to John Lander's deed at Pascataquack in 1639; gave "bale" in court at Strawberry Bank in 1643. Juryman in 1646. Could not have been the son of William, and probably was not the person who sold land in Cape Porpoise 2 Jan. 1687-8? Compare with John, of Watertown, Mass. in 1635.

William, Plymouth, one of the party with John Howland at Kennebeck in the Hocking affair in 1634. Received land on Duxbury side Feb. 6, 1637. Owned cattle in 1638; sold in 1640. He m. 30 Aug. 1638, Ales Kitson. Rem. to Cape Porpoise; took oath of allegiance to Mass. govt. 5 July, 1653. Was then allowed to keep a ferry at Kennybuncke, and to have 3 pence a passenger. With wife Alice made deed of gift 12 April, 1675, to son John, conditioned on life care of the parents. Ch.: John, Samuel, Job, William, Mary (m. James Langley), Jane (m. Thomas Wormwood).

RICE, RYCE, RISE, RYSE,

Thomas, husbandman, Kittery, came at an early day; worked for John Treworgy, brewing for the fishermen; to this he deposed in the Gunnison case 21 April, 1654, being of the age of 38 years. Took oath of allegiance to Mass. govt. 16 Nov. 1652. Land granted him in that year was confirmed to him by the selectmen 4 Dec. 1655. [York De. L.] Sold land 14 Sept. 1660.

Thomas, [presumably his son], m. Mary, dau. of Thomas Withers.

RICHARDSON, RICHERSON,

John, sued for falling timber on Mr. Larkham's lands in Dover court in 1642.

See Clifford.

RICHMOND,

Mr. John, a sea-captain trading here, brought suit in Maine court Feb. 7, 1636, to recover wages for the labor of a servant of his, who had been let out to another person. Other suits. Sold powder to Winter in trade for beaver as per testimony in 1640.

RIDDAN,

Thaddeus, Strawberry Bank, bought house of Wm. Palmer 4 Sept. 1651; sold it to Richard Cutt 10 June, 1653.

RIDER,

Phinehas, Falmouth, bought 55 acres of land of Cleve 25 March, 1658.

He died, "of Great Island"; inventory of his estate was taken 30 April, 1681, and brought into court 7 June by his widow Alice, who was appointed administratrix; the court gave her the whole estate; no land and no children mentioned.

RISHWORTH, RUSHWORTH,

Edward, bapt. at Saleby, co. Linc. Eng. May 5, 1617. Came to Exeter, signed the combination 5 (4) 1639. Removed to Wells; proprietor and purchaser of land in 1640. With Boade and Wheelwright was authorized by Thomas Gorges, Esq. to allot lands in Wells 14 July, 1643. [York De.] Had a grant of land at Cape Nuttacke river for a saw-mill 20 Oct. 1651.

Took oath of allegiance to Mass. govt. at York 22 Nov. 1652, and was appointed commissioner for minor trials at York and secretary of the General Assembly of Lygonia 14 Aug. 1658. Magistrate, deputy.

He was one of the commissioners of Charles II in 1664. Gave deed of property 17 Oct. 1682, to his son in law John Sayword, husband of his daughter Mary, and received promise of life care, etc.

His son Edward m. Susanna, daughter of Rev. John Wheelwright. Having had charge of the records of the province of Maine 30 or 40 years, a petition, signed by many of the justices and people July 6, 1686, desired that he keep them, rather than have them go to Dover, etc. [Bax. MS. VI.]

See also Cross, Gaile, Haborne, Hocking, Pierce, Saward, Wheelwright.

ROBERTS, ROBARTS,

Gyles, Black Point, made will 25 Jan. 1666, prob. 20 June, 1667, inventory taken 30 Jan. 1666; beq. to his 3 children that were with him and the 2 that lived with his brother Arthur Auger (Alger). Henry Jocelyn and bro. in law William Sheldon overseers.

John, planter, Dover, taxed Oct. 19, 1648.

Selectman in 1665.

With wife Abigail sold land 29 June, 1665. She received a bequest from her father, Hatevill Nutter in 1675. Signed petition to Gen. Court Oct. 10, 1665.

He conveyed to his son John 20 April, 1680, a tract of land which he had received from his father in law.

Thomas, Mr. Dover, signed the combination in 1640; had lawsuit in 1641; proprietor in 1642; juror, 1646; taxed Oct. 19, 1648. "Thomas Roberts, Newe England," is in list of fishmongers in Tax Roll of London, 1641. See Hilton.

His will dated 27 Sept. 1673, probated 30 June, 1674, bequeathed to children John, Thomas, Hester, (now wife of John Martyn "of New Jarze,") Anne (wife of James Philbrooke), Elizabeth, (wife of Benjamin Heard of Cochechock), son in law Richard Rich, husband of daughter Sarah.

William, in court at Strawberry Bank in 1643.

He died before March 29, 1676, when admin. on his estate was granted 27 Aug. 1677, when a list of his debts was filed;

mention was made of claims of William R. Jr. and the care of the "widow and girl" 18 months past; but their names are not given.

See also Crockett, Layton, Nutter, Weare.

ROBIE, ROBY,
 Henry, planter, Exeter, signed the combination in 1639; signed petitions of inhabitants Sept. 7, 1643, and 29 (3) 1645. [Mass. Arch. 112, 8 and 39.] Clerk of the market and commissioner for minor trials; sworn at Salisbury court 24 (2) 1649. Had grant of land for a sawmill with others in 1649. Town officer. Rem. to Hampton; deposed about Wall's selling his mill to Colcord, Oct. 18, 1658. Sold house and lands to Wm. More of Ex. 20 Sept. 1653. Town officer, 1656. He deposed 13 (12) 1656, ae. about 50 years. [Norf. court Files, 49.] A judge of the Court of Sessions in 1684.

 Wife Ruth died May 5, 1673; he m. 2, Jan. 19, 1673-4, Elizabeth, daughter of Thomas Philbrick, and widow of Thomas Chase and John Garland. He m. (3) Sarah —, who died Jan. 23, 1703. Children, Thomas b. 1 (1) 1645-6, John b. 2 Feb. 1648, [Judith,] Ruth b. 3 (1) 1654, Deliverance b. 22 (1) 1657, Samuel b. 4 (6) 1659, Ichabod b. 26 (9) 1664, Sarah b. April 19, 1679.

 He d. April 22, 1688. Will Jan. 10, 1686, codicil April 3, proved June 5, 1688; Sarah, my now wife; ch. Thomas, Samuel, Ichabod, Judith, John, Ruth Roby and Mary ffoulsham.

ROBINSON,
 Francis, Mr., Saco, magistrate in 1631, as he deposed Sept. 6, 1670, being then 52 years old. [Bax. MSS.] He deposed in a case in Maine court April 4, 1637. Grand jury man, 1640. Sold wheat to Winter in 1643. Witness of Mary Allen's deposition in 1647.

 John, blacksmith, Haverhill, bought house and land in 1644, which he sold 5 Aug. 1651, wife Elizabeth joining. Gave letter of attorney 17 (8) 1650 for the collection of a legacy left by his father John Robinson, blacksmith, of

Mapersall, co. Bedford, Eng. [A.] Bought house and land in Exeter 20 (12) 1651-2. As "planter," Exeter, sold house and lands 24 (2) 1654; mortg. land 3 Nov. 1674, to secure contract for delivery of boards and pipe staves. He deposed 26 June, 1661, ae. about 45 years. [P. Files.] He died 10 (9) 1675; administration May 30, 1676; account rendered 6 (2) 1677 by his widow Elizabeth and son David. See also Treworgy.

ROE, ROW,
George, Portsmouth, lands assigned him in 1660.
Nicholas, Portsmouth, with wife Elizabeth, in court at Dover 3 (8) 1648, charged with slandering certain persons. He sold to Richard Shortridg 5 (8) 1659, half of a block of land which was granted by the town to him and Edward Burton.
See Mussall.

ROGERS,
Christopher, servant to Sir Ferdinando Gorges, came early to Piscataqua; became a planter. Received a grant of land in York from Mr. Thomas Gorges, and sold the same to John Gooch July 21, 1645.
George, Richmond Island, one of Winter's fishermen, 1639. Kittery, proprietor, 1641. [York Deeds and Court Records.]
See Bragdon, Gunnison.

ROPER, ROAPER,
Walter, carpenter, Ipswich, Mass.; removed to Hampton. Frm. May 13, 1642. Proprietor in 1641; selectman, 1644. Sold house to Robert Saward in 1647. Removed to Topsfield, Mass. Agent for Wm. Payne in 1653. He deposed in 1661, ae. about 48 years.
Child Mary bapt. at Hamp. Aug. 22, 1641.
Will dated 15 July, prob. 28 Sept. 1680, beq. to wife Susan, sons John and Nathaniel, daus. Mary, Elizabeth and Sarah,

grandchildren Elizabeth, Susan, Margaret, Rose and Sarah Sparkes, and Elizabeth and Susan Dutch.
See also Dalton.

ROUSE,
Nicholas, of Wemberry, Eng. came to Casco and dwelt with Thomas Alger about 1630. [Trel.]

ROWLEY,
William, Dover, one of the "Shrewsbury men," q. v.; a witness to Obediah Bruen's deed in 1642.

ROSS, ROOSE,
James, claimed in petition to Andros in 1687 that he and his father had occupied about 30 years at the Back cove in ffalmouth. [Bax. MSS.]

ROYAL, ROYALL, RYALL, RIALL,
William, cooper and cleaver of timber, was engaged March 23, 1628, by the Mass. Bay Company in England to come to New England and work for them. Came to Salem that year — 1628-9. Some time later he removed to Casco Bay, Maine; had a lawsuit in court at Saco 25 March, 1636. Received a patent for the land on which he was living 27 March, 1643. His land included part of that through which "Royall's river" flows, which was named for him. He was a deputy to the Maine assembly Sept. 14, 1648.

He married Phebe, daughter of Margaret Green, the second wife of Samuel Cole of Boston, Mass. She signed with him in witness of a deed of John Smith of Casco in 1646. He deeded to his sons William and John, 28 March, 1673, certain property, on condition of life care for himself and wife. Children, John, Samuel, Isaac, Joseph, Mary and Mehetabel. About 1675 he removed to Boston, where he died June 15, 1676. The widow died July 16, 1678.
[Gen. by E. D. Harris in Reg. XXXIX, 348.]
See also Winter.

SAMBORNE, SANBORN, SANDBORNE, SANDBURN, etc.,

John, married, probably in England, Ann, daughter of Rev. Stephen Bachiler. Three of their children, John, Stephen and William, came to Hampton, either with or soon after their grandfather.

John, Hampton, proprietor, signed the petition about Howard March 7, 1643.

He deposed 14 (2) 1668, ae. about 48 years.

He m. 1, Mary, daughter of Robert Tuck; she died 30 (10) 1668. He m. 2, Aug. 2, 1671, Margaret, daughter of Robert Page, and widow of Wm. Moulton. Children, John, Mary, b. 12 (2) 1651, Abigail b. 23 (12) 1653, Richard b. 4 (11) 1654, Mary b. 19 (1) 1657, Joseph b. 13 (1) 1659, Steven b. 12 (9) 1661, d. 24 (12) 1661-2, Ann b. 20 (9) 1662, Nathaniel b. 27 (11) 1665, Benjamin b. Dec. 20, 1668, Jonathan b. 25 May, 1672.

He died Oct. 20, 1692. Inventory taken 2 Nov. following.

Stephen, Hampton, proprietor, signed Howard petition in 1643. Sold house and land in Kittery 29 Aug. 1650.

Wife Sarah; children, Sarah b. 12 (4) 1651, Dorothia b. 2 (1) 1653.

William, yeoman, Hampton, signed the Howard petition in 1643. Proprietor; sold land 17 May, 1647. On the 8th of the seventh month following he and his brothers John and Stephen and Nathaniel Bachiler received a deed of certain land from their grandfather, Rev. Stephen Bachiler. Frm. 8 (8) 1651.

Wife Mary; children, Mephibosheth b. 5 (9) 1663, Sarah b. 10 (12) 1666.

He died 18 Nov. 1692; inventory filed 22 Feb. following by "Nath[ll] Bachiler Senr."

He beq. his estate to wife Mary, sons Stephen, Josiah, William, Mephibosheth.

Genealogy.

See also Cutts.

SAMSON, SAMPSON,
Thomas, brewer, Richmond Island, in the employ of Winter; returned to England in 1637. Wife there. [Trel.]

SANKEY, SANCKY,
Robert, ae. 30, "sent away by Robert Cordell, goldsmith, Lombard street, London," came in the *Increase* April 14, 1635. Settled at Saco. Was constable at court in Saco Jan. 9, 1636-7. Sold pork to Winter in 1639.
He died before 2 Aug. 1642, as appears from reference in a deed of land adjoining his. [York De. I.]
Was he the fishmonger of London, enrolled in 1641? See Hilton.

SANDERS, SAUNDERS,
Edward, "of Watertown," was "sick at Piscataqua" when called before Mass. Gen. Court 5 (1) 1638-9. Presumably the same, agent for Capt. Francis Champernowne, sold a house and land at Great Bay on south side of Pascataway river, to Mr. Francis Norton of Charlestown 20 Sept. 1644. Had a judgment upon Capt. C.'s house and lands, and sold the same to Mrs. Sarah Lynne Aug. 1 following. Mass. Gen. Court punished a person of same name 19 Oct. 1654. Same name a soldier in Naragansett war from Scituate, Plym. Coll. in 1645.
John, Ipswich, proprietor, 1635; removed to Salisbury 6 Sept. 1638; rem. to Hampton; admitted inhabitant Dec. 13, 1639. Rem. to Wells; sold house and lands at Hamp. 27 (7) 1644. Bought house and land 20 Aug. 1643; was appointed sergeant 5 July, 1653, and lieutenant before 1657. [York De.] Of Cape Porpoise, sold land 9 Oct. 1663, wife Ann joining. Commissioner. Peter Turbat married his daughter Sarah.
Will dated 13 June, prob. 24 June, 1670, beq. to wife Ann, son Thomas and his son John, and to "all my children."
John, joiner, worked for Winter at Richmond Island 4 weeks in 1641 or 1642. [Trel.]

Robin, Richmond Island, in service of Winter June 22, 1640.

Robert, perhaps the same as the above, husbandman, of Plymouth, England, contracted with Trelawney and Winter 22 Nov. 1642, to work for them at Richmond Island or elsewhere in fishing, planting, etc. [Trel.]

William, carpenter, indebted to Mr. Bellingham and Mr. Gibbins contracted 19 (10) 1636, to serve them 3 years. [W.] One of the founders of Hampton, 6 (7) 1638. See Munjoy, Turbat.

SANDERSON, SAUNDERSON,

Robert, goldsmith, silversmith, settled first at Hampton, 1638; had land grants in 1639 and 1640. Town officer in 1639. Removed to Watertown, Mass. [See P. of M.]

SANFORD, SANDFORD, STANFORD, STANNIFORD, STAMFORD,

Robert and *Thomas,* of Falmouth, petitioned Gov. Andros 9ber 27th, 1687, deposing that they had been in actual possession and improvement of lands on the southward side of Casco river about 35 years (i. e. from about 1652) and asked to have the land surveyed for them. Thomas subscribed by his mark ("Stanford") to the oath of allegiance to Mass. Bay July 13, 1658, and signed a petition to the king in 1665. Robert also signed the latter.

SARGENT, SERGEANT,

John, fisherman, Isles of Shoals, proprietor; mortgaged his house and lands for the payment of 40 li. Aug. 28, 1658. Removed to Winter Harbor about 1661; and to Great Island in 1677. Deposed Aug. 13, 1668, aged "neere 36." [Bax. MSS.]

Stephen, master of one of the crews of fishermen at Richmond Island, 1638-40. Wrote reports to Trelawney. See Heyman.

SATTERLY,
   Roger, fisherman, Richmond Island, in service of Winter, 1639-40. Wife in England. [Trel.]

SAVAGE, SAVIDG,
   Henry, Haverhill, proprietor, 1644. Removed to Portsmouth; for work done in Ambrose Lane's sawmill, he received a deed, 29 May, 1655, from Richard Tucker, attorney for Lane, of two houses and certain lands. Was fined in 1663, for declining to serve on the grand jury.
   He m. Elizabeth daughter of Thomas Walford.
   She made will Nov. 13, 1708, prob. 1709; son John and dau. Easter Savage, dau. Deborah Wills and her children; son in law Edward Wills, exec.
   See Brookins, Spencer.

SEAWARD, SAWARD, SEWARD, SAYWARD, SAYWORD, SAWERS,
   Henry, millwright, Hampton, proprietor, had grant of land to set a wind-mill on Sept. 2, 1642. Rem. to Strawberry Bank; sold Hampton land about Nov. 2, 1650. Rem. to York; land laid out to him April 20, 1661. Exchanged marsh land near his saw mill with Edw. Rishworth July 7, 1669. Mortg. land and mill on Mousam river etc. to Simon Lynde, of Boston Sept. 2, 1673; was in partnership with Bartholomew Gedney of Salem in mill, logs, etc. in 1674. [York De. II.] He deposed Oct. 15, 1669, that he had been an inhabitant in this country 32 years and upwards since he came from England; that he lost 1000 pounds by the burning of his mills at York. The court gave him permission to cut timber on Cape Porpoise river.
   Wife Mary; ch. Joseph, b. at Hampton 16 (9) 1655; probably also John, who m. Mary dau. of Edw. Rishworth, and Samuel who was attorney for John Knowlton of Ipswich in 1679. Admin. of his estate was granted April 6, 1682, to his widow Mary; the inventory mentions saw-mills and cornmills at York, Cape Porpoise, Mousam and Casco. [York De V.]

Richard, Portsmouth, had 10 acres of land assigned him in 1652.

His will, dated Feb. 21, 1662, proved July 1, 1663, gave to son Richard Seaward and son [in law] Richard Jackson and their children. Refers to brother Roger Seaward; owned a vessel and cargo. Land at Drake Point.

Robert, Exeter, signed the combination in 1639; removed to Hampton, "signed" in 1640. Bought lands of Lieut. Howard and sold the same to Nathl. Boulter Sept. 25, 1646. His purchase of a house from Walter Roper was acknowledged in court at Dover in 1647.

See also Crawley, Fryer.

SCADLOCK,

William, planter, Cape Porpoise, "came with Vines in 1630." [Hist. Kpt.] Was before the Court at Saco March 25, 1636. Grand Jury man in 1640. Took oath of allegiance at Saco July 5, 1653. Clerk of the writs. Res. at West Saco. [Bax. MSS.]

Will dated Jan. 7, 1661-2; proved July 3, 1662; wife Ellner; ch. William, Susanna, John, Rebecca, Samuel and Sarah. Some articles specified for each, religious books, etc. included. Stephen Kent and Bryan Pendleton execs.

SCAMMAN, SCAMMON,

Nicholas, Dover, witness to Obediah Bruen's deed in 1642.

SCOTT, SKOT, SKOTE,

James, Portsmouth, before the Court June 27, 1656; had a lot of land, half an acre, at Great Island assigned him Jan. 1, 1656-7.

SEALY, SEELEY,

George, Isles of Shoals, signed petition of inhabitants 18 (3) 1653.

John, fisherman, Isles of Shoals, chosen constable in 1646; the court ordered that he take oath of office before

Mr. Smyth. Witnessed Crockett's deed of land at Kittery in 1648. He conveyed, 20 June, 1651, to his brother William S. all money due him, and gave him power of attorney for collection, etc. [Court Rec.] Administration of his estate was granted 30 June, 1670, to his brother William Seeley, for the benefit of his heirs, executors, or wife or children.

Mr. Dover, taxed Oct. 19, 1648. Perhaps this was John.

Richard, Isles of Shoals, signed petition of inhabitants 18 (3) 1653. Appointed one of the commissioners for settling controversies there.

William, fisherman, Isles of Shoals, chosen ensign of military company in 1652. [Bax. MSS.] Signed the petition 18 (3) 1653. Bought house, stage, flakes, cables, shallop, etc., 24 June, 1653. Sold his house and land 10 April, 1666.

His widow Elizabeth, as administratrix of his estate, sold 15 Nov. 1673, a house and land which he had bought of Richard Carle in 1666.

See Benill, Brown, Swadden.

SEAVEY, SEAVY, SEVY,

William, Strawberry Bank and Isles of Shoals, sold fish to Winter in 1642. Sold house and land at Strawberry Bank 6 June, 1648. Was one of the commissioners to try minor cases in 1649. Signed with four others a petition of S. B. people for full rights, Oct. 20, 1651. [Mass. Arch. 112, 38.] Took oath of allegiance July 2, 1657.

Was Thomas his son, who had lot assigned him at Portsmouth in 1652; was a juryman in 1656, and with wife Tamason sold land 4 Oct. 1667?

See also Ellen, Hutchinson, Lane, Tucker, Turpin, Wiley.

SELLERS, see Sealy,

William, was sued in Piscataqua court in 1642.

SEWARD, see Saward.

SHAPLEIGH, SHAPLEY,

Alexander, merchant, from Kingsweare, co. Devon, came to the Piscataqua valley at a very early day. He is said by some writers to have been an agent of Gorges; but of this no evidence appears in our records. He carried on a large amount of fishing, trading, and his grandson, John Treworgy, called at Richmond Island in 1640, doing business in Mr. Shapleigh's name. [Trel.] He was a resident of New England when he sold to his son in law James Treworgy all his lands, boats, houses, etc. in N. E. May 26, 1642. While his dwelling may have been at Strawberry Bank, he had grants of land at Kittery; and finding that Nicholas Frost had received too little marsh for his stock of cattle, he gave him the 5 acres of marsh which had been allotted to himself. Testified 31 May, 1643. [York De. I.]

Children: i. Katherine, m. (1) James Treworgy; m. (2) Edward Hilton. She must have been much older than her brother Nicholas, as she said in a petition on his behalf to the General Court of Mass. Bay, May 7, 1674, referring, probably, to his being deprived of a mother in infancy, "I nursed him at my breast (which I canot forgett)"; she also refers to her father thus: "About 38 years since, in a time of great scarcity, our ffather laid out a good estate for the supply of this Countrey and the settling some part of it. & in a season of there want supplyed them soe reasonably with provisions, that it was thankfully receipted, & acknowledged by the authority then in being," etc. [Mass. Arch. 106.]

ii. John, who remained in England while his son John came over here and acted as agent for his grandfather; iii. Nicholas, also a merchant at Kingsweare, Devon, who came over here as early as 1641, when he bought lands, houses, fishing coast, etc. of his brother in law Treworgy. He lived at Boston and Charlestown from about 1645 till about 1648, when he was a citizen and a town officer of Kittery. He was "instrumental by an order to some of Road Iland to make seizure of certain persons" about 1674, in consequence of which he was arrested and imprisoned at Boston in 1674; and at that time his sister sent down the petition mentioned above. He was soon released. His descendants have been numerous.

See also Amerideth, Chadbourne, Godfrey, Gunnison, Johnson, Lane, Small, Taintor, White, Withers.

SHAW,

Edward, sued Matthew Giles in Dover Court 30 Jan. 1657, for wages. A man of the same name, a sawyer, lived at Duxbury, Plym. Col. 1632; was before Plym. Court 2 Oct. 1637, hired for a year with Robert Bartlett Dec. 1, 1638.

John; a suit was brought against him in Strawberry Bank Court in 1646, others in 1649 and 1650.

Roger, husbandman, yeoman, Cambridge, proprietor, 1636; frm. March 14, 1638-9; town officer. Rem. to Hampton. Bought house and land 15 Nov. 1647; sold land in 1658. Deputy; juryman.

He married, first, Anne —; he m. second, Susanna, widow of William Tilton of Lynn, Mass.; she died 28 (11) 1654. Children, Joseph, Benjamin, Esther b. (4) 1638, Mary d. 26 (11) 1639, Mary b. 29 (7) 1645, Margaret, Ann. His "son in law" [step-son] Abraham Tilton was apprenticed 5 Dec. 1653, to John Hood, weaver, of Lynn; whose wife Elizabeth, acting under a power of attorney from her husband then in England, released the apprentice 10 Nov. 1656, although she had previously sent him to Peter Tilton, living in Connecticut. [Norf. Rec. I.] Samuel Tilton, another of the children of "my late wife Susanna," received a tract of land from Mr. Shaw April 6, 1660, and receipted in full for his portion 12 June, 1661, and for that of his brother Daniel Tilton 13 July, 1663.

He died 29 (3) 1661. Will dated 25 Aug. 1660, codicil dated 20 March following, probated 10 (8) 1661, beq. to sons Joseph and Benjamin, daughters Margaret Ward, Ann Fogg, Hester, and Mary; sons Abraham and Daniel Tilton to have their portions when they come of age according to covenant.

See also Bachiler.

SHEHEE,

Dermond, Portsmouth, deposed 28 (4) 1660, ae. about 50 years.

SHELDON, SHELLDEN,
 Godfrey, planter, Black Point.
 He made will 13 March, 1663-4, ae. about 65 years; beq. to wife; to eldest son William and his wife Rebecca; to son John and to "daughters." Prob. 3 April, 1670.
 Gyles Roberts, in his will in 1666, calls William Sheldon his son in law.

SHEPARD, SHEPHERD,
 Thomas, Richmond Island, one of Winter's fishermen, 1638-42.

SHERBURN, SHERBORN, SHERBURNE, SHEARBORNE,
 Henry, yeoman, Portsmouth; it was ordered by Piscataqua court in 1642 that he keep a ferry from the great house to the great island, one to the province, one to Strawberry Bank, one to "Rowes," and "other ferryes," with specified fares for each route; and that he "keep an ordinary, at 8d a meale." He was appointed commissioner and clerk of the writs in 1649. Signed petition of inhabitants to Gen. Court 20 Oct. 1651. [Mass. Arch. 112, 38.] Took oath of fidelity July 2, 1657. Deputy to Gen. Court in 1658. [Mass. Arch. 39, 47.] Sold houses and land at Isles of Shoals in 1660, his wife Rebecca signing with him. He conveyed land 29 Sept. 1659, to Richard Slooper (Sloper) in consideration of his marriage to his daughter. He deposed 25 June, 1662, ae. about 48 years. [P. Files.]
 He married Rebecca, daughter of Mr. Ambrose Gibbons, bequeathed in 1657 to their children, Samuel, Elizabeth, Mary, Henry, John, Ambrose, Sarah and Rebecca, the boys to receive their portions at 21, and the girls at 18 years of age. He m. (2) Sarah, widow of Walter Abbot.
 He died before Sept. 8, 1681, when the inventory of his estate was presented in court by his sons Samuel and John S. The daughter Elizabeth married Tobias Langdon about 1662.

John, Strawberry Bank, sued in court in 1642, juryman in 1650. Took oath of fidelity in 1659. He married Elizabeth, dau. of Robert Tuck of Hampton, q. v. See also Hutchinson, Sloper, Walling, Wedge, Woodward.

SHERES, SHEIRES, SHIRRES,

Jeremy, Kittery, had lawsuit in Dover court in Oct. 1650. He and Elizabeth were witnesses in court in 1652. Took oath of allegiance 16 Nov. 1652. Rem. to Cape Nottocke. With wife Susanna sold land 14 Nov. 1664. See Johnson.

SHILAND,

John, before Piscataqua court in 1652.

SHORT, SHORTE,

Clement, Kittery, married in Boston 21 Nov. 1660, Faith, daughter of Mr. Thomas Munt; had a grant of land in 1662, which was sold 25 Dec. 1706, by his son Thomas, of Boston, printer.

Tobias, Richmond Island, a servant of Winter, 1639-1643.

SHORTRIDG,

Richard, fisherman, Portsmouth, bought land of Nicholas Row 5 (8) 1659, and sold it in 1661.

SHURT, SHIRT, SHORT,

Abraham, merchant, came from Bristol, Eng. as the agent for Aldworth and Elbridge, the patentees of Pemaquid and vicinity. Samoset's deed to Brown, 15 July, 1625, was made before him.

He brought letters to Richmond Island in 1635; was trading along the coast to Boston in 1639 and 1643. [Trel.] Brought suit in Maine court May 20, 1637. His son Adam Shurt, on behalf of his mother Mrs. Mary Shurt, brought a suit in 1647.

He gave a general receipt to Giles Elbridge of Bristol, merchant, exec. of the will of Robert Aldworth, merchant, late of the same city, deceased 14 (9) 1646, and put himself "a covenant servant" with Elbridge "to serve, dwell & abide in New England . . . . dureing the terme of fyve yeares," etc. Made Robert Knight, merchant, now residing in Boston, his attorney 27 (7) 1647. [A.] We have but few glimpses of his career.

See Brown, Cocks.

SHUTE,

Robert, planter, "of Winnegansett," gave bond in March, 1640-1, with Matthew Norman for a debt of the latter. [L.] He was one of the associates of Robert Morgan in Purchase's suit 31 May, 1641.

SHREWSBURY MEN, The, or The Shrewsbury Merchants,

From various sources we gather the names of some of these men who received a patent of the land in the Piscataqua valley, where the towns of Dover, etc. now stand. William Walderne was one. Richard Percyvall, draper, was one; he sold his share May 4, 1640, to Obediah Bruen, who came here and resided several years. Richard Hunt was another, a signer of the Piscataqua combination in 1640, one of the defendants in the suit brought against the company by Colcord on behalf of Parker in 1650; William Rowley, here in 1642, was another of the defendants in this suit; Capt. Thomas Wiggin was asserted by Colcord to have been the agent of the company at the time they employed Parker. Rev. George Burdett seems to have been imported or at least employed by them, hence Colcord sued them for wages due him. "Ye estate att Quamscooke belonging to ye Shrewsberie men" was appraised by Robert Page and Lieut. Christopher Hussey at the request of Capt. Thomas Wiggin; inventory filed in Norf. court 12 (2) 1659; cattle, 128 pounds; land, 3 miles square, much of it rough and wet, lying in the wilderness, 100 pounds. [Norf. Rec. 1, 17 and 81.]

SIMMONS, SYMONS, SYMONDS,

John, Richmond Island, in the fishing company in 1636.

John, yeoman, Kittery, owned land adjoining that of Robert Beedle in 1641. Took oath of allegiance to Mass. govt. 16 Nov. 1652. Selectman. He deposed 25 June, 1662, ae. about 47 years. [P. Files.] He conveyed house and lands to his son in law William Hilton as a dowry to his daughter Rebecca, Hilton's wife, 18 April, 1667. He m. (2) Welthian, widow of John Goddard; with her he sold land 23 July, 1669.

SIMPSON, SIMSON,

Henry, York, married Jane, daughter of Lieut. Col. Walter Norton, one of the patentees of the plantation; received a deed of land as a marriage portion from Mr. William Hooke, the second husband of Jane's mother, 13 March, 1638. As attorney for William Hooke, he laid out and sold lands to purchasers from April 15, 1640 onward.

His widow Jane married second — Bond; she deeded her lands 16 June, 1688, to her only son Henry Simson, who had cared for her about 15 years. [York De. I, III and VI.]

Patrick, Dover, juryman in 1660.

See also Plaisted.

SINGLEMAN,

Henry, Cape Porpus, his land that of Morgan Howell in 1648.

SINKLER, SINCLAIR, SINCLARE,

John, Senior, Exeter, bought land 6 Jan. 1659; sold land 27 April, 1667.

Wife Mary; children, James b. 27 July, 1660, Mary b. 27 June, 1663, Sary b. 15 Sept. 1664. [Norf. Rec.]

He made will 27 Jan. 1699-1700; prob. 14 Sept. 1700; beq. to wife Deborah according to contract before marriage; to sons James and John; daughters Mary Wheeler, and Meribah Loll; grandsons John and Benjamin Jonson.

SKILLING, SKELLING,
   Thomas, Falmouth, bought 55 acres of land of Cleave 25 March, 1658.
   Will dated 14 Nov. 1666, prob. 2 Oct. 1667, beq. to wife Deborah, sons Thomas and John, and "all my children." See Ingersoll.

SKOT, see Scott.

SLEEPER,
   Thomas, weaver, Hampton, proprietor, June, 1640. Bought land in Boston 15 (5) 1645; sold land in Hamp. 10 (8) 1657, his wife Joannah consenting; bought house and land in Haverhill, Mass. 27 June, 1657, and removed thither. Returned to Hamp. Bought land in Hamp. of N. Bachiler 20 June, 1660.
   First wife Jemina, second wife Joannah; children, Elizabeth (m. Abraham Perkins), Mary, Ralf b. 1 (4) 1650, John b. 10 (7) 1652, Naomi b. 15 (2) 1655, Moses b. at Hav. 13 (1) 1657-8, Aaron b. 20 (12) 1660, at Hamp. Luther b. Nov. 14, 1668, d. 19 (3) 1670.
   He died 30 July, 1696.

SLOOPER, SLOPER,
   Richard, Portsmouth, received a tract of land from Henry Sherburne Sept. 29, 1659, in consideration of his marriage to Sherburne's daughter. [N. H. Deeds.] Had town lands in the divisions of March 22, 1660-1. Was a juror in 1662 and 1668. Took oath of fidelity Oct. 2, 1666. Conveyed lands to son Ambrose March 27, 1706, his wife Mary signing with him. Made will Oct. 26, 1711, proved Dec. 28, 1714. Ch. Ambrose, Richard, Henry, Elizabeth, Martha (m. Obediah Morse, Jr.) and Tabitha (Bridgman).

SMALL, SMALE,
   Edward, Isles of Shoals, grand jury man in court held at Saco 25 June, 1640. Bought 100 acres of land 25 July, 1643,

and sold it 23 June, 1647. Signed petition of inhabitants 18 (3) 1653.

Francis, fisherman, Dover, taxed in 1648. Removed to Scarborough. Bought land of Sciterygusett of Casco Bay, Sagamore, 27 June, 1657. Took oath of allegiance to Mass. govt. at Spurwink 13 July, 1658. He deposed 16 June, 1677, ae. about 50 years, concerning what Trustrum Harris said when they were together "impressed to goe upon ye Countrys service to Ossaby." His wife Elizabeth, ae. about 49 years, deposed with him 10 May, 1683, as to his being employed about 23 or 24 years before to purchase a certain island from the Indians for Maj. Nicholas Shapleigh. He deposed 8 Sept. 1685, ae. 65, about servants of Mason's plantation being left by Francis Norton in 1640 and appropriating what possessions remained, goods and lands. Had lived in New England upwards of 50 years.

James, Exeter, signed petition of inhabitants Sept. 7, 1643. [Mass. Arch. 112, 8.]

Samuel, deposed at Kittery, Nov. 11, 1637, aged about 73 years, that in his youth he was a servant to Henry Joslin, Esq. several years at Pemaquid; was often at Damariscotty; knew the land from which Walter Phillips, the owner, had been driven away. [Eastern Claims.]

See Champernowne, Maverick.

SMART,

John, Hingham, Mass. proprietor, 1636. Resident of Exeter in 1643, signer of town petition that year. Suit against him and his wife Margaret in 1647, and one against him and Rob: Smart 24 (2) 1649.

Lived in the part of town now Newmarket. [Hist. Ex.]

SMITH, SMYTH,

Bartholomew, Dover, signed the combination in 1640; proprietor — "Smey," in 1642. Of Kittery, bought land March 21, 1648.

George, Dover, a resident about 1635; made use of lands about Lamprill river which had been bought of the Indians; so he deposed 18 (8) 1652. [Mass. Arch. 112, 44.] Witness to Walderne's deed 11 (5) 1645. One of the committee to end controversies in 1648. Associate judge. Sold land in Kittery 18 Dec. 1650, on behalf of John Newgrove.

James, of "Wayquait," an associate of Robert Morgan in a lawsuit in 1641.

John, Hampton, about 1640; wife Deborah, a near relation and legatee of Mrs. Ruth Dalton. Removed to Nantucket or Martha's Vineyard. His daughter Deborah married Nathaniel Bacheller; his son John, cooper, of Hamp. sold to his brother in law Stephen Hussey, 9 June, 1674, one half of all the lands belonging to him on the island of Nantucket, "as owned by my father John Smith late of the Vineyard deceased."

He made will 14 Feb. 1670; bequeathed his land on Nantucket to sons John and Samuel, who were to pay to their sisters Deborah and Abigail 5 pounds apiece; all his land at "Martin's Vineyard" to son Philip, not then in good health; wife Deborah executrix; friends Mr. Thomas Mayhew and Thomas Macy overseers.

John, carpenter, Saco, had lawsuit in court at Saco Feb. 7, 1636-7; grand jury man, 1640; bought land of Vines 8 April, 1642; residing at "Casko Mill under the Govt. of Mr. George Cleeve," 8 June, 1646, he and wife Joane, sold land in York. Took oath of allegiance to Mass. govt. 5 July, 1653. His lands in York specified by the townsmen Feb. 2, 1654. [York De. I.] He bought lands on which he had resided several years, of his brother in law Edward Wanton, in 1657. John, Senior, with wife Joane, deeded land 23 Oct. 1657, to son John, on condition of his rendering certain services to them. He deposed June 23, 1685, ae. about 73 years, respecting a case which occurred under him as marshall "40 yeares ago." [York De. IV.]

Nicholas, Exeter, bought house and land 8 Sept. 1658.

Children, Nathaniel b. June 9, 1660, Nicholas b. Sept. 3, 1661, Ann b. 8 Feb. 1663, Theophilus b. 14 (12) 1667. [Norf. Court Rec.] He d. June 22, 1673; Mary Smith, widow, admin.

Robert, tailor, Exeter, signed the combination 5 (4) 1639, and the petitions of 1645 and 1647. One of the commissioners of the town to end small causes in 1643. Took freeman's oath 17 (2) 1644. Rem. to Hampton; was executor of the will of Mrs. Susanna Leader in 1657. His wife Susanna was killed by lightning June 12, 1680. Children, John, Meribah, Jonathan, Joseph. [Dow.]

He died Aug. 30, 1706. Will dated March 22, 1699 or 1700, proved Sept. 3, 1706; sons John, Jonathan, Asahel, Joseph, dau. Meribah.

Thomas, Hampton, proprietor in 1640.

Thomas, tailor, residence not stated, sued in court at Strawberry Bank in 1642.

Thomas, residence at West Saco, [Bax. MSS.], juryman in Saco court in 1640.

William, planter, Black Point, was sworn in as constable for the region from Cape Elizabeth Eastward, in Saco court, 25 March, 1636.

He signed petition to the Gen. Court of Mass. to secure a fair trial of the claims which he and Jocelyn and others maintained, in 1653. He deposed 2 (5) 1664, ae. about 69 years, concerning a payment of money. [York De. I.]

Made will 20 Sept. 1661, "aged 72 years or thereabouts"; bequeathed Bible, 2 oxen, and 2 cows to Mr. Henry Jocelyn; the rest to his brother Richard Smith, living at the city of Westchester in England, and sisters Elizabeth and Mary in England. The inventory was returned 18 July, 1676, by Mr. Jocelyn, who stated that the testator was aged 88 when he died, in March, 1675-6.

See Bachiler, Brown, Bulgar, Dalton, Frost, Godfrey, Haborne, Hussey, Marston, Palmer, Royal, Wanton, White, Ugroufe.

SPARKS,
  John, West Saco, 1653; [Bax. MSS.], may be the "Mr. John Sparke" to whom money was paid for John Libby by Mr. Trelawney about 1643. See Page, Roper, White.

SPENCER, SPENSER,
  Mr. John, was asociated with Mr. Dummer in the grant of the "plantation at Winnacannet" (afterward Hampton) by the General Court of Massachusetts Bay March 3, 1638; and they had "power to presse men to builde a house forthwith at some convenient place & what money they lay out aboute it shalbe repaide them againe out of the treasury, or by those that come to inhabit there." This building, called "The Bound House" was soon erected, but it is not known by whom it was occupied, nor exactly where it stood. Neither Spencer nor Dummer were *bona fide* inhabitants of the region, however.

  Roger, Charlestown; had liberty from town of Biddeford to put up a saw-mill Sept. 27, 1653. He bought land at Saco of Robert Jordan, and sold it 13 Aug. 1658, to Bryan Pendleton. Rem. to Saco. Mortg. his share in sawmill etc. 28 Jan. 1657. Rem. to Boston; sold all lands to Thomas Savage 26 May, 1669.

  Thomas, Cambridge, Mass. proprietor, 1633; frm. May 14, 1634. Rem. to Kittery; lawsuit in Maine court March 6, 1636-7. Took oath of allegiance to Mass. govt. 16 Nov. 1652.

  His wife Patience signed with him deed of land (undated); witnessed a deed in 1648. His son William paid a debt for him 15 Aug. 1663, and the father deeded him "the timber in Tom Tinkers swamp" 20 Dec. 1669. He gave a dowry of land to his daughter Margaret, and afterward confirmed it to her husband, Daniel Goodwin, 14 Aug. 1667. Nicholas Hodsden, and his wife, ae. 40 years and upward, testified 18 April, 1670, that Spenser gave Goodwin one half of his part of the mill and timber, being a quarter part of the whole.

He died 15 Dec. 1681; will dated 5 June, 1679, prob. 1 May, 1682, beq. to wife Patience, eldest son William, daus. Susanna and Elizabeth; rest to be divided by wife among the other children; refers to his gift to Thomas Etherington who had m. dau. Mary, with Patience Atherton, their dau. and John Gattinsby who had m. dau. Susanna; John Wincoll, Jr. son of John Wincoll by his wife Mary, now deceased, who was a daughter of the Etheringtons. The widow Patience gave to her youngest son Moses a tract of land adjoining parcels already given to sons in law Goodwin, Etherington and Gattensby, and her second son Humphrey Spencer, etc. 30 June, 1682. Inventory in York De. V. The widow died in 1683; her children, William, Humphrey and Moses Spencer, Ephraim Joy and Thomas Chicke, chose Richard Nason and James Emery to divide the estate; who reported 15 Nov. 1683.

See also Easton.

SPINNEY, SPYNNY,

Thomas, yeoman, Kittery, took oath of allegiance to Mass. govt. 16 Nov. 1652. Bought land of John Symonds 23 July, 1669.

Will dated 9 July, 1701, prob. 23 Sept. following; "aged and very weak"; beq. to sons Samuel, James, Thomas, and John, daughter Hannah (wife of Nathaniel) Fernald, and grandchildren Mercy and Margery, (daus. of son John) and others.

SPURRELL, SPURWELL,

Christopher, Cape Porpoise, took oath of allegiance to Mass. govt. 5 July, 1653. Bought land of John Lea and Ralph Trustrum and sold it to Richard Ball before Dec. 11, 1655.

SQUIRE, SQUARE,

Bernard, Portsmouth, creditor of the town 4 Feb. 1660-1.

John, Accomenticus, made sale of pork and fish to Winter in 1642.

STACY,
Thomas, Portsmouth, inhabitant, 1656.

STANFORD, STAMFORD, see Sanford.

STANYON, STANION, STANYAN, STANYELL, STANIELL,
Anthony, glover, planter, ae. 24, came in the Planter April 6, 1635. Took freeman's oath at Piscataqua court 17 (2) 1644. Settled at Boston. Removed to Exeter. Resident in 1645; rem. to Hampton; selectman; one of the commissioners for minor trials in 1651. Bought one third of a mill 27 Nov. 1654. He deposed 13 April, 1675, ae. about 68 years.
First wife Mary; child John, born at Boston 16 (5) 1642. He m. Jan. 1, 1655, Anne widow of William Partridge of Salisbury, Mass.
He secured to her children John, Hannah and Elizabeth P. 11 June, 1659, the payment of a legacy left them by their grandfather, John Partridge, of Olney, Bucks, England. [See P. of M.]
He died before 21 Feb. 1688-9, the date of the appraisal of his estate.
The widow Anne died July 10, 1689.
See Bradbury, Wilson.

STARBUCK,
Edward, Dover, had suit in court in 1640; proprietor in 1642; one of the men appointed by the town 20 (2) 1644, to have control and management of the fisheries in the river. Taxed in 1648. Was charged with being an Anabaptist, and was sent to Boston for trial in 1648.
With wife Kathren he sold land 20 (5) 1653, to his son in law Peter Coffyn of Dover, and made over to him all his property 9 March, 1659.
See also Phillips.

STARR,
   Edward, Piscataqua, signed the combination in 1640. [See Cutt, John.]

START, STIRT,
   Edward, fisherman, York, took oath of allegiance 22 Nov. 1652. Bought land and house in 1653; sold land 24 Nov. 1666, to John Card, cooper, of Kittery, wife Wilmot signing with him.

STEPHENS, STEVENS,
   Benjamin, husbandman, of Lanrake, co. Cornwall, Eng. made contract 22 Nov. 1642, with Trelawney and Winter, to come to New England and serve them 3 years in planting, fishing and other labor. He had previously served them 3 years at Richmond Island, as their books show; had sent money to his wife in Eng. during the years 1638-1641.
   See Heard.

STEVENSON,
   Thomas, Dover, had lawsuit in 1642; taxed in 1648.
   His wife Mary died 26 Nov. 1663; he died 7 Dec. 1663. [Dov. Hist. Coll.]
   Administration of his estate was granted 28 June, 1664, to his son Joseph; he chose Wm. Follett guardian, who gave bonds for the payment of portions to Joseph and his brothers and sisters. Brother Bartholomew admin. on estates of Thomas and Joseph in 1694.

STILEMAN,
   Elias, son of Elias, Sen. of Salem, Mass. (and probably of his surviving wife Judith) came early to Salem. Child Elias born March 15, 1639-40, (m. April 10, 1667, Ruth Mannyard). Town officer at Salem. His father carried on business in the Portsmouth region and he removed thither about 1658; one of the commissioners for the town Oct. 12, 1658. Was chosen clerk of Pisc. court 30 June, 1659. With wife

Mary he sold land in Ports. to Christopher Jose 29 Sept. 1662. He appears to have been much in Salem within the next few years, but was settled fully at Ports. (Strawberry Bank) 18 Jan. 1671-2, when he sold a house and land there. Was chosen captain. Deeded land to Richard Stileman 22 May, 1678. His wife died after 1684 (when she was a witness), and he married second, Lucy, dau. of James and Katharine (Shapleigh) Treworgy, widow, successively of Humphrey Chadbourne and Thomas Wills (Wells). He deposed 13 Aug. 1686, ae. about 70. [Es. Court Files.]

He died Dec. 19, 1695. Will names children of wife Lucy by her former husbands, dau. in law Elizabeth Allcutt ana Ruth Tarlington (Tarlton), dau. of his deceased son Elias, with her children Elias and William. [Reg. XXVIII, 206, and LI, 346.]

Richard, scrivener; Cambridge, Mass. 1644. Removed to Salem; sold house and land there 9 Aug. 1647. Rem. to Portsmouth; had grant of lands 4 Feb. 1660-1; deposed in Jan. 1662, aged 51 years, that he formerly bought a piece of ground, a house and a mill at Salem of Mr. Friend and afterward sold it to Mr. Wm. Hathorne. First wife Hannah; children, Samuel b. 23 (3) 1644, at Camb. Samuel bapt. 20 (5) 1651, at Salem, Mary b. Jan. 6, 1657, (m. Nathaniel Fox), Elizabeth b. May 8, 1658, (m. John Jordan). He m. second at Andover 4 Oct. 1660, Elizabeth, dau. of John Fry; child Richard b. March 20, 1667, (d. before 1707; no family known).

He died Oct. 11, 1678.

See Jose.

STIMSON,

Thomas, had lawsuit in Piscataqua court in 1655.

STONE,

Richard, Kittery, ae. about 19 years, testified in behalf of Hugh Gunnison 21 Dec. 1653. [Bax. MSS.]

STORER, STORY,

George, party to a lawsuit in court at Strawberry Bank in 1643.

William, Dover, signed the combination in 1640; proprietor in 1642 and 1648. Sworn into office as clerk of the train band at Dover court 10 (6) 1650; was also chosen marshall; see Crowther.

He died, and his widow Sarah married, second, Samuel Austin, to whom the court gave the administration of his estate June 27, 1661, he giving bonds to make good the sum of 130 li. to the 4 children. He deeded certain lands 31 Jan. 1670, to Joseph and Benjamin, the two eldest children, for which they gave receipt and engaged to maintain 5 neat cattle for their father in law and mother. He deeded land to the son Samuel 8 Oct. 1674.

STORRE, STORRS,

Mr. Augustine, Exeter, was owner of lands which John Legat sold in 1650. He signed the combination 5 (4) 1639; was selectman in 1640.

He is said in the Hist. of Exeter to have been a brother of the first wife of Rev. John Wheelwright and the husband of a sister of his second wife (which would make him a brother in law of Mrs. Anne Hutchinson).

STOVER,

Sylvester, fisherman, York, had grant of land at Cape Neddicke 3 July, 1649, with John Ball and others, for the fishing trade. Took oath of allegiance to Mass. govt. 22 Nov. 1652. Proprietor in 1655. [Bax. MSS.]

Will dated July 21, 1687, prob. 14 Feb. 1689-90; was "bound by the grace of god into old England"; bequeathed to wife [Elizabeth], sons John, Dependance, Josiah and George, and "the rest of my children." Josiah, of Tiverton, R. I. one of the sons, sold his share to his brother Dependance 19 April, 1709.

SWADDEN,

Philip, in the employ of Robert Seeley of Watertown 14 June, 1631; was set free on payment of 10 shillings Aug. 16. [Mass. Col. Rec.] Resided "neare the river of Pascattaquay" 9 (5) 1639. [L.] Rem. to Strawberry Bank; signed the combination in 1640; had lawsuit 10 (9) 1642. His wigwam on the north side of Piscataqua river was mentioned in the bounds of a tract of land sold to Johnson for Treworgy in 1636.

He deposed Aug. 27, 1673, ae. about 73 years, concerning land titles in Kittery "38 or 39 yeares ago." [York De. III.]

SWAIN, SWAINE,

Richard, planter, Hampton, 6 (7) 1638. Commissioner for the ending of small causes, and lot-layer in 1639. Signed petition in Howard case in 1643. Signed petition of Exeter inhabitants 29 (3) 1645. [Mass. Arch. 112, 39.] Owned a house and land at Exeter in 1650. Gave part of his house lot in Hampton to his daughter Grace and her husband, Nathaniel Bolter, Sept. 4, 1660; another tract to Hezekiah, eldest son of his son William, deceased, 12 (5) 1663. Was fined by Gen. Court Nov. 12, 1659, for entertaining Quakers. Deposed 10 (7) 1662, ae. about 67 years. He rem. to Nantucket; sold his remaining estate at Hamp. to son in law Bolter 6 July, 1663.

Name of first wife not found by the writer; he m. [2] Jane, widow of George Bunker of Topsfield, with whom he sold land in T. July 5, 1660. Children, Francis and Nicholas, (signers with him of the Howard petition in 1643), William, (sergeant, lost in a vessel that sailed from Hamp. for Boston Oct. 20, 1657), Grace, (m. Nathaniel Bolter), Elizabeth, (m. Nathaniel Weare), Richard b. Jan. 13, 1659-60, [Dorothy, John].

SYMONDS, SYMES, see Simons,

John, Spurwink, gave bonds for a man in court in 1648; constable, 1650, took oath of allegiance 13 July, 1658.

William, Wells, witnessed deed 25 Sept. 1655; commissioner, 1659. Grand jury man, 1663.
See Gooch.

TAINTOR, TAYNTOR,
Michael, Mr. set the bounds between his land and that of Nicholas Frost about 1640; witnessed Shapleigh's deed of Isles of Shoals property in 1642.

TAPRILL, TAPERELL,
Robert, Portsmouth, mariner, proprietor, 1660. Wife Abisha, d. leaving a nuncupative will dated Jan. 25, 1678-9, left children, not specified by names. Alexander Waldren, who d. at Great Island in 1676, bequeathed a house in Boston to Abisha for her life and 10 li. to her dau. Alice Taprell; the latter was also a legatee of George Walton, Sen. in 1686, to 8 acres of land jointly with her sister Priscilla, while he gave their sister Grace "the house her mother died in."
William, Dover, in the employ of George Walton, testified in Hampton court 1 (8) 1650. Had land, at Portsmouth in 1660.

TARE, TAYRE, [Thayer?]
John, had lawsuit in Piscataqua court in 1642; was a juryman in 1646; brought suit against John and Hester Marten in 1647.

TART,
John, Dover, taxed in 1648.

TAYLOR, TAILOR, TAILER,
Anthony, felt maker, Hampton, proprietor, June, 1640. Signed petition in Howard case in 1643. Bought land of John Cass in 1648.
Wife Phillippa died Sept. 20, 1683; children, John, Lydia, Martha, Sarah. [Dow.]
He died Nov. 4, 1687, ae. 80 years. [Dow.]

Henry, brought suit in Piscataqua court in 1646. Was presented in court 3 (8) 1648, and sent to Boston Jail. Administration of his estate was granted by Dover court 5 (5) 1649, to John Webster; division to be made to creditors.

George, ae. 31, came in the *Truelove* in Sept. 1635; settled at Lynn; proprietor before 1638; freeman May 2, 1638; constable 31 (6) 1647. Opposed Infant Baptism. [Es. Files.] He deposed in Salem in 1654 about bringing beaver from Saco to Boston for Francis Johnson about 1636. Some George Tailor died in S. 28 (10) 1667. Compare this with

George, planter, residing at Black Point; he took oath of allegiance to Mass. govt. 13 July, 1658. He married Margaret, widow of Philip Hinkson, q. v. He deposed 25 July, 1681, ae. about 70 years. [York De. IV.] His son Andrew, of Boston, gave receipt 20 March, 1685, for the payment of money due on account of sale of land by his father 29 July, 1679.

John, mariner, from Jalme, [Yealmpton?] Eng. was a boat-master for Winter about 1630. [Trel.]

John, planter, Damariscove River, gave bond for the payment of money in company with Nathaniel Draper, 2 June, 1651. [Suff. De.]

See also Cass, Legat, Page, Reading.

TEDDAR, TEDER,

Stephen, was reported by Ambrose Gibbons in 1633 as being with him at Newichewanick. He signed the Piscataqua combination in 1640. Had suit in court in 1642.

TENNEY, TENNY, TINNY, TYNNY,

John, (Tynny), Spurwink, took oath of allegiance to Mass. govt. 13 July, 1658.

John (Tenney), of Kittery, with wife Margaret, sold land 4 June, 1700, on the north side of Saco river, which he had bought of John Waddock. [York De. VIII, 206 and X, 245.]

Compare with John, son of Thomas of Rowley.

THOMAS, see Rice, Billing, Goddard.

THING, THYNG,
 Jonathan, before the Gen. Court of Mass. in 1641. In the service of Henry Ambrose [Charlestown], as per court record 29 May, 1644. Rem. to Exeter. Had suit in Hampton court in 1650. Rem. to Wells, Me.; took oath of allegiance to Mass. govt. 4 July, 1653. Was appointed sergeant. He deposed in 1667, ae. about 46 years. [Es. Files.]
 Children born at Exeter, Elizabeth b. 5 June, 1665, John b. 20 Sept. 1665, (sic rec.), d. 4 Nov. 1665, Sam: b. 3 (4) 1667.
 He died before 29 April, 1674, when the inventory of his estate was taken; an agreement was concluded 9 Oct. 1676, between the widow Johannah and the son Jonathan to manage the estate jointly, bring up and educate the younger children Samuel, Elizabeth and Mary, and pay them their portions when they come of age. The inv. shows carpenter's tools, etc.
 See King.

THOMPSON, THOMSON, TOMPSON, TOMSON,
 Mr. David, who, with the Hiltons, *founded* New Hampshire, was a fishmonger at London, though of Scotch birth, and came to Piscataqua in 1623 "to begin a plantation," as Hubbard tells us. The phrase implies that he had such companions and furnishings as would be adapted to shore life as well as the fishing business; probably none of the company brought their wives and children at first but had them brought over on later voyages of the ships which carried fish and other commodities back to England. Captain Thompson doubtless made many voyages across the ocean as well as coastwise. Bradford tells of his going along with some Plymouth men to "Damarinscove" to traffic for the goods of a ship-wrecked Frenchman in 1626, mentioning him as then dwelling at Piscataqua. Not far from that time he went to Boston harbor and bought an island called

Trevour's Island, which was afterward called by his own name, and erected a habitation there. He died not long after that date, according to testimony given in Court when the title of the island was confirmed to the son in 1648.

He married at Plymouth, Eng. July 13, 1613, Amyas Colle (Amias Cole) who survived him and married second Mr. Samuel Maverick, who was at Boston Bay about 1625 and came into possession of the island called Noddle's Island, now East Boston. Mrs. Maverick joined her second husband in a deed in 1632; in 1633 she wrote a letter to Mr. Robert Trelawney, alluding to her first husband's friendship for him and to her "fatherless children" by Mr. Thompson. The only one of these children known to us is John, who obtained the island above-mentioned after it had been in the possession of citizens of Dorchester and its income the foundation of the free school of that town in 1641. So the name of Thomson was prominent in the pioneer annals of two colonies.

It is particularly suitable that New-Hampshire people should honor the memory of this enterprising man.

Miles, Senior, carpenter, Kittery, signed the petition to Cromwell in 1657; was one of the selectmen in 1659. Bought land adjoining to some previously possessed of John Morrall, plasterer, 12 May, 1663; bought other land in partnership with Israel Hodgsden, of Abraham Tilton and Mary his wife. Deeded land Dec. 4, 1694, to sons Bartholomew and Thomas, the latter to maintain himself and his wife Ann.

Rev. William, some time curate of the church at Winwick, Eng. came to this land in 1636 or 1637. Joined the church of Dorchester, Mass. of which his friend Rev. Richard Mather was pastor. Preached a while at Accomenticus, [Kittery]; removed to Braintree, Mass. and was installed as pastor with Rev. Henry Flint as teacher, Nov. 19, 1639. He was "a very gracious, sincere man, — an instrument of much good, — a man of much faith." [W.] See P. of M.

Note. In Piscataqua Files there is a well written letter from "Sam: Thomsonn," dated at "Taunton, March, 27th,

1660," addressed to "Deare Brother & Sister." He had received letters from them 4 and 2 years since, but none this spring. They had ordered cloth of him, which was to be sent by Mr. John Payne. He had rode to Cheriton to confer with his uncle White about sending it. He now sends "3 karsyes," i. e. pieces of kersey cloth; directed to one Mr. Reynes in New England for them. He supposes that they "and all my cousins and their little ones are in good health, though my cousin William Thompson writt not a word of it." Hopes "my cousin John's children are with you, and that you are a father and mother to them." Is sorry to learn of the death of "cousin Esther." His own son Samuel is in school in Ilminster, and almost "fitt for Oxford"; his "daughter Mall is a religious and vertuous young woman."

This letter may prove very valuable as a means of discovering the relationship of several American families to their English connections. The great variety in the spelling of names at that period is here illustrated by the "Thomsonn" of the signature and the "Thompson" of a cousin's name. The "cousin William" who had recently written but failed to give all family news, calls to mind the Braintree parson, though without any real evidence of identity.

"*A maid*," of this name came to Richmond Island about 1639; was drowned. [Trel.]

THORPE,
    Rev. John, Scarborough, witnessed a deed of Robert Jordan 9 Oct. 1658. Was complained of by Jordan and others for misconduct, and was forbidden by the Gen. Court 2 (3) 1661, to preach till further notice.
    [See Register XIII, 193.]

TIBBETTS, TIBBETT, TIBBET, TIBBOT, TYBBOTT, TIPPET, TIPPITS, TYPIT,
    Henry, shoemaker, ae. 39, with Elizabeth, ae. 39, Jeremy, ae. 4, and Samuel, ae. 2, and Remembrance, ae. 28, came in the James in July, 1635. Settled at Dover. Name on list

of proprietors in 1642. Testified in the suit of John Ault against Thomas Wiggin in 1645, that the time of service of [his sister] Remembrance began March 1, before she came to this country. Had lawsuit in 1647. He — planter, sold land in Dover to John Tuttle 6 June, 1657. Was sealer of leather in 1661. Joined in petition of inhabitants to Gen. Court 10 Oct. 1665. [Mass. Arch. 106, 160.]

The inventory of his estate taken Dec. 10, 1683, specifies the bill of John Tucker for care in sickness and cost of burial. See also Allen, Canney, Nock, Twambly.

TOBY, TOBEY,

Henry, Exeter, proprietor, one of those who signed "the Combination" 5th day, 4th month, 1639, and re-affirmed it in 1640; his land was sold 12 (8) 1649, by John Bursley. [Pisc. court rec.]

TOPP, TOP,

Mary, Kittery, summoned to court at Strawberry Bank in 1642. Took oath of allegiance 22 Nov. 1652.

TOWLE, TOLL,

John, fisherman, gave testimony in Piscataqua court about George Walton in 1651, and corrected it in 1652.

Philip, Hampton, proprietor, 1657. Bought house and land in 1664.

He m. Nov. 19, 1657, Isabel, [said by Dow to be a daughter of Francis Austin]; children, Philip b. 3 (3) 1659, Caleb b. 17 (3) 1661 (killed by the Indians in 1677,) Joshua b. 29 (4) 1663, Mary b. Nov. 12, 1665, Joseph and Benjamin b. May 4, 1669, Francis b. Aug. 1, 1672, John b. July 23, 1674, Caleb b. May 14, 1678.

He died Nov. 11, 1696, ae. 80. Will proved May 25, 1697, beq. to wife "Esabell," sons Phillip, Joshua, Benjamin, Joseph and Caleb.

TOZIER,

Richard, Kittery, had land granted to him by the town

16 Oct. 1659; bounds between him and William Pyles settled 23 April, 1668.

He died before 30 March, 1683, when the estate of his widow Judith, administratrix to his estate, was appraised; inventory presented by her son Richard. [York De. V.]

TREBY,
    Edward, Richmond Island, one of Winter's fishermen, 1639-1642.

TRELAWNEY,
    Mr. Edward, merchant, a man whose letters show strong Puritan sentiments, brother of Robert Trelawney, below, wrote from Boston, Mass. 10 Jan. 1635, to his brother Robert; letter given in the Trelawney papers. Was named in the records of the Maine court at Saco, 7 (7) 1636. Spent some months or years in New England; returned to England.
    Mr. Robert, merchant, Plymouth, England, patentee of Casco, Richmond Island, etc.; article on Winter.
    See Cleve, Hinkson, Neale, Vines.

TREWORGY, TREWORTHY, TRUEWORTHY,
    James, on the grand jury at Saco in 1640; one of the assessors. He sold all his fishing gear, buildings, etc. in N. E. to his brother in law Nicholas Shapleigh April 2, 1641; had deed of similar property from his father in law in 1642. His wife's application for a share in her father's property was denied 6 July, 1650, on account of previous bestowment of her portion.
    He married Katharine, daughter of Mr. Alexander Shapleigh; she survived him and married Edward Hilton. Children: John, (who was a merchant at Dartmouth, Eng. and came to New England as an agent of his mother's father as early as 1636), Elizabeth, (m. Capt. John Gilman), Joanna, (m. John Amerideth or Merida), Lucy (married (1) Humphrey Chadbourne (2) Thomas Wells, and (3) Elias

Stileman), and Samuel, (to whom the mother conveyed land 2 Nov. 1674).

Mrs. Katharine Hilton, dau. of Alexander Shapleigh, wife, first of James Treworthy, second of Edward Hilton, made nunc. will, attested at Hampton Court 30 May, 1676. Beq. to James, son of Samuel Treworthy, a silver beaker, to be kept in the hands of her dau. Elizabeth Gilman till he comes of age; to James, son of John T.; to Edward Hilton, Jr.; to gr. ch. Samuel, and Mary G. and Joanna Merideth; to Mr. Samuel Dudley; to daus. Joanna M. and Elizabeth G.; to Abigail, wife of Edward G.; to Betty, Katharine, Sarah and Lydia G.; to Katherine Paul, Mrs. Lucie Wells, goodwife Robinson and Jane H. Son in law Capt. John Gilman exec. Mrs. Wells to be paid. Rest to be divided among all her gr. ch. Proved May 30, 1676.

Nicholas, witnessed a deed of Alexander Shapleigh, conveying property at Isles of Shoals, in 1642.

See also Johnson, Reeves, Rice, Swadden.

TRICKEY, TRICKY, TRICKETT,

Francis, Dover, proprietor, 1649. With wife Sarah in court for "slander" in 1656, probably for mentioning some unwelcome facts.

The inventory "of the estate of Mrs. Sarah Tricky and of her son John Tricky, deceased," taken May 17, 1686, was presented by the mother in York court. [York De. V.]

Thomas, Bloody Point, joined in the petition for annexation to Dover about 1642. [Mass. Arch. 3, 438.] Had lawsuit in 1643. He and his wife Elizabeth before the court in 1646. Prosecuted Michael Brand for slander in 1652. Was taxed in Dover in 1648. Was building a vessel of 30 or 40 tons at Piscataqua for George Dod of Boston in 1650. [Suff. De.] Lawsuit in Hamp. court in 1650.

Inventory of his estate, taken 3 Dec. 1676, was presented by his widow, Elizabeth, to whom the court gave it "for her comfort and Livelyhood."

TRIMMINGS,
Oliver, before Piscataqua court in 1643 for cleaving clapboards where he had no right; again in 1652 for alleged *trimming* in his testimony. Lot of land assigned him at Portsmouth Jan. 13, 1652.

TRISTRAM, TRUSTRUM,
Ralph, Cape Porpoise, had cattle of John Lee's in his care in 1647. [Suff. De.] Residing at Saco, he took oath of allegiance to Mass. govt. 5 July, 1653. Constable; house at West Saco. [Bax. MSS.] Children, David, Hannah, (m. Dominicus Jordan), Nathaniel, Benjamin.

He died before March 4, 1678-9, when inventories of his estate and that of his son Nathaniel were filed by Dominicus Jordan; that of his son Benjamin was presented by Sylvanus Davis 25 Jan. 1678-9. David and Hannah sold land formerly their father's 17 Oct. 1684.

See Spurrell.

TROTT,
Simon, Cape Porpoise, took oath of allegiance to Mass. govt. 5 July, 1653. Stephen Batson in 1673 bequeathed to grandchild John Trott and to Mary Trott.

TUCK, TUCKE, TOOK,
Robert, vintner, Watertown, proprietor, 1636; a pioneer at Hampton (7) 1638. Frm. Sept. 7, 1639. Signed petition in 1643. Clerk of the writs in 1649; selectman.

Wife Johannah; children, Robert, Elizabeth, (m. John Sherborne), Mary, (m. John Sanborn), Edward, (signed petition about Howard in 1643; d. 6 April, 1652; estate given to widow and sons Edward and John;) William. She married second James Wall.

He died 4 (8) 1664; 17 Nov. 1664, the appraisal of his estate was made and admin. granted to the widow for herself and the three children Robert Tuck, Elizabeth Sherburne and Mary Sanborn and John Tuck son of Edward Tuck. The

widow Johannah died 14 Feb. 1673; double inventory rendered in April, 1674. John Samborne, administrator, and John Sherbourn, part heir to the estate, made an agreement 25 (12) 1674, with William son of said Robert (now of Gorlston, near Yarmouth, Eng.). John Tuck, of Hampton, carpenter, son of Edward, recd. a share 26 (12) 1673.
See also Philbrick.

TUCKER,

John, fisherman, Kittery, deposed 21 Dec. 1653, about the Gunnison affair, where he had been an assistant of the marshall. Lived on the Isles of Shoals.

Will dated 31 (8) 1670, prob. 3 Jan. 1670-1, beq. to Thomas Wells, minister at Kittery, and to friend John and Johanna Amerideth.

Richard, gent. bought the patent of Richard Bradshaw at Spurwink; he became a partner of Cleve, and they recd. a patent from Gorges Jan. 27, 1627, of 1500 acres "from Machegonne Point to the Falls of Pesumsca." He had a lawsuit in Saco court 25 March, 1636. Was a member of grand jury in 1640. Deed of Alexander Rigby, Esq. to him and Cleve was dated 23 May, 1643. Wife Margaret joined him in a deed in 1661.

The inventory of his estate was brought into court at Portsmouth 30 Sept. 1679, taken 11 days before by Nathaniel Drake and William Seavey; attested by the widow, Margaret, admx.

See also Bickford, Cleve, Heard, Leavitt, Lewis, Moses, Peverly, Savage, Tibbetts, Wall.

TUCKERMAN,

Otho, Portsmouth, proprietor, 1660; he died and admin. of his estate was granted to his widow Eme May 24, 1664; the children's portions to be secured.

TURBAT, TURBUTT,

Peter, Cape Porpoise, took oath of allegiance to Mass. govt. 5 July, 1653. Sold 12 Feb. 1660, land he had bought of his father in law John Sanders and John Bush, which they had bought of Sosowen, the Indian sagamore. He and his wife Sarah apprenticed their son Peter to Capt. Francis Champernowne Nov. 8, 1661.

Will probated 19 Oct. 1669, beq. to wife Sarah, sons John and Peter; father in law John Sanders to bring up daughter Elizabeth. The widow married second Daniel Goodwin of Berwick; sold land in the "Coxhall" tract June 29, 1687, her eldest surviving son, Nicholas Turbat, and her daughter Elizabeth, his wife, consenting.

TURPIN,

Thomas, fisherman, Isles of Shoals, in company with Richard Commins, bought a plantation at Salt Creek on Piscataqua river 6 (10) 1645. [Suff. De.] Sold cattle to William Seavey 7 Feb. 1648.

He died before 8 (8) 1650, when Wm. Payne was appointed administrator of his estate; R. Commings paid 14 li. for half of the property above mentioned in 1652. The widow Jane married second Thomas Furson, and adjusted matters with Cummings in court June 27, 1656.

See also Drake.

TUTTLE, TURTLE,

John, planter, Dover, proprietor in 1642 and 1648. Bought land of Henry Tippets 6 June, 1657.

Admin. of his estate was granted 30 June, 1663, to his widow Dorothy; eldest daughter already portioned and married; son John to have his part at 21 years of age; youngest daughter to have hers at 18; the widow to have her thirds.

TWAMBLY, TWAMBLE,

Ralph, Dover, sued for a debt by Ralph Hall in 1660. Was excused from training 28 June, 1670.

His will dated 28 Feb. 1684, was proved 7 (8) 1686; bequeathed to wife Elizabeth and children John, Joseph, Ralph, Elizabeth, Hope, Sarah, Esther and William Twambly and Mary Tibbetts.

TWISDEN, TWISDALE, TWISDELL,
  John, Senior, planter, York, received 20 acres of land of Wm. Hooke July 19, 1645; sold land 7 May, 1664. He deposed to his signature to a deed 24 June, 1678, ae. about 54 years.
  His widow Susanna and sons John and Samuel joined in a deed of land 10 April, 1685.
  [Same name at Scituate, Mass. 1638-1649.]
  Peter, fisherman, Isles of Shoals, signed petition in 1653. Bought land in York 23 April, 1662.

UNDERHILL,
  Capt. John, Boston, adm. chh. 1630; was paid by Gen. Court for military service 7 Sept. 1630; frm. May 18, 1631. Deputy 1634. Rem. to Dover. Became governor of Piscataqua plantation; and there made utterances which gave offence of Mass. Bay authorities. For this and other charges he was summoned to Boston; came 29 (11) 1639, and apologized to the church. Was restored to fellowship 3 (7) 1640. Wife Helena, a Dutch woman, adm. chh. Bo. 15 (10) 1633; dism. to chh. of Exeter 22 (6) 1641; ch. Elizabeth bapt. 14 (12) 1635, John bapt. 24 (2) 1642, ae. about 13 days.
  He rem. to the Dutch settlement, (New York) in 1642. [W.]

UGROUFE, UNGROUFE, see Yougroufe.

UREN, EURIN, YORINE, YURRING,
  William, Portsmouth, 1653; house lot, 1658; Isles of Shoals, signed petition of inhabitants 18 (3) 1653.
  Admin. of his estate was granted 28 June, 1664, to Jonathan Wade and others. The widow married Richard Woolcomb and had her thirds of the estate in 1672.
  She made her will Sept. 19, 1699, bequeathing to son John Muchemore and (son) Joseph Yurring. John Urin, son to Eleanor Wilcome late of the Isle of Shoals, widow, petitioned that John Muchemore might administer on her estate Dec.

25, 1699, he having married Uren's sister by the mother's side; Zaccheus Wilcome was another of her children. [N. H. Prob. Rec.]

VARNEY, John, Dover, inhabitant 6 (4) 1659.

VEERIN,
John, "of the town of Harwick on the west side of Kenebeck River," petitioned Andros May 1, 1688, for confirmation of title to a tract of about 200 acres of land which he bought and had possessed "nere twenty Six yeares since . . . it being on a Nek of Land between wisswell[s] Cove & Kenebeck River," etc. [Bax. MS. VI.]

VESEY, VEAZIE,
George, Dover, proprietor; before the court in 1659 for being more than half an hour at the tavern; a technical violation of a recent ordinance.

He married Mary, daughter of Capt. Thomas Wiggin, bapt. at Hampton Sept. 2, 1641.

VICARY,
Andrew, [Black Point?] signed petition with Jocelyn and others to the Gen. Court in 1653, asking for trial of claims to territory, etc.

VINES, VYNES,
Mr. Richard, gent. in company with John Oldham, received a patent of land in Maine, issued 12 Feb. 1629; possession given 25 June, 1630. This he sold Oct. 20, 1645, to Dr. Robert Child. Dec. 1, 1631, he was appointed one of those who should give possession of the Goodyear and Trelawney tract in Maine. Gave possession in July, 1632. Was attorney for similar purpose several other times. Resided at Saco. He and Isaac Allerton and others traded along the coast; "landed goods at Machias and there he set up a small wigwam, and left five men and two murderers, [small can-

non,] to defend it, and a shallop," in 1633; the goods were soon after taken, two of the men killed, and the rest sent as prisoners to France by La Tour, and his men. The case was tried before Gov. Winthrop at Boston in 1643; when La Tour was visiting and trying to conciliate the authorities. [W.] Made a voyage to St. John the next year with Wonerton and Shurt. [Folsom.]

He was one of the commissioners who held court at Saco 7 (7) 1636. Was "Steward General" of Sir Ferdinando Gorges "for the province of New Somersetshire" in 1640, and governor under Mass. Bay Colony in 1645.

Mrs. Joane Vines appealed to the Court at Saco 28 March, 1636, concerning the island where she formerly planted, and requested that her husband might now have liberty to plant there.

He removed in 1646 to Barbadoes whence he wrote friendly letters to Gov. John Winthrop in 1647. He "practised physic" beside carrying on two plantations.

See also Brown, Cleve, Field, Wiggin, Winter, Withers.

VOUCKLIN,

John, brought suit in Piscataqua court in 1642. Court ordered in 1644 that money be sent to Christopher Holmes for him.

VOYSEY,

Simon, brought suit in Piscataqua court in 1644.

VIVION,

John, servant of Trelawney, came to Richmond Island and worked with Winter from 1637 to 1641.

WADDOCK,

Henry, Biddeford, one of the Commissioners who held court there 1 March, 1653-4.

Admin. of his estate was granted to his widow Jane; inventory was taken June 16, 1679. [York De. V.]

See Tenney.

WADLEIGH, WADLY, WADLOW, WODLEY,

Edward, shipwright, worked for Winter at Richmond Island 10 days in 1641 or 1642. [Trel.]

John, planter, Saco, assessed for the "rate for the minister" 7 (7) 1636; grand jury man in 1640; removed to Wells. Had a grant of land from Vines "in Yeapskessett river" April 1, 1639. Bought land of Indians 18 Oct. 1649. Took oath of allegiance 5 July, 1653. Was one of the first selectmen of Wells. With wife Mary sold land 19 Dec. 1663. Son Robert joined with the father in purchase of land from Indians and in sale of same March 13, 1659.

WAKEFIELD,

William, ae. 22, and Anne ae. 20, came in the Bevis in May, 1638. Settled at Hampton. Received a house lot as "a young man"; frm. March 13, 1638-9. Chosen town clerk Oct. 31, 1639; clerk of the writs in 1641. Rem. to Newbury, Mass. Certain lands he had owned passed to Stephen Pent, who sold the same 14 (2) 1652.

See Littlefield.

WALDERNE, WALDRON,

Captain Richard, Dover, signed the Combination in 1640; had lawsuit in 1641; recorded proprietor in 1642; selectman. 1647 and 1665. Joined with William Waldron in a bond June 12, 1645. Removed to Boston; his servant Elizabeth Tilston d. Sept. 2, 1658. With wife Ann he sold land at Dover April 13, 1660. Was appointed to join persons in marriage in 1662. Returned to Dover. He deposed in June, 1664, ae. about 48 years. Signed petition to Gen. Court Oct. 10, 1665. Ch.: Elnathan, b. in Boston 6 July, d. 10 Dec. 1659; Esther, b. Dec. 1, 1660; Mary, b. Sept. 14, 1663; Eliazer, b. at Dover 1 May, 1665; Elizabeth, b. 18 Oct. 1666; Marah, b. 17 July, 1668. [Dov. Hist. Col.] His wife Anne d. 7 Feb. 1684-5. He was killed by the Indians 28 June, 1689. [?]

William, Dover, "partner with the Shrewsbury men,"

[Mass. Col. Rec. IV. Pt. II.] Signed the combination in 1640; was a proprietor and recorder of lands for the town in 1642. Frm. Mass., 1642; deputy, 1645-6. Gave bonds 12 June, 1645, for payment of money to Mr. William Whiting for the use of "The Adventurers in Piscataqua River" and for "The Shrewsbury merchants." [Suff. De.] "A good clerk and a subtle man." Went to Saco, and on his return in September, 1646, was drowned in attempting to cross a small river at Kennebunk. [W.] Dau. Prudence m. Richard Scamman. They petitioned the Gen. Court in 1664.

The court of Dover ordered his creditors to present their accounts at the General Court at Boston, and the estate was settled by Capt. Thomas Wiggin and Edward Rawson; then left in the hands of Hate Evill Nutter and John Hall until May 22, 1666, when it was given to Richard Scamman for his wife Prudence.

WALFORD,
Thomas, blacksmith, came to Charlestown, Mass. before 1628; was living in a thatched and palisaded house on the arrival of the Spragues and others from Salem in the Spring of 1628-9. In some unexplained way he incurred the displeasure of the authorities and was arrested, ordered to pay a fine of XL shillings and to leave the jurisdiction with his wife; the charge alleged is "contempt of authority and confronting officers"; this edict was given 3 May, 1631. He paid the fine by killing a wolf. He soon departed, as his goods were sequestered for debts Sept. 3, 1633. [Mass. Col. Rec.] He removed to Portsmouth.

Wm. Payne brought suit against him concerning lumber 26 (6) 1646. He and his wife Jane brought suit in Dover court 3 (8) 1648. He was a grand jury man in 1650. 50 acres of land assigned to him in Portsmouth Jan. 13, 1652. He took oath of fidelity July 2, 1657. His wife was accused of witchcraft in 1656; son Jeremy gave bonds for her; she was discharged July 2, 1657.

He died in 1667. Will dated 15 Nov. 1666, probated 27

June, 1667; beq. wife Jane; to grandchildren Thomas and Jeremiah W., John Westbrook, Mary Hingson, Mary Homes, (wife of John H.), Sara and Samuel Jones, and Mary and Hester Savidg; to daughters Peverley and Westbrook; to John Peverley and John Westbrook; to John Homes; servant John Read to be at the disposing of son in law John Westbrook. Refers to land which son in law Thomas Hingson formerly possessed.

The widow Jane deposed 27 June, 1667, ae. 69 years, that he gave a piece of land to his daughter Elizabeth Savidg (Savage) 9 years before he died, and that it was commonly called Bess Savidge's marsh. His daughters Mary, wife of Will Brookings, ae. 32, and Martha Westbrook, ae. 22, with his son Jeremiah W. and grandson John Homes, ae. 26, confirmed her testimony. The widow's thirds were laid out by order of court 27 June, 1671. The daus. Jean Goss, Hanna Jones, Mary Brookin and Eliza Savage petitioned the court to give them the overplus of the estate Sept. 7, 1681.

See Bachiler.

WALKER,

Joseph, Portsmouth, proprietor, 1660. He d. Nov. 7, 1683.

Admin. of his estate was granted to his widow Hannah and son George Dec. 10, 1683.

Samuel, Exeter, signed the combination in 1640; town officer, 1643; on a com. to distribute corn to the needy, 1644. Took oath of freemanship at Pisc. Court 17 (2) 1644.

Compare with Samuel Walker of Woburn, Mass. who had m. the widow of Arthur Alger of Scarborough; also with Samuel Walker, mariner, of Boston, who petitioned Andros in 1688, jointly with Benj. Blackman, of Saco, for confirmation of title to land there.

WALL, WALLES,

James, carpenter, millwright, deposed 21 (3) 1652, that about the year 1634 he and his partners William Chadbourne and John Goddard, carpenters, came over to Mason's land on his account and their own; that "Mr. Joislin," Mason's agent, brought them to certain lands at Asbenbedick Falls, as the Indians called the place, where they carried on a sawmill and a stamping mill for corn 3 or 4 years; that he built a house there, and that Chadbourne built another. [Mass. Arch. 3, 437, 8.]

Witnessed deed in Exeter April 3, 1638; signed the combinations of Exeter settlers in 1639 and that of Piscataqua settlers in 1640. Was a proprietor also at Dover in 1642. Town officer. Rem. to Hampton. Bought mill and rights at Quachecho Falls 2 (8) 1647. Second wife Mary, widow of Edward Tuck; children, Mary b. 8 (11) 1655, Hannah b. 17 (1) 1658.

He died 3 (8) 1659. Will dated Sept. 20, proved Oct. 4, 1659; wife Mary, eldest daughters Elizabeth and Sarah Wall and the children he had by present wife, viz. Mary, and Hannah. The latter were placed under the guardianship of their uncle Thomas Philbrick.

The widow died in Oct. 1702; inventory taken 5 May, 1703. Agreement made 12 Feb. 1702-3, between her children John Tuck, Mary Marston and Benjamin Moulton (in the right of his wife Hannah).

See also Colcord, Listen, Redman.

WALLING, WALLIS,

John, Spurwink, took oath of allegiance to Mass. govt. 13 July, 1658. He petitioned in 1687 for confirmation of title to lands in Falmouth which he and his predecessors had possessed "neere fifty years."

Nathaniel, also took oath of allegiance at Sp. 13 July, 1658.

Peter, was sued by Henry Sherburne of Portsmouth in 1660, for keeping his boat upon Sherburne's mooring-place.

WALTON,

George, ordinary keeper, vintner, tailor, before Gen. Court at Boston 4 (10) 1638. Rem. to Exeter; signed the combination 5 (4) 1639. Bought land on Great Island of John Hord 1 March, 1649; acknowledged in 1655. Taxed at Dover in 1648. Assessed for wine sold in his ordinary. Had land assigned to him at Portsmouth in 1652. Rem. to Kittery. Bought land in Back Cove 16 Aug. 1659; Abishag* Walton a witness. Rem. to Portsmouth. Sold his houses and lands to Henry Robie 1 Aug. 1662. Was licensed 14 Oct. 1662, to keep the ordinary upon the great island in Pascattoquack river. [Norf. rec.] Suffered from "Stone-throwing" imposters. [Magnalia.] A child of his was found drowned in 1657. [Inquest].

He made his will Feb. 14, 1685, proved March 9 following. To present wife Alice; to son Sidrach Walton; to Sam: Walton; to Alice and Priscilla Taprell each 8 acres of land; to Grace Taprell the house her mother died in; to Thomas and Walton Roby and Elizabeth Treworgy.

John, brought suit against George Walton in 1651, for cutting timber on his land. Had land assigned him at Portsmouth in 1652.

See Bulgar, Disher, Hilton, Taperill, Towle, West.

WANNERTON, WONNERTON,

Thomas, gent. captain, had charge of Gorges and Mason's house at Pascataqua in 1633, as Gibbons wrote. Lived later at Strawberry Bank; engaged in trading along the Eastern coast. He was brought before the Gen. Court of Mass. Aug. 4, 1635, on complaint of John Holland and others,

---

*The occurrence of this name "Abishag Walton" leads us to compare this man George Walton with "Alexander Waldren" (Walden, Waldron), a "sojourner on the Great Island near piscataqua River," who, in his will dated 7 June, 1676, proved 27th same month beq. to bros. Isaac, of Boston, William, George, Edward ("in the kingdom of Old England") ; to Joan Barker of Coventry, Eng.; and his house and land at Boston to "Abisha, wife of Robert Taperell mariner during her life"; he also gave her two gold rings, and to her daughter Alice Taprill 10 pounds. Have we here *George Walton, Sen.* and his brothers and sister? Names were *so* confused in those days!

for violent attacks on them and abusive language against the Mass. Bay people. Witnessed the deed to Johnson 5 May, 1636. Had suit in Maine court May 20, 1637. Mortg. house and lands 25 April, 1644. [Suff. De.] Was fined at S. B. in 1643 for striking his wife with a stool. He led a party of the French adherents of La Tour in an attack upon D'Aulnay's farm house at Penobbscot in the summer of 1644; and was killed in the first onset. [W.] Administration of his estate was ordered by Piscataqua court.

His widow Ann married second Thomas Williams.

See also Champernowne, Gee, Goddard, Johnson, Knight.

WANTON,

Edward, York, bought land on the south side of Cape Nedacke river 13 Nov. 1651, and sold the same 11 Nov. 1657, to his "brother in law John Smyth who hath beene severall yeares in possession of the same."

WARD, WARDE, WORD,

Rev. John, son of Rev. Nathaniel, of Ipswich, Mass. and grandson of Rev. John, of Haverhill, England, came to Accomenticus about 1641, to be their minister. Was lost two days and one night with Revs. Peter and Dalton and a York man on the way from Dover through the woods.

Was called to Haverhill, Mass. and settled there in October, 1645. There he remained till the close of his useful life.

He married Alice. Children, Elizabeth, b. April 1, 1647, (m. Nathaniel Saltonstall), Mary b. 24 June, 1649, (m. Rev. Benjamin Woodbridge, whose dau. Elizabeth m. 1, Rev. John Clark and 2, Rev. John Odlin, of Exeter, N. H.)

He and his wife Alice deeded a tract of land in Hav. 17 May, 1654, to Elizabeth, wife of Thomas Lilford, and their heirs.

His will is on file, dated 27 May, 1680, headed "O Lord into thy hand commend I my spirit. *Credo languida fide tamen fide."* He bequeathed his estate to his son Benjamin

Woodbridge and daughter Mary, his wife; to daughter Elizabeth and her husband Nathaniel Saltonstall. Final date in the document Jan. 23, 1692-3, probated March 28, 1694.

Thomas, planter, yeoman, weaver, Hampton, proprietor, June, 1640. Selectman, 1651. Bought land of Isaac Perkins 7 (8) 1652.

Wife Margerite; children, Elizabeth b. 10 (10) 1651, Mary, Hannah b. 2 (9) 1655, Thomas b. 3 (11) 1665.

Will dated 18 June, 1678, prob. 7 Sept. 1680, beq. to wife Margritte; son Thomas Ward; daughter Hannah Ward; dau. Elizabeth, wife of John Mason; dau. Mary, wife of John Dearborn.

Note one Thomas Ward, juryman in Gen. Court of Mass. 28 Sept. 1630; same name proposed for a proprietor at Dedham in 1638. No evidence connects these persons; yet the name and dates suggest identity.

See Fogg, Shaw.

WARDELL, WARDALL, WADDELL, WARDWELL, WODDELL,

Thomas, shoemaker, Boston, admitted church 9 (9) 1634, frm. March 4, 1634-5; proprietor Jan. 1635-6. Was dismissed to the chh. of Exeter with the Wheelwright party 6 (11) 1638. Proprietor; town officer; commissioner for local trials; sergeant. Returned to Boston.

Wife Elizabeth; children, Eliakim bapt. 23 (9) 1634, Martha b. (6) 1637, Benjamin b. at Exeter Feb. 1639-40, Samuel b. 16 (3) 1643.

He died in Bo. Dec. 10, 1646. "Mis. Wardel, an ancient wido," died 2 Feb. 1697.

William, servant to Edmund Quinsey, was admitted to the chh. of Boston 9 (12) 1633. Proprietor. Was dismissed to Exeter 6 (11) 1638. Proprietor; signed the combination. Rem. to Rhode Island, whence he was brought for trial in 1643 with Gorton and others, on charge of heresy, etc.; was confined at Watertown. Rem. to Wells, Me. When the commissioners of Mass. were summoning the inhabitants to take the oath of allegiance, he was charged with contempt of court, as dissuading neighbors from the act; but plead that he was absent from the meeting, endeavoring to get his neighbors to join in allegiance; he took the oath 5 July, 1653. [Bax. MSS.] Returned to Boston.

Wife Alice died; he m. second, Dec. 5, 1657, Elizabeth, widow of John Gillitt, (Jellett,) with whom he contracted to bring up her daughter Hannah, then 2 years old, in consideration of the widow's house. [Suff. Prob.; Reg. XII, 275.] Children, Meribah, bapt. 25 (4) 1637, (m. Francis Littlefield,) Usal b. 7 (2) 1639, Elihu bapt. 5 (10) 1641, Elihu b. (9) 1642, Mary b. (2) 1644, (m. Nathaniel Rust,) Leah b. 7 (10) 1646, (m. William Tower,) Abigail b. April 24, 1660, d. 23 Aug. 1661.

Will prob. 18 April, 1670, beq. to wife Elizabeth one half of the house in Boston for her life; to daus. Hannah and Deborah Gillett; to eldest son Uzzal and son Elihu; to daus. Leah, wife to William Tower, Meribah, wife to Francis Littlefield of Wells, and Mary, wife to Nathaniel Rust. [Reg. XLVIII, 458.]

See Mingay.

WARE, see Weare.

WARNER,
Thomas, Cape Porpoise, may be the person who was before Gen. Court at Boston 3 Sept. 1639; legatee of James Woodward in 1648; took oath of allegiance to Mass. govt. at Wells 5 July, 1653.

WARREN, WARRIN,
John, planter, cardmaker, Exeter, 1650.

He sold his house and land "upon Shrewsberry pattent" to John Foss 29 Sept. 1668. Rem. to Boston; sold one eighth part of a sawmill in Exeter 20 May, 1673.

He married 21 Oct. 1650 Deborah daughter of Thomas Wilson, b. at Roxbury (6) 1634; she died 26 (4) 1668. He

m. (2) Elizabeth, widow of John Coomes, who died in 1671 and beq. to her children Sara Barlowe, Elizabeth and Sara Coomes and Nathaniel Warren. Her husband administered on her estate (11) 1671. He m. (3) Elizabeth —. He died in July, 1677; will dated 10, prob. 31 July, 1677, beq. to wife Elizabeth, who is to bring up his children Nathaniel and Abigail according to contract made before marriage; to son Joshua "the engine I cut tobacco with;" the shop, not the land, to son Thomas; "to the rest of my children."

WARRINER, WARRENER,
 Thomas, sued in Dover court in 1651; did not appear.

WARWICK, WARWICKE, WADWICKE, WADDOCK,
 Henry, Saco, taxed in 1636; grand jury man in 1640. Sold wheat to John Winter in 1643. Had lawsuit in Maine court June 5, 1637.
 See Cammock.

WASHINGTON,
 Margaret, Portsmouth, had land assigned 22 March, 1660-1.

WATTS,
 Mr. Henry, fishmonger, Black Point, [L.] His name appears in a London Tax Roll of 1641 among fishmongers. See Hilton. Newe England identifies him.
 One of those who witnessed the giving possession of land in Maine to Lewis and Bonython June 28, 1631. Petitioned the court at Saco 25 March, 1636; taxed there 7 (7) 1636. Bargained with Thomas Wallis of Plymouth, N. E. about fish, in March, 1640-1. [L.] He testified 8 Sept. 1640, that Casco river had borne that name for nine years or thereabout. Was deputy to the Lygonia Assembly in 1648. Took oath of allegiance to Mass. govt. 13 July, 1658. Deposed 29 June, 1675, ae. about 71 years, as to John Mills mowing a certain piece of marsh. [York De. IV.]
 See Downing.

WAY, WAYE,

Thomas, fisherman, York, had a grant of land at Cape Neddicke 3 July, 1649, in partnership with John Ball and others.

WEARE, WIER, WYER, WYRE, WARE,

Nathaniel, [son of Nathaniel, of Haverhill in 1645?] born about 1631, married 3 Dec. 1656, Elizabeth, daughter of Richard Swain, of Hampton. Children, b. at Newbury, Elizabeth b. 5 Jan. 1657, Peter b. at Hampton 15 Nov. 1660. He died 13 May, 1718, ae. nearly 87. [Coffin]

Peter, York, had lawsuit in Piscataqua court in 1640. Proprietor; witness to an Indian deed to Humphrey Chadbourne in 1643; bought land at Cape Nuddocke beach 18 Oct. 1644. Had land grant from the town in 1646. [York De. I.] Took oath of allegiance to Mass. govt. 22 Nov. 1652. He deposed 7 Dec. 1658, ae. about 40 years, relative to land grants made 14 or 15 years before. Was a faithful friend of the Mass. govt. and was imprisoned in 1668 by the royalist authorities for that cause; petitions describe his sufferings; had been lame many years. [Bax. MSS.]

He died before April 18, 1692, when the inventory of his estate was taken; the widow Mary presented it in court Nov. 1, following. [York De. V.] She made her will 21 Jan. prob. 7 April 1719; beq. to children Hopewell and Daniel Wear, Mary Roberts and Sarah Nowell, and to son in law Nowell.

See Brooks, Davis, Gooch, Swain.

WEBB, WEBBE,

George, Dover, signed the combination in 1640; proprietor in 1642 and 1648.

He died before 8 (2) 1651, the date of granting admin. on his estate to George Smith.

WEBSTER,

John, Senior, brewer, Strawberry Bank, had liberty from Norf. court 24 (2) 1649 to sell wine. Brought suit concerning house and land 3 (8) 1648. Made deed of gift 20 Jan.

1650, to son John, conveying all his estate, house, brew house, furnace, vessels, furniture, etc. [Piscataqua court rec.] Juror in 1650.

Signed a petition of inhabitants to Gen. Court 20 Oct. 1651. [Mass. Arch. 112, 38.] Exchanged land with John Jones 24 May, 1656; acknowledged 15 July, 1659. With wife Rachel sold land on Great Island 28 Jan. 1660. Licensed to keep house of entertainment renewed in 1660 and 1661.

He died before June 24, 1662, when the widow Rachel declined to admin. on estate; June 30, 1663, Richard Waldren was appointed. The son John brought suit against Richard Cutts concerning the estate 27 June, 1665.

Thomas, planter, Hampton, bought land of Wm. Cole, adjoining land of Philemon Dalton and Robert Drake 17 Oct. 1656. Sold a tract 4 April, 1660. Dea. William Godfrey made a bequest to "son in law Webster" in his will in 1667. Upon this genealogists have built the theory that he was a son of Margaret, second wife of Dea. Godfrey, and have found records in England relating to the case.

He married 2 (9) 1657, "Sarah Bruer"; children Mary b. 19 (10) 1658, Sarah b. 22 (11) 1660, Hannah b. and d. 1663, Thomas b. 20 (11) 1664, Ebenezer b. Aug. 1, 1667, Isaac b. April 12, 1670, John b. Feb. 16, 1673-4, Joshua b. Nov. 8, 1676, Abigail b. Jan. 1, 1678-9.

He died Jan. 5, 1715, ae. 83. [Dow.]

Note. Thomas Webster, born in Boston, Jan. 11, 1661, was son of James Webster, brewer, "Scotchman," of Bo. and "Mary Hay, an Irish maid," who were married 14 Feb. 1658. Thomas, innholder, of Exeter, N. H. sold his interest in the estate of said James to a brother William W. shopkeeper, of Bo. Dec. 15, 1715. [Suff. De.]

See Cole, Taylor.

WEDGE,
Thomas, Strawberry Bank, in court at suit of Henry Sherburne 8 (8) 1650. Ordered to go to his wife.

See Hinkson, Monke.

WEDGEWOOD,
  John, planter, husbandman, Ipswich, proprietor, 1637. Before Gen. Court 3 (7) 1639. Rem. to Hampton. Proprietor June, 1640. Sold land 29 Jan. 1648-9.
  Wife Mary; children, John, Jonathan, Mary Abigail b. 12 (7) 1650, d. 19 (5) 1669, David b. 12 (10) 1652. He died 9 (10) 1654. Will dated 24 Nov. 1654, prob. 10 (2) 1655, beq. to eldest son John house and land at Exeter, part of which adjoined that of Edward Hilton; this John is to have at the death of his grandmother; to wife Mary; to sons Jonathan and David and daughters Mary and Abigail. Wife Executrix. Wm. Fifield and Henry Moulton overseers. The widow died Aug. 24, 1670.
  See Haborne.

WEEKS,
  Oliver, sailor, was in the service of Winter at Richmond Island in 1633; deposed 20 Nov. 1640. Worked for Winter 1642-3.

WELBY,
  Thomas, Dover, signed petition to Mass. govt. in 1654.
  See George, from Northamptonshire, Eng. settler at Lynn, Mass. and Southampton, L. I. [P. of M.]

WENBOURNE, WINBOURNE, WEN, WIMBOURNE, WENBORNE,
  William, husbandman, Boston, 1635-8. Rem. to Exeter; signed the combination 5 (4) 1639, and the petition of 1647; frm. May, 1645. Clerk of the writs and commissioner. Returned to Boston; bought house and lot 14 (12) 1644; sold Aug. 11, 1662.
  Wife Elizabeth; children, John b. 22 (9) 1635, John b. 21 (7) 1638.

WENTWORTH,
  William, Exeter, signed the Combination 5 (4) 1639. Proprietor. Lawsuit about a house in 1649. Selectman of

Wells; juror, 1647-9. Constable, 1648. Removed to Dover; proprietor in 1650; juryman, 1650. Lands in what has since been known as Rollinsford. Selectman; commissioner to try "small causes." Signed petition to Mass. Bay govt. in 1654 and Oct. 10, 1665. [Mass. Arch. 3, 447, and 106, 160.] Took oath of allegiance to Mass. Bay govt. 22 Nov. 1652. He was the "ruling elder" of the church; preached sometimes, particularly at Exeter during the period 1683 to 1693. Resisted an Indian attack at Dover in 1689 with remarkable vigor. His wife Elizabeth signed a deed with him in 1666; she survived him. For discussion of his ancestry and family see Genealogy. He d. March 15, 1696-7, "ae. 81."

WEST,

John, husbandman, West Saco, i. e. Biddeford, leased mansion and land lately occupied by Thomas Cole or John Andrews 20 Nov. 1638. His corn referred to in records of Maine court April 4, 1637. Lawsuit in Piscataqua court June 21, 1641. Took oath of allegiance 5 July, 1653. One of the town commissioners. [Bax. MSS.] Selectman. Had share of marsh in 1653.

Will dated 29 Sept. 1663, prob. 5 Oct. 1663; beq. to Ann, Lydia, Samuel and Thomas Haly, in care of William Coole, to whom he gives "all the iron Towles" etc.; to Thomas and Francis Littlefield and their mother; to Frances Woolfe and Mary Reade.

WESTELL, WARSELL,

John, Dover, signed the combination in 1640; proprietor in 1642.

WEYMOUTH, WAYMOUTH, WAIMOTH,

James, Isles of Shoals, in court in 1656.

He made will 10 April, 1678, prob. 25 June following; beq. to sons William, George and James, and daughter Elizabeth; rest to wife Mary. Desired to be buried on Star Island. Elizabeth m. Richard Currier. The widow m. Thomas Diamond.

Robert, Kittery, took oath of allegiance 16 Nov. 1652. Admin. on estate of his brother William Weymouth 27 June, 1654.

William, known only by this settlement of his estate. See Fabes.

WHARTON, WHORTON,

Edward or Edmond, sued in Piscataqua court in 1642 and 1644. Came to court 30 June, 1663, "to bear witness to the truth," as he said; was placed in the stocks and told by the judges that they looked upon him as "a Vagabond Quaker"; they sentenced him to be passed from constable to constable to Salem, the place of his habitation, etc. [See P. of M.]

WHEELER,

Roger, perhaps son of John, of Newbury, had lawsuit in Piscataqua court in 1657. John beq. in 1668 to Mary and Joseph, children of his son Roger.

WHEELWRIGHT,

Rev. John, graduated at Cambridge university, England, in 1614; vicar of Bilsby, Lincolnshire, 1623-1631; came to Boston, Mass. with wife and family in 1636. Was received to church 12 (4) 1636. Preached at Braintree, and sometimes at Boston. Because of his sympathy with his famous sister in law, Mrs. Ann Hutchinson, which greatly scandalized the ministers and magistrates of Mass. he was compelled to leave the colony. Removed to Exeter, N. H. where he with Samuel Hutchinson and Augustine Stor, of Boston, Edward Colcord and Darby Field of Piscataqua, John Compton of Roxbury, and Nicholas Needome, of Mount Wollaston purchased the rights of the Indian sagamore Wehanownowit and his son to the territory of Exeter April 3, 1638. Was the leader in the foundation of that town where he filled the office of pastor of the church and an active citizen.

Bought land near Ogunquett river in Wells, Me. 17 April, 1643, and removed thither, becoming minister to the people of that new community. He petitioned the Gen. Court of Maine 15 Oct. 1650, for leave to erect a sawmill at the falls of the Ogunquat; granted. From 1647 till 1658 he was pastor at Hampton; he served the church of Salisbury, Mass. from Dec. 9, 1662, till his death. In the interval between the Hampton and Salisbury pastorates he visited England. He deeded, 22 Oct. 1677, to his daughter Sarah Crispe of Boston, Mass. land and tenement at Mawthorp in the parish of Willoughby, co. Lincoln, Eng. referring to Belleaw, same co. as his former residence.

He obtained for a house-maid one Elizabeth Evans of Bridgend, co. Glamorgan, Wales; an abstract of the "covenant" for 3 years' service from June 25, 1639, wages 3 li. per an. and passage paid for by J. W. is given in Lechford.

He married 1, [Nov. 8, 1621,] Marie, [daughter of Rev. Thomas Storre, vicar of Bilsby;] she died in Eng.; he m. 2, Mary, dau. of Edward Hutchinson, mercer, of Alford, Eng. and his wife Susanna; children, [John], Samuel, Susanna, (m. Edward Rishworth, Jr.) Katharine, (m. 1, Robert Nanney, 2, Edward Naylor,) Mary bapt. 25 (4) 1637, (m. 1, Edward Lloyd or Lyde, 2, Theodore Atkinson,) Elizabeth, (m. George Person,) Rebecca, (m. 1, Samuel Maverick, Jr. 2, Wm. Bradbury,) Hannah, (m. — Checkley,) Sarah, (m. Richard Crispe,) Thomas. The son Thomas and six daughters are mentioned in the will of their uncle Samuel Hutchinson of Boston in 1667.

He died 15 Nov. 1679; made will 25 May, 1675, "aged"; it was proved 26 Nov. 1679. Beq. to gr. son Edward Lyde estate in Mumby, Langham and Minge, co. Linc. to be delivered to his mother, Mary Atkinson; to gr. dau. Mary Mavericke other lands in Eng.; to son in law Edward Rishworth and his dau. Mary White; to gr. ch. Thomas and Jacob Bradbury; to son Samuel lands at Craft near Waneflitt, Eng. and at Wells, N. E.; to his latter wife's children all his plate.

See also Haborne, Wiggin.

WHITE, WHYTE, WHITTE, WHIT,

John, yeoman, with James Phipps, (father of Gov. William Phipps,) bought of Edward Bateman of Kennebec "a certain large tract of land near the river of Kennebec at a place called Negwusset, lying between that and the river called Munsweague which was the easterly bound; there they lived many years, built houses and otherwise improved it, and died seized of the whole except a certain neck of land called Jeremiah Squam's Neck which they sold in 1679 to Sr. Wm. Phipps."

His wife died and he m. before Oct. 4, 1679, Mary, widow of his partner James Phipps.

Sir Wm. Phipps' legatee Mary claimed the tract —"Cherysequamy neck" — "as by deed from John White and Mary his wife formerly the wife of James Phipps of Kennebeck deceased; dated Oct. 4, 1679." [Me. H. and G. Reg. VIII, 202.]

He died before 1722, when his son Peter, then of Milton, Mass. sold one half of his portion, which was two fifths of the moiety or half of the tract, to Paul Dudley. He testified to the foregoing facts and that his father had eight children of whom four had died without issue. His portion was that of the eldest son. [York Deeds XI, 15.] Perhaps Paul White, taxed at Milton, Mass. 1681-3, was another of those children. Peter gave his age as 67 in 1727, which places his birth about 1660; as William Phipps is known to have been born in 1650 we may locate the partners on the tract before that date.

John, Kittery, about 1638; servant of Alexander Shapleigh; knew of the setting of bounds between Shapleigh and Nicholas Frost at Sturgeon Creek meadow. So he deposed 19 Dec. 1662, being then about 58 years old. Deposed also in 1679. [York De. I and V.]

John, Strawberry Bank, 1643, died before 26 (6) 1646, when inventory of his estate was presented and administration granted to John Reynolds and Robert Mussell. He had been in partnership with Robert Mussell.

Nicholas, Richmond Island, one of Winter's fishermen 1638-1640. Money paid [in England] to his sister and to his master, John Sparke.

Nicholas, Spurwink, took oath of allegiance to Mass. govt. 13 July, 1658. Sold his right in House Island 23 Oct. 1661.

Paul, Pemaquid, captain, merchant, bought in Dec. 1648, of Capt. Francis Champernowne, one half of the land in Maine which had been granted to Capt. C.'s father. [Suff. De.] Rem. to Newbury, Mass. Mrs. Bridget White, supposed to have been his wife, d. Dec. 1664. He m. March 14, 1665, Mrs. Ann Jones, widow, to whom he bequeathed, in will dated 14 Aug. 1674, his estate for herself and children, specifying Mary, wife of Thomas Woodbridge. He d. 20 July 1679, ae. 89. [Coffin.]

Philip, "mariner, of Pascattaquay," was made the attorney of William Grey for the collection of money from Jeremiah Willis 26 (9) 1639.

William, was brought from Derbyshire by Dr. Child before 1648 to work mines; reported that "the spirit of solidity and fusion was not in them." Complained that his family was not cared for according to contract. [Mass. Hist. Soc. Coll. IV, 198.]

See Conley, Frost, Jose, Pierce, Reading.

WICKS, WEEKS,

Leonard, Portsmouth, land assigned him Jan. 29, 1656.

WIETH, WYETH,

Benjamin, Hampton, proprietor, 1644. See Greenfield.

WIGGIN, WIGAN, WIGGINS, WIGON,

Captain, Thomas, gent. [L.] whose birth-place has eluded search, may be the person of whom Sir John Drake wrote from Barnstaple, England, Jan. 6, 1627; "Captain Thomas Wigan desires a letter of marque against the French"; this was addressed to the secretary of state, and is noted in Index to Parl. Docs. Dom. ser. Charles I, vol. XLVII, 7. But the Piscataqua man stands clearly before us as one of the witnesses to the possession of land under patent to Oldham and Vines, in Maine, 25 June, 1630. Another proof of his presence here at that time comes in the letter of John Humphrey, Esquire, one of the Massachusetts Bay company, to his brother in law, Isaac Johnson, Esquire, from London, Dec. 9, 1630: "For Mr. Wiggin & your thoughts concerning him & those who set him on worke, I think you will hear little more. Yet your letter shall be delivered, . . . I purpose this morning to goe to Mr. Downing to advise about it." [Winthrop Letters, Mass. Hist. Coll. XXXVI, 3.] The historian Hubbard says that "Bristol and Shrewsbury men" planted a colony on the upper part of the Piscataqua in 1631, "under Captain Wiggans." The Captain again witnessed the giving of possession of a patent, this time to Lewis and Bonython, in Maine, Jan. 28, 1631-2. "Captain Wiggans went back for England the next year," Hubbard continues, "and soon after returned with more ample power and means to promote what was in hand. The Bristol men had in the mean time sold their interest (which was two thirds) in the said plantation to the Lord Say and the Lord Brook, one to Mr. Willis, and Mr. Whiting, who likewise employed Captain Wiggans to act in their behalf for the space of seven years next following; the Shrewsbury men still retaining their own share. After the time was expired, the advance not being much, the whole was prised but at 600 li. and sold to Captain Wiggans; which he paid at a very easy rate, as some of his neighbors have used to say."

Captain Wiggin remained in charge of the "Dover and Squamscot" patent, including Dover, Exeter and outlying lands, till about 1639, when Rev. George Burdett, (successor of Rev. William Leverich, the first minister of the colony) worked himself into the favor of the people, and assumed control, though with no legal authority. The coming of Rev. John Wheelwright and his associates to settle Exeter, together with the agitation by Mass. Bay people of the question whether that town was not within their jurisdiction, all operated to incline the Captain toward acknowledgement of their claims; and he became the most important factor in the extension of the Mass. government over both New Hampshire and Maine. But this was no sudden freak. As far back as the year 1632 when in England on business connected with his own colony, Captain Wiggin had written two memorable letters, one to Mr. Downing, touching Sir Christopher Gardiner's fiasco and another matter of some importance to New England; the other to Sir John Cooke, principal secretary, testifying to the great value of New England as a profitable place for plantations, and especially showing the high character of Gov. John Winthrop and the people of "the Mattachusetts." [Mass. Hist. Coll. 3d. S., VIII.]

This testimony was given at a critical moment in the affairs of the Bay colony. Gov. Winthrop, in his History, thus describes it: "Feb. 22, 1632-3, .. We had intelligence from our friends in England that Sir Ferdinando Gorges and Captain Mason (upon the instigation of Sir Christopher Gardiner, Morton and Ratcliffe,) had preferred a petition to the lords of the privy council against us, charging us with many false accusations; but through the Lord's good providence and the care of our friends in England, (especially Mr. Emanuel Downing who had married the governor's sister,) and *the good testimony given on our behalf by one Capt. Wiggin, who dwelt at Pascataquack and had been divers times among us,* their malicious practice took not effect."

The friendly service thus voluntarily rendered by Capt. Wiggin was never forgotten. And when Massachusetts needed a man to superintend the pacification of the colonists about the Piscataqua and along the coast of Maine, they naturally turned to him. He was commissioned first as an Assistant, then as a presiding judge, then as commissioner for adjustment of all manner of problems arising in the assumption of authority in new plantations. It is fair to say that he was the most important man in the whole business of uniting the colonies of upper New England.

He was also a deputy to the Gen. Court at Boston, and in his magisterial capacity performed the marriage ceremony, attested documents, etc. in Massachusetts as well as in New Hampshire and Maine. He had grants of land from the Gen. Court in addition to what he had recd. from the Patentees and had purchased. He carried on milling and farming operations. 23 May, 1656, "Captain Wiggan, having been imployed by the Gen[ll] Court with other gent., to bring in the easterne plantations, as a gratuitie in respect of his service, hath the grant of two hundred acors of land uppon the river that leads up to Cochechawicke," etc. The committee appointed to lay out his tract reported April 28, 1659, that they had laid it out "near the head of the littell river caled the back river."

He and his son Thomas sold land April 25, 1662; he made a power of attorney to Thomas March 21, 1662-3. With wife Katharine he gave a marriage portion to son Andrew 4 June, 1663. The 30th of that month he attended court for the last time; a year later he was unable even to reach the "ordinary" without help, as a neighbor testified who had failed to reach his place in the grand jury that day by reason of assisting "his worp." i. e. "his worship," the title of the magistrate.

He kept his lands apart from any town association many years, holding aloof from participation in town meetings or in the support of the ministry or other public affairs; probably deeming his state duties and charges heavy enough, and owning a tract large enough to constitute a "plantation" of itself. But at length public opinion prevailed against him, and he became a tax-payer in Exeter.

He married Katharine —, who may have been a sister of Mr. William Whiting of Hartford, one of the proprietors of the Squamscot patent. At all events, Mr. Whiting made a bequest "to my sister Wiggen 5 li. and unto her children 3 li. apiece," in his will dated March 20, 1643. Children, Thomas, Andrew, Mary, all bapt. at Hampton Sept. 20, 1641. The latter married George Vesey.

He made will 16 June, 1664, which was probated in Hampton court in "1666." He bequeathed to his wife Katherine certain articles and whatever debts were due him and all goods not heretofore or herein given; certain bequests to sons Andrew and Thomas who have already had their portions, and to daugher Mary, for whom 150 pounds had been previously set apart in the deed to Andrew.

See Ault, Burdett, Chesley, Colcord, Commins, Duncan, Emery, Leverich, Lewis, Purchase, Shrewsbury, Tibbett, Vesey.

WIGHT, WEIGHT, (WRIGHT?)

Thomas, Exeter, proprietor, signed the combination 5 (4) 1639; Censured and fined by town for "contemptuous carriage and speeches against the court and magistrates" in 1642. Signed a petition of inhabitants Sept. 7, 1643. [Mass. Arch. 112, 8, 9.] Admin. on his estate granted April 11, 1665, to Israel Wight.

WILKINSON.

John, had lawsuit in Maine court June 5, 1637. He deposed in 1641 that he was a servant to John Winter at Spurwink in 1633. Residence not stated.

WILLEY, WILLY,

Thomas, Dover, proprietor, taxed in 1648; resigned rights in "Champering island" to Richard Kinge 13 Aug. 1649. [Portsmouth records.]

He married Margaret, widow of Stephen Crawforde; they brought suit in 1649 against William Seavie to recover 50 li. which was the money of Susan, one of Crawford's daughters; Sarah, another daughter, was a party to the suit. His son Samuel d. in 1679; admin. granted to the father June 24, 1679.

He died before Sept. 7, 1681, when admin. on his estate was granted to the widow Margaret and son John.

See also King.

WILLIAMS,

Francis, gent. "a prudent man, of better quality than the rest, was chosen governor of the lower Piscataqua in 1633 after Captain Neal went away." [Hub.] Brought over his wife and nine other members of his family about 1636. Recd. grant of 900 acres of land from Gorges, recorded 13 Aug. 1644. He signed a grant of glebe lands with Ambrose Gibbons, Assistant, May 25, 1640. [See the book, "Capt. John Mason."]

The Gen. Court of Mass. appointed him one of the associate justices for Piscataqua 7 Oct. 1641.

He sold, 6 (10) 1645, his plantation near Salt River, being a point of land railed in by William Berriffes, etc. [Suff. De.]

Matthew, before Piscataqua court in 1646; his estate was administered upon June 25, 1667, by John Bickford and others.

Thomas, in court at Portsmouth in case of Judith Ellyns 3 (8) 1648. He m. Ann, widow of Thomas Wanerton; they brought suit for possession of land 27 June, 1671.

Thomas, Saco, in court 28 March, 1636; juryman in 1640. Took oath of allegiance 5 July, 1653. Commissioner of the town, selectman. Resided at West Saco i. e. Biddeford; selectman, 1653. In consideration of a promise of life maintenance, he deeded land 17 Dec. 1681, to his "grandson in law," Phineas Hull and his now wife Jerusha.

William, planter, Dover, constable in 1657. Bought land of John Goddard in 1659.

Wife Margaret; children, William b. 22 Dec. [1662], John b. 30 March, 1664, Elizabeth b. 25 Oct. 1665. [Dov. Hist. Coll.]

See also Bonython, Clifton, Coham, Drake, Ellen, Goddard, Wanerton, Woodward.

WILLINE,

Roger, Cape Porpoise, his land adjacent to that of Morgan Howell in 1648.

WILLS,
   Bennett, of Plymouth, Eng. boatswain, was one of Winter's fishermen about 1630 at Richmond Island. Sold goods to W. in 1643.
   See Abbot, Chadbourne.

WILLIX,
   Balthasar or Belshazer, Exeter, proprietor in 1640; signed petitions in 1643 and 1647. His wife was robbed and murdered between Dover and Exeter in 1648. He married second, Mary, widow of Thomas Hawksworth. Rem. to Salisbury.
   He died March 23, 1650-1. Admin. of his estate was granted 8 (2) 1651, to his widow Mary, who was also made admin. of the estate of her former husband, who had died in Salisbury in 1642.
   She rem. to Hartford, Conn. [A.]
   See Dalton.

WILSON,
   Gowen, Exeter, bought land of Thomas Jones; failing to obtain possession, he brought suit in court 7 (8) 1651. [Norf. Court rec.]
   Rem. to Kittery; took oath of allegiance to Mass. govt. 16 Nov. 1652. Resided "further northward." Testified in the Gunnison case 24 April, 1654, ae. about 36 years. [Bax. MSS.] Gave marriage portion 2 June, 1684, to daughter Deborah, on her union with Andrew Haley.
   Thomas, miller, Roxbury, arrived in New England (4) 1633. [Rox. rec.] In court 4 (10) 1638. Was undoubtedly the brother to whom Edward W. of Boston beq. property in 1638; may be the brother to whom William of Bo. and Braintree referred in bounds of land at Dunnington, Lincolnshire, near that of his father William W.
   He was dismissed 12 (4) 1642 to the church of Hampton, having removed in 1639 to Exeter, where he signed the combination and built the first grist-mill in 1640, the inhabitants

regulating by vote the amount of toll he should receive. Was chosen "ruler" of the town 20 (8) 1642.

Wife Ann; children, Humphrey, Samuel, Joshua, Deborah b. at Rox. (6) 1634, m. John Warren; Lydia b. (9) 1636.

He died in 1643. Will dated 9 (11) 1642, prob. Suff. and Ipswich courts, beq. to wife, eldest son Humphrey and four younger children. The widow m. second John Legat, who made over to Anthony Stanyan certain cattle for the benefit of her dau. Deborah 5 (12) 1644.

See Cornish, Elson, Garland, Legat, Rayner, Warren.

WINCOLL, WINCALL, WINCHELL, WINCHILL,

John, yeoman, Watertown, proprietor, 1636; frm. May 6, 1646; surveyor in 1647. Rem. to Kittery; took oath of allegiance to Mass. govt. 16 Nov. 1652. Signed petition to Parliament respecting Mr. Leader 20 Dec. 1652, — "John Wincoll." Selectman, 1654. Captain. Engaged in 1659 to build a sawmill upon the salmon falls of great Mewichawannock river for Walter Price and Richard Cooke. The town gave him the timber on a certain tract of land in connection therewith; this he mortg. in 1666. [York De. VI.] He deposed 6 July, 1671, relative to contracts he had made for the sale of lumber; referred to his "brother" Thomas Broughton. Associate judge in 1673.

"Captain John Wincol falls off his horse and killed Oct. 22, 1694. Captain Hammond of Kittery, appointed by the Lt. governour and Council, Dec. 4, 1694, clerk and register, vice Capt. Wincol, dec." [S.]

See also Cutt.

WINDSOR, WINSER,

Walter, "son of John Winser of Hemick, co. Devon, Eng." apprenticed May 3, 1660, to John Deaman for 5 years. Of Portsmouth, deposed 5 Jan. 1685, ae. about 64 years, as to a fence set up "a great many years since," when he was in the employ of John Cutt.

WINGFIELD,

Thomas, Dover, witness to a deed of Obediah Bruen in 1642.

WINTER,

John, mariner, of Plymouth, England, deserves to be honored as one of the most efficient and persevering pioneers who came forth from old England in the seventeenth century. Intense in his convictions, severe in his antagonisms, rugged in manners, he was yet deeply devoted to what he regarded as the principles of divine and human right.

Mr. Robert Trelawney, holding a patent for the island which had somehow received the name "Richman" or "Richmond" Island, remained in Plymouth to receive whatever profits could be made from the land and water over which he had received control; but Mr. John Winter, who had passed that apprenticeship of years by which alone a man in those days could be termed "mariner," bade adieu to the easy life of home and sailed across the ocean, then so broad — and toiled at the head of a band of toilers. He not only superintended the fishing operations, by which several ships a year were laden and sent home; he also looked to the cultivation of the soil on the island and ashore, training many men for their own farming, and making that island the nursery of Maine's grand husbandry and the pioneer shipyard of the state. More; he and Trelawney corresponded in a style that shows the good business habits of both; and the letters thus written form the first book of real history of the people of "The Pine Tree State."

Right here let respect be paid to that citizen of Maine, Mr. James Phinney Baxter, by whose scholarly research and munificent use of well-earned wealth these "Trelawney Papers" were brought out of their hiding in England and placed in fitting form before historical students; and let passing tribute be given to the Maine Historical Society, whose Collections, so rich in treasures of this class, have embraced this remarkably valuable compilation.

John Winter received a power of attorney with Thomas Pomery 18 Jan. 1631, and in the summer following, — July 21 and 30, 1632, he received possession of the Casco land and islands from Richard Vines. His letters extant begin 11 July, 1633; but he had been here before, as we must infer from many notes in the letters and accounts. Really the year 1630 may be taken as the beginning of Winter's operations on this coast, probably.

He left his family in England at first; asked Mr. Trelawney to pay money to his wife and daughter Mary Coulinge; referred to his daughter Sarah. Mrs. Winter and Sarah came over in 1639. He drew on Trelawney 15 June, 1642, for 15 li. to be paid to his daughter Mary Hooper, to whom he wrote 13 June, 1644; tells of the marriage of daughter Sarah to Rev. Robert Jordan 5 months before; mentions his son John Winter, and tells of receiving a letter from him since he came from the East India to England.

The inventory of his estate was taken and appraised by George Cleve, William Ryall and Henry Watts 10 Oct. 1648, by order of the Lygonia Assembly, at the request of Rev. Robert Jordan; it was attested before the commissioners of Massachusetts July 16, 1658.

See Brown, Cleve, Jope, Jordan, Trelawney.

WISE,

Thomas, Casco, petitioned the court at Saco 25 March, 1636. Gave testimony in the case of Winter in 1640.

WITHERS,

Thomas, gent. Kittery, grand jury man in 1640. "In consideration of faithful services and long aboad [abode]" he received from Gorges 1 March, 1643, 400 acres of land on the Northeast side of Piscataqua river, two islands near his house, and 40 acres of meadow. Also had deed from Vines, steward of Gorges, a tract of 600 acres of land at the head of Spruce Creek. [York De. I, and Bax. MSS.] Was agent of Francis Champernowne, 1650-1652. Took oath of allegiance to Mass. govt. 16 Nov. 1652. Was chosen

deputy to Gen. Court 24 March, 1656. [Mass. Arch. 48.]
He was one of the royal commissioners in 1664. He deeded
one half of his farm 25 April, 1671, to his daughter Sarah
on her marriage to John Shapleigh; and other lands 30 July,
1675, to daus. Elizabeth and Mary.

He and his wife Jane, "being of great age," and "waxing
antient," gave their cows and sheep to their daughter Elizabeth 22 Dec. 1684; William Heynes testified 13 April, 1685,
that this deed was written by him and signed by Mr. Withers but little while before his death.

Wife Jane; children Mary, (m. Thomas Rice), Elizabeth,
(m. — Berry), Sarah, (m. John Shapleigh).

His will dated 26 Sept. 1679, was certified to 30 March,
1685; beq. to wife, daughters Elizabeth, Mary Ryce, son in
law John Shapleigh and grandchildren Alexander and Alice
Shapleigh.

The dau. Mary Ryce deposed 30 March, 1685, ae. about
25 years. The widow conveyed land April 1, 1691, to dau.
Elizabeth Berry. She m. William Godsoe before Oct. 6,
1692, and joined with him in a deed of land formerly possessed by Withers in 1707.

See Champernowne.

WOODEN, WODEN, WOTTEN,
John, husbandman, before Saco court 25 March, 1636.
Of Hampton, signed the anti-Howard petition March 7, 1643.
Before Piscataqua court in 1644; case "put to reference."
Bought of widow Mary Hussey a "joint possession" of certain lands 25 (2) 1648. Reference to an absent wife in court
in 1650.

Rem. to Haverhill; rem. to Salisbury; bought land 15 (2)
1659. Had a grant of land from Mass. govt. in 1667, on his
petition, stating that he had been 32 years an inhabitant of
the land, and had many children.

Wife Mary; children, John, Mary b. in Hav. March 6,
1652-3, Martha b. at Hampton (12) 1654-5, Sarah b. at Salis.
Feb. 29, 1656-7, John b. at Salis. Oct. 7, 1659.

WOODWARD,

James, before Piscataqua court in 1646; died previous to 10 (7) 1647, when an inventory of his estate was exhibited at Dover court and a memorandum of "instructions" from him. He had worked a year for Mr. Williams of Saco; had accounts with him, with John Sherburne and Thomas Warner. Bequeathed his estate to Lydia Williams, Mr. Bachiler and William Chatterton.

WORMESTALL,

Arthur, Wells, took oath of allegiance to Mass. govt. 5 July, 1653. Rem. to Saco. With wife Susanna sold land 23 Sept. 1681. Gave land to son in law William Daggett, carpenter, as a portion to his daughter Rebecca, Daggett's wife. Other ch.: Susan, b. 1658; Arthur, b. 1661; John, b. 1669. [Hist. Ken. Port.]

WORMWOOD,

William, Kittery, a witness to John Lander's deed in 1639. Lived on Star Island; accused of improper dealings with sailors, and ordered to leave the island and dwell on the main land in 1647. Sold land to Thomas Crockett before 1647.

Anne [his child] was freed from the service of John Crowther and his wife 3 (8) 1648. Katherine, (his first wife?) testified in court in 1650. Son Jacob.

Inventory of his property, taken by Arthur Came and John Hovie, was presented in court by Mary Wormwood (his widow?) Dec. 3, 1690. [York De. V.]

WRIGHT, see Wight.

YORK,

Richard, planter, Dover, taxed Oct. 19, 1648. Signed petition to Mass. Gen. Court in 1654. With wife Elizabeth sold land 7 Aug. 1661.

Elizabeth, his daughter, m. at Exeter 23 Sept. 1668, Philip Carte. [Norf. Rec.]

He made will 23 April, 1672, "well stricken in years"; beq. to sons John, Samuel and Benjamin; daughters Elizabeth Cartie, Rachel Halle and Grace York; grandchildren Richard and Benjamin York; and to his wife. Brought into court 30 June, 1674, and administration granted to the widow Elizabeth and son John. The widow m. (2) William Graves; they made an agreement with John 7 June, 1681.
See Branson.

YOUGROUFE, [YEWGROVE,] UGROUFE, NUGROVE, NEWGROVE,

John, mariner, Kittery, signed the Piscataqua combination in 1640. Had lawsuits in 1640. Owned ground and house which he asked George Smyth to sell for him, etc.; letter received 19 April, 1641; Smith sold the land 18 Dec. 1650.

Administration of his estate was granted to his daughter in law Sarah Morrill of Boston; and John Pickering, as her attorney, filed claim to certain lands 27 Sept. 1695. [York De. III and V.]

See also Jenkin.

YOUNG,

Rowland, Senior, York, an inhabitant there about 1637, according to the deposition of his son Rowland in petition to Andros in 1688; "brought up a great family of children." [Bax. MS. VI.] Took oath of allegiance to Mass. govt. 22 Nov. 1652. With wife Johanna he conveyed land 18 April, 1682, to son Samuel; and to son Rowland 25 Aug. 1685, a tract formerly the homestall of their father Robert Knight, and a tract adjoining land of their son Robert Young.

Will prob. 6 Nov. 1685, beq. to wife Johannah; in her will prob. 20 June, 1698, she beq. to sons Rowland and Job, and daughters Mary Moulton and Lydia Haines. [Me. Wills 124, and York De. IV and V.]

See Batson.

INDEX

Index

INDEX

Other Names

ACREMAN
  Sara 138
ADAMS
  Abraham 131
  Ammi 56
  John 56
  Margaret 56
  Nathaniel, Jr... 165
  Sarah 131
ALDEN
  Elizabeth 162
  John 161
  Nathaniel 146
ALDERSEY
  John 51
ALDWORTH
  Robert 189
ALLINE
  Edward 167
ALMERY
  Hannah 155
AMBROSS
  Abigail 52
ARNALL
  Joseph 52
  Phebe 52
APPLETON
  Wm. S......... 20
ASHLEY
  Elizabeth 14
  Sarah 14
ASPINWALL
  Elizabeth 161
  William 161
ATHERTON
  Patience 196
ATKINSON
  Mary 130
  Theodore 130, 162, 230
AXALL
  Humphrey 85

BABB
  Peter 33
BACKUS
  Francis 49

BAKER
  Sarah 155
  William 155
BARKER
  Joan 220
BARNARD
  Matthew 54
BARNS 169
BARROW
  James 2
BARTLETT
  John Heard ... 92
  Nathan 92
  Robert 92
BASS
  Peter 154
BATHORNE
  Roger 118
  Wrath 118
BATTEN
  Arthur 14
BAXTER
  James Phinney, iii, v, 240
BEAL
  Edward 46
BEEX
  John 123, 147
BELCHER
  Mr. 146
BELLINGHAM
  Mr. 165, 181
BENMORE, BINMORE
  Philip... 2, 149, 150
BENNETT, BENNITT
  George 161
  Richard 161
  Samuel 101
BENWICK
  Arthur 80
BETTS
  John 1
BEWFORD
  John 86

BLACK
  Daniel 2
  Elizabeth 2
  Sarah 2
BLACKMAN
  Benjamin 218
BLACKSTONE
  William ... 108, 126
BLAKE
  James 9
BLAND
  Isabel...... 59, 125
  Joane 125
  John 59
  Joshua 125
BLANEY
  John 167
BLANOE
  John, Sen...... 148
BULLEN
  Mary 20
BONNER
  Marie 136
BOUEN
  Ambrose 91
BOYCE
  Antipas 96
BOYES 172
BRACKETT
  Thomas 140
BRAWN
  John 57
BRENTON
  William 51
BREWSTER
  William 142
BRIDGHAM
  Elizabeth 166
  Jonathan 166
BRIDGMAN
  Tabitha 191
BROOKHOUSE
  Mary 14
BROUGHTON
  George 152
  Thomas.... 63, 239

247

BRUER
  Sarah 226
BRYERS
  Elizabeth 11
  John 11
BULKLEY
  Edward 63
BUNDY
  John 142
BUNKER
  George 201
BURT
  Henry 11
BURTON
  Thomas 51
BUSHNELL
  John 117
BUSS
  Elizabeth 23
  John 23
BUTTON
  Matthias 60

CAME
  Arthur 243
CANE
  Mary 53
CARD
  John 112, 198
CARLE
  Richard 184
CARRINGTON
  James 68
CARTE
  Elizabeth 243
  Philip 243
CARTER
  Mary 53
  Thomas 53
CHADWELL
  Thomas 114
CHAPMAN
  Elizabeth 76
CHECKLEY
  Hannah 230
CHICKE
  Thomas 196
CHICKERING
  Francis 7
CHIPMAN
  John 30
CLARKE
  Elizabeth 222
  Frances 172

John 221
Thaddeus 140
Thomas....75, 102
CLAYDON
  Richard 89
CLOUTMAN
  Thomas 148
CLOYCE
  Hannah 128
  John 139
  Nathaniel 139
  Peter 128
COLE
  Amyas 205
  Samuel 178
COOKE
  John 234
  Richard 41
COOLIDGE
  John 154
COOMES
  Elizabeth 224
  John 224
  Sarah 224
  Thomas 15
CORBET
  Abraham 49
CORDELL
  Robert......3, 146
COTTON
  John...... 93, 136
  Seaborne 136
CRANCH, CRUNCH
  Andrew 130
  Elizabeth 130
  Frances 146
  John......130, 146
CRISPE
  Richard 230
  Sarah 230
CROMWELL
  Philip 122
CROSSE
  Susanna 114
CURRIER
  Richard 228
CUSHING
  Daniel 79

DABYN
  Robert 104
DAGGETT
  Rebecca 243
  William 243

DANFORTH
  Thomas 146
DANIEL
  Thomas 51
DAVENPORT
  Captain 87
DAVIS
  Elizabeth 6
  Sylvanus 210
DAVISON
  Nicholas 5
DEATH
  Mary 156
DERBY
  Edward 102
DILL
  George 153
DOD
  Elizabeth 54
  George 209
  Mary 54
  Mehitable 54
DOLHOFF, DOLHORT
  Christian 117
DOWNING
  Emanuel 234
DRAKE
  John 232
DUDLEY
  Paul 231
  Samuel 209
  Thomas 112
DUGLASSE
  Henry 107
DUMMER
  Thomas 38, 61, 195
DURGIN
  William 70
DUTCH
  Susan 178

EATON
  Mary 96
  Theophilus 96
EDEN
  Alice 144
EDGERLY
  Rebecca 7
EDMUNDS
  Ann 84
  William 84
ELBRIDGE
  Giles 189

248

ELLIOT
  Humphrey 35
ELY
  Richard 123
ETHERINGTON
  Mary 196
  Thomas 196
EVANS
  Elizabeth 230
EVERILL
  Abiel 162
  Elizabeth 162

FEILD
  Mary 161
FLINT
  Henry 205
FORETT
  James 119
FOSTER
  Mary 156
  Reginald 156
  William 100
FOTHERGILL
  Gerald 97
FOWER, FARR
  Barnabas 122
FOULES
  Thomas 90
FOX
  Nathaniel 199
FREDERICK
  Christopher ...146
  Mary 146
FRENCH
  Judith 104
FRY
  Adrian 44
  John 199
FULLFORD
  Richard 157

GARD
  John 168
GARDINER
  Christopher 167, 234
GATTINSBY
  John 196
  Susanna 196
GEDNEY
  Bartholomew
    63, 148, 182
GENDALL
  Walter 132

GILE
  James 53
  Samuel 53
GILLETT, GILLITT
  Elizabeth 223
  John 223
GILLIN
  Zachary 161
GLOVER
  Ralph 145
GODSOE
  William 242
GOODENS
  Adam 144
GOODYEAR
  Moses 148
GOOSE
  Susanna 114
  William 114
GORDON
  Nicholas 128
GOSS
  Jean 218
GOWINE alias
  Smyth
  William 72
GRAVES
  Ann 140
  Elizabeth 244
  William 244
GREENE
  John 85
  Margaret 178
  Phebe 178
GREGORY
  Jonas 58
GREY
  William 232
GRISE
  Samuel 85
GROOPE
  Jane 43

HACKETT
  William 90
HALEY
  Andrew 238
HALLE
  Rachel 244
HALSTON
  Susan 136
HAMMETT
  Thomas 30
HARRIS
  Trustram 192

HARVY
  Mr. 140
HASSAM
  John T.........99
HAWKESWORTH
  Mary 238
  Thomas 238
HATHORNE
  William ...123, 199
HAY
  Mary 226
HAYWOOD
  Robert 78
HELMES, see
  HOLMES
HERRICK
  Sarah 169
HIGGINSON
  John 14
HINCKS
  John 71
HOBBERT
  Elizabeth 50
HODSDON,
  HODGSDEN
  Francis 170
  Israel 205
  Joseph 170
  Nicholas 195
HOGG
  Peter 85
HOLDEN
  John 66
HOLLAND
  John 220
HOLMES, HOLMS
  HOMES
  Christopher ...215
  Daughter 160
  Jane 73
  John 218
  Mary 218
  Thomas 73
HOOD
  John 186
HOOPER
  Mary 241
HOVIE
  John 243
HOW
  Samson 156
  Sarah 156
HOWLAND
  John 173

HUBBARD, see
  HOBBERT
  William ...97, 204
HUDSON
  William 162
HUMPHREY
  John 233
HUTHINSON
  Mrs. Anne (Marbury)
  62, 119, 143, 200, 229

ISAAC
  Elizabeth 54

JACOBS
  Lydia 141
JAGO
  Thomas 120
JAMES
  Henry 122
  Thomas 122
JANVERIE
  Thomas 31
JELLISON
  John 85
  Nicholas 85
JOHNSON
  Isaac 233
JOY
  Ephraim 196

KENDALL
  Margery 14
KENNEY
  Jane 39
KENT
  Stephen 183
KEY
  Mrs. 81
KITSON
  Alice 173
KNOWLES
  Jemima 125
  Sarah 125
KNOWLTON
  John 182

LANG
  John 25
LANGLEY
  James 173
  Mary 173
LANGWORTHY
  Nicholas 117

LARRIFORD,
  LEREFET
  Brother 134
  John 134
LAWRENCE
  Antoine 81
LEATHERS
  Edward 16
LERABY (LARRIBEE)
  William 66
LILFORD
  Elizabeth 221
  Thomas 221
LITTLEBURY
  John 148
LITTLEJOHN
  George 105
LOCKE
  William 54
LOLL
  Meribah 190
LOOMAN
  Mrs. Anne.....142
LORD
  Rebecca 161
  Robert 161
LUDLOW
  George 101
LOUGIE
  Ellen 5
LYFORD
  John 98
LYNDE
  Simon 182

MACY
  Thomas 77, 84, 193
MAKENTYRE,
  MACINTYRE
  Makem 162
MAGOUN
  Alexander 128
MANN
  Michael 135
MANNYARD
  Ruth 198
MARCH
  Thomas 235
MARSH
  George 74
MARSHALL
  Thomas 130
MARTIN
  Hester 175

John 175
Samuel 157
MASON
  John 67, 77, 80, 112,
  222, 234, 237
MATHER
  Cotton 164
  Richard 136
MAVERICK
  Moses 137
  Samuel....102, 230
MAYHEW
  Thomas 193
MEADER, see MEDD
  Sarah 147
MERCER
  Hester 10
MERCHANT
  Matthew 150
MERRIE
  Elizabeth ...52, 96
  Joseph...... 52, 96
MESANT
  Ann ...29, 80, 112
MILLBURY
  Henry 57
MORRALL, MORRILL
  John 205
  Sarah 244
MORSE
  Martha 191
  Obediah 191
MUNT
  Faith 188
  Thomas 188

NAYLOR
  Edward 230
NOBLE
  Martha 160
NORDEN
  Samuel 165
NORRIS
  Sarah 47
NORTON
  Joseph 77
  Susanna 77
  Walter 102
NOWELL
  Sarah 225

ODLIN, AUDLYN
  John 221

OLDHAM
  John 214
ORCHARD
  Thomas 72
PAINE, PAYNE
  John 206
  Thomas 9
  William....177, 217
PALMER
  Christopher 98
  John 3
  Richard 30
PARKHURST
  George 52
  Joseph 52
PEARCE
  Justinian 43
PEARSON
  Ann 114
PENHALLOW
  Samuel 50
PENNY
  Ellene 171
PERLEY
  Lydia 156
PERSON
  George 230
PETER
  Mr. (Hugh) ...221
PHILLIPS
  Walter 192
PIKE
  Dorothie 94
  John 94
  Robert 94
POLLARD
  George 128
POMERY
  Thomas 241
POPE
  John 47
PORTER
  Roger 154
POTUM
  Charles 108
POWELL
  Mary 141
  Robert 141
PRESSON
  John 170
  Susannah 170
PRICE
  Walter 239

PULLMAN
  Jasper 6
  John 57
POWSSLEY
  Richard 40
QUINSEY
  Edmund 222
RACHELL
  Robert 90
RAINKING, RAN-
    KIN
  Andrew 24
RAINSFORD
  Priscilla 77
  Solomon 77
RAMSAY
  Mrs. 94
RATCLIFFE 234
RAWSON
  Edward 217
RAY
  Hephsibah 156
RAYES
  John 27
RICH
  Richard 175
RICHARDS
  William 10
RICORD
  Mary 32
RIGSBY
  Alexander 39
ROBINSON
  John 176
ROE, ROWE
  Richard 146
ROGERS
  Grace 154
  Rebecca 132
  Thomas 24, 154
  William 86, 132
RUSSELL
  Martha 141
RUST
  Nathaniel 223
  Mary 223
SALTONSTALL
  Elizabeth 222
  Nathaniel 222
SANFORD, SANT-
    FORD
  Bridget 162
  John 162

SCAMMAN,
  SCAMMON
  Prudence 217
  Richard 217
SCARLET
  John 71
SCRIVEN
  Bridget 35, 51
SEARLE
  John 84
SEVERANS
  John 52
SHATREDG
  Ann 55
SHAW
  Samuel 9
SHERMAN
  John 153, 154
  Martha ..153, 154
SHIPWAY
  Ann 51
SIVERT
  Johanna 116
SMITH, SMYTH
  Daniel 154
  Capt. John......98
  Joane 28
  John 28, 30
  Richard 80, 194
SNELL
  George 105
SNOW
  Samuel 142
SOUTER
  Hannah 170
  John 170
SPARKES
  SPURKES
  Edward 153
  Rose 178
  Sarah 178
STANLEY
  Christopher ...161
  Sussannah 161
STANWOOD ..139
STARR
  Dr. (Comfort)..84
STILLSON
  James.......26, 83
  Margaret 26
STOCKBRIDGE
  Mary 94
STOWERS
  Richard 73

251

STRATTON,
    STRATTEN
  Bridget 162
  Elphell 162
  John 6
STUBBIN
  John 46
SWEETSER
  Seth 161
SYMONDS
  Harlekenden ... 19

TARLINGTON,
    TARLTON
  Ruth 199
TARRETT
  Ruth 155
TAYLOR
  Katherine 153
  John 171
TEED
  John 86
THOMAS
  Elizabeth 18
  James 89
THORNER
  Henrie 12
THURSTON
  Martha 161
THURTON
  Thomas 73
TILDEN
  Nathaniel 166
TILLEY
  Alice 127
  Sarah 87, 127
  William ... 87, 127
TILSTON
  Elizabeth 216
TILTON
  Abraham.. 186, 205
  Daniel 186
  Mary 205
  Samuel 186
  Susanna 186
TOBEY
  James 90
TOMLINS
  Edward 119
  Timothy 119
TOWER
  Leah 223
  William 223

TRAFTON
  Elizabeth 141
TRUE
  Henry 23
  Jane 23
TURNER
  Ephraim 161
  Habbakuk 162
TYTHERLEY
  William 145

VAUGHAN,
    VAHAN
  George 126
  Margaret 51
  William 51
VITTERY
  [VICARY]
  Margery 105

WALES
  John 54
WALLIS
  Thomas 224
WALTON
  Henry 28
WANTON
  Edward 193
WATERS
  Henry F........ 99
WATSON
  Elizabeth 15
WAYTE
  Richard 32
WEBBER
  Mary 155
  Thomas 47
WEDGE
  John 99
WELCOME, WIL-
    COM, WOOL-
    COMB
  Eleanor 213
  Sarah 141
  Richard 213
WELLS, WILLS
  Deborah 182
  Edward 182
  Lucy...... 199, 208
  Thomas
        199, 208, 211
WHIDDEN
  Samuel 33

WHITE
  Richard 98
WHITEHOUSE
  Elizabeth 53
WHITING
  William
        217, 233, 235
WILKINSON
  Elizabeth 66
  Prudence 66
WILLARD
  Simon 63
WILLIAMS
  John 167
WILLIS
  Jeremiah 232
  Mr. 232
WILSON
  John 172
WINESLEY
  Samuel 19
WING
  John 10
WINGATE
  Mary 151
WINSLOW
  Edward 109
WINTHROP
  John
    19, 111, 167, 215, 234
WOOD
  Daniel 156
  John 104
WOODBRIDGE
  Benjamin 221
  Dorothy 71
  Elizabeth 221
  John 71
  Mary...... 221, 232
  Thomas 232
WOODMAN
  John 170
WOODMANSEY
  John 162
WOOLCOMB, see
    WELCOME
WOOLFE
  Frances 228
WYMAN
  John 9

YALE
  Thomas 96